Alan Silverstein's

Home-Buying Strategies
for Resale Homes

Alan Silverstein's

Home-Buying Strategies for Resale Homes

The Smart-Money Guide to Canadian Home Ownership

Published in 1997 by Stoddart Publishing Co. Limited
34 Lesmill Road, Toronto, Canada M3B 2T6
Tel. (416) 445-3333 Fax (416) 445-5967
Email Customer.Service@ccmailgw.genpub.com

01 00 99 98 97 1 2 3 4 5

First published in hardcover in 1986 by Stoddart Publishing
First paperback edition published in 1989

Stoddart Books are available for bulk purchase for sales promotions, premiums, fundraising, and seminars. For details, contact the **Special Sales Department** at the above address.

Canadian Cataloguing in Publication Data

Silverstein, Alan, 1951–
Alan Silverstein's home-buying strategies for resale homes : the smart-money guide to Canadian home ownership

Rev. pbk. ed.
ISBN 0-7737-5868-2

1. House buying - Canada.   I. Title.   II. Title: Home buying strategies for resale homes.

HD1379.S553 1997   643'.12'0971   C97-930292-7

"Zero Lot Line" illustration: Jane Edmonson
Cover design: Bill Douglas @ The Bang
Text design: Tannice Goddard
Computer graphics: Mary Bowness

Printed and bound in Canada

Contents

Preface

Buying a home should be an exciting and fulfilling experience. From the first house-hunting expedition until closing and beyond, prospective purchasers should experience feelings of happiness, enthusiasm and anticipation about themselves, their new dwelling and their futures. While this heady euphoria cannot continue indefinitely, no buyer wants to suddenly encounter the unanticipated, the unexpected and the unforeseen just before closing. Concern easily can turn to crisis, totally demoralizing a buyer. How can the peaks and valleys — the mixed emotions — be smoothed out, so that the initial buoyancy can be maintained throughout?

Buying a home has remained basically the same over the years. Too often it has been a "learn by doing" proposition, with buyers wishing they knew at the beginning what they know at the end. Typically, buying a home began by signing an Offer to Purchase. Only in the interval between acceptance and closing were fundamental questions asked — many of them concerning finances and closing costs — and crucial information sought. Few buyers ever challenged this approach; it was simply the way things had always been done.

Not any more! Today, a new consumer awareness prevails when buying a home. More and more purchasers realize that all the key decisions must be made *before, and not after,* the offer is signed. *The interval between acceptance and closing is the time to implement those decisions, not initiate them.* Signing the offer is the climax of the process, not the first step. By restructuring the home-buying process, these purchasers are giving themselves more time to investigate, make inquiries and seek out answers before becoming legally committed to a property. Armed with more information, obtained much earlier than usual, they are less likely to face the unanticipated, the unexpected and the unforeseen. They put pen to paper better prepared than their predecessors, having carefully analyzed their needs, wants and financial ability to pay for that house and carry it each month. In short, little is left to chance.

Reflecting this new approach to buying an owner-occupied home is what I call HOBS — Home-Buying Strategies. In its simplest form, HOBS emphasizes the need to plan and arrange every aspect of a transaction before signing an offer to purchase. Buyers must have a particular understanding of what they are committing to, before making that commitment. In the commercial world, it's called "due diligence." For children in school, it's called "doing your homework." Whatever the terminology, it's all the same: being prepared before making any final decisions. Once the offer is signed, everything should simply fall into place, the important tasks having already been completed.

Alan Silverstein's Home-Buying Strategies for Resale Homes examines in great detail the information buyers need to know, the pitfalls to avoid, the questions to ask and the answers to seek, so that buyers can create and implement their own unique home-buying strategy. And that is one of the key elements of a home-buying strategy. Everybody's HOBS will be different. What one person or couple needs and wants from a house will differ from everyone else's needs and wants. The means to pay for that house, and cover its ongoing expenses each month, will again vary from person to person, couple to couple.

Alan Silverstein's Home-Buying Strategies for Resale Homes has been written with two goals in mind. The first is to unravel the mysteries associated with buying a house, making people more comfortable with the topic. Because our schools don't offer courses such as "Home-Buying 101," too many people learn about buying a house via hearsay, through someone else's painful experiences or in the "School of Hard Knocks." This book provides Canadian home buyers — both first-time and move-up buyers (those who currently own a home, who must sell it to buy another) — with a straight bill of goods on what to do, what to avoid, who to consult and when. Buyers will be guided through every step of the transaction, from the time a decision is made to start looking for a home until well after closing.

The second goal of *Alan Silverstein's Home-Buying Strategies for Resale Homes* is to help buyers rethink and constantly refine their home-buying strategy as they proceed along the path of purchasing a house. Much information must be assembled, and many decisions must be made beyond merely selecting a house. Properly applied, the strategies developed using this book will help buyers make the right decisions, so that they will acquire the right home at the right price — the house that best satisfies all of their needs and as many wants as possible, a house they can afford to buy and carry each month.

With the bulk of the work in buying a house to be done at the pre-contract stage, a considerable portion of this book is devoted to the preliminary issues buyers must examine before looking for a house. Detailed discussions follow on the selection of real estate professionals, mortgage financing and the con-tents of the offer — all before the question of signing the offer is even raised! The commentary on the post-contract period understandably is considerably slimmer, the transaction at that stage being etched in stone and unalterable.

This revised edition also brings readers up to date on recent developments in real estate, covering issues as diverse as the impact of the GST on residential real estate, buyer brokerage, seller disclosure, government incentive programs and the tax laws on home offices.

Just as buying a used car differs dramatically from purchasing a new one, so too with buying a home. Purchasers of newly built (or yet-to-be-constructed) homes must deal with numerous issues that purchasers of resale homes never face: purchasing from plans; new home warranties; onerous contractual terms; and delayed closings. Mixing a discussion of resale and newly built homes would do justice to neither. Therefore, the focus of this book is the purchase of a resale home — one that has been previously owned and occupied. Readers who want a thorough review of the process when buying a brand-new home from a builder, and the unique concerns they will encounter, should read another of my books, *Alan Silverstein's Home-Buying Strategies for Newly Built Homes.*

Alan Silverstein's Home-Buying Strategies for Resale Homes is a companion volume to *Hidden Profits in Your Mortgage, The Perfect Mortgage* and *Save! Alan Silverstein's Guide to Mortgage Payment Tables,* all published by Stoddart Publishing. These last three titles provide an in-depth analysis of mortgage financing and mortgage strategies, all designed to help Canadians cut the cost of home ownership. Together, this library of books forms an invaluable reference tool, whether a first-time or move-up buyer is purchasing, financing or refinancing a resale or brand-new home. The message throughout is the same: in order to deal with the complex issues of home buying and mortgage financing, a sound, personalized and well-thought-out strategy is a must.

The home-buying strategies appearing here have been developed and refined over 20 years from my background as a real estate lawyer, broadcaster and lecturer on real estate topics, as well as from the incidents, good and bad, that clients have encountered over the years. Experience is such a valuable teacher, yet gaining it can be so difficult. Readers of this book are learning from other people's experience. Can we benefit from yours? Have you faced a particular problem not addressed in this book, or do you have a home-buying strategy that other Canadians should know about? If so, then drop me a line. Address your correspondence to me, c/o Stoddart Publishing, 34 Lesmill Road, Toronto, Ontario M3B 2T6.

Acknowledgments

In any major undertaking, the contributions of the people who play vital roles behind the scenes must be acknowledged.

First, I offer my sincere appreciation to all the staff at Stoddart Publishing, especially Angel Guerra, Don Bastian, Stephen Quick and Nelson Doucet. Since our relationship began in the early 1980s, Stoddart Publishing has been committed to providing Canadians with the most comprehensive information about home buying and mortgage financing anywhere. No simple task, considering the rough ride that real estate endured during the first half of the 1990s.

But the most important and meaningful thank-you always belongs to my family: my wonderful wife Hannah, and my dear sons Elliott and Darryl. Over the years my family has always encouraged me in my endeavours, and has always been so understanding despite the considerable time commitments. As always, I dedicate this book to them. Their strength and support helped make this book a reality.

1
What Is HOBS?

Buying a resale house is not something done overnight. It takes time — a lot of time. And thought. Many questions must be asked and the answers carefully analyzed before any commitment to buy can be made. Sports teams prepare a game plan before taking to the ice or the field, to help guide them through the game. Doesn't it make sense for home buyers to do the same?

Think for a moment about buying a car. With so many different models, options and features available today, would anyone ever think of submitting an offer to purchase without first doing considerable homework? By the time most car buyers are ready to sign, hours have been spent doing preliminary research, investigating the marketplace, dealerships, the product and car loans. They have clearly spelled out their needs, their wants and what they can afford to pay. Only then will they start negotiating. Should the situation be any different when those same people buy a house, for a price anywhere from five to ten times the cost of a car? How can anyone even consider buying a home without having done that same degree of homework?

To avoid rushing headlong into the purchase of a house, potential buyers must understand what they are committing to, before making any commitment. Key decisions on buying a home can only be made after going on a fact-finding expedition, asking pointed questions and obtaining satisfactory answers. Acknowledging this need for information, two questions must then be asked:

1. What are these critical preliminary decisions?
2. When should they be made?

HOBS stands for Home-Buying Strategies. A modern, practical and educated approach to buying a home, it requires that all important decisions be made *before* signing and submitting an Offer to Purchase. These decisions, in the past too often left until after the purchase papers were signed, include the selection of real estate professionals (agent, home inspector and lawyer), pre-approval for mortgage financing, and a detailed examination of a buyer's financial ability to buy a house and pay for it monthly. Buyers armed with a HOBS will also demand complete and timely disclosure of all costs they will face when buying a home — including the so-called hidden closing costs. Only in this way can they plan and budget early for these expenses. Signing a contract is the climax of the whole scenario, not the first step. Properly executed, a home-buying strategy will take the guesswork out of acquiring a principal residence.

Each buyer will ask a multitude of questions and demand thorough answers in designing his or her own HOBS. That strategy will be constantly refined and updated over time, based on the many different answers received and decisions reached along the way. Understandably, then, each buyer's HOBS will be unique, reflecting his or her needs and wants.

HOBS is the master plan that buyers should prepare at the outset, to guide them through the home-buying process. By the time pen hits paper, relevant information affecting the *entire* transaction has been obtained and all the fundamental decisions have been made. The remainder of time until closing is anticlimactic, a buyer's major task then being to pack. In short, developing and applying a home-buying strategy represents the commonsense approach to buying a house in Canada.

Why is HOBS so important? Contrast it with the (far too common) situation where buyers, caught up in the emotion and excitement of buying a house, sign first and ask questions later. For example, suppose the selection of a lawyer is left until after the offer is signed. How can the lawyer review and revise the contract, when it is a *fait accompli*? Does that make sense? The same is true with mortgage financing. Too often buyers do not even think about arranging a mortgage (although they know they will need one) until after the contract is signed. With very little time to get a mortgage, buyers are hard-pressed to shop around adequately for a loan. Too often they must accept whatever financing package is presented, simply because it is available. Is that wise?

Given the costs involved in closing a real estate transaction — legal fees (plus GST), disbursements (plus GST), title transfer taxes, adjustments, costs associated with arranging a mortgage and other expenses — how can a buyer sign a contract without first learning more about these charges? How can a buyer properly budget funds for closing, oblivious to these outlays? How can a buyer know how large a mortgage to book without knowing what these expenses will total?

For potential home buyers who lack a HOBS, time becomes their greatest enemy. Critical decisions must then be made quickly, and under pressure. Choose a lawyer. Choose a home inspector. Choose a lender. Budget finances. If any item is overlooked or underestimated, a shortfall of funds for closing is a real possibility.

As part of their HOBS, buyers will also learn more about the "state of the market." Is it a buyer's market (generally the case when the market is slow), when purchasers can negotiate from a position of strength? Is it a seller's market (during busier times), when the reverse is true? Or is it a balanced market (the healthiest type of market), when the pendulum rests midway between buyer and seller, meaning that neither side has the upper hand in negotiations? In the spring and fall there is usually a seller's market, while in winter and summer there's more of a buyer's market. But the pendulum can swing into buyer or seller territory at any time, and stay there for an extended period of time.

A home-buying strategy also demands that buyers take stock of themselves first and seriously analyze their own distinctive situation before signing any contract. Is that such a bad idea? What buyer wants the high hopes and expectations experienced on signing an offer to be ruined soon afterwards because they can't qualify for a mortgage loan? Who wants their bubble of enthusiasm to burst days before closing, on learning that they lack sufficient funds to complete the transaction?

The key to success when buying a home is advance preparation and planning: checking out *everything* ahead of time, making the signing of the offer one of the last steps in the home-buying process — not the first. That allows buyers to move quickly when they find their "ideal" house — one that satisfies all their needs and as many wants as possible, one they can afford to buy and carry each month — because all the preliminary work has long been completed.

Developing a home-buying strategy will obviously require a considerable investment of time and effort, to thoroughly investigate every step to be taken. Yet a HOBS is an easy-to-use and inexpensive method of ensuring that the ultimate decision made is the correct decision. With a home-buying strategy, the buyer's initial level of optimism and excitement can grow throughout the transaction, climaxing when the deal is completed and the keys are received on the day of closing.

2
Rent or Buy?

Rent or buy? — an age-old dilemma. And the answer is not a simple one. Primarily it depends on very individual factors like your financial health — your ability to purchase and then "carry" a property each month — your lifestyle, and other personal considerations.

A home serves two purposes. It's a place to live, and a place where funds are invested. For most people, buying a home is probably the biggest single investment they will ever make. As rental accommodation can satisfy the first goal, the investment side of home ownership should never be overlooked.

Obviously, home ownership is not for everyone. Your lifestyle may not require the facilities, or allow some of the benefits, offered by home ownership. Like Steve and Ruth, some people prefer to rent because of the freedom from responsibility it provides. From shovelling snow in the winter and cutting the grass in the summer, to being at home when an electrician or plumber is needed, home ownership requires a regular expenditure of time and money on maintenance, repair and upkeep. People needing mobility can relocate much more quickly and easily if they rent their premises. Tenants can also avoid both the long-term mortgage obligations and the commitment of funds that home buyers face.

Renting has a unique advantage in those provinces where some form of rent regulation is in effect. While mortgage rates, taxes, utilities and repairs may increase dramatically over time, rent increases will be kept to fixed maximums. During the days of double-digit mortgage rates, renting was often viewed as being cheaper than owning, from a monthly cash-flow point of view. (As interest rates fell in the mid-1990s, however, affordability of ownership improved to record levels.) Security of tenure, which permits tenants to remain in possession of their apartments on a long-term basis, is another important factor encouraging people to continue as tenants.

Aside from the mortgage commitment, owner-occupied homes are not a "liquid" investment, either. The reason: homes cannot be readily converted into cash, as is the case with Canada Savings Bonds and term deposits.

Despite all these factors, buying real estate during the second half of the 20th century has traditionally been an excellent hedge against inflation. According to a study from Canada Mortgage and Housing Corporation, resale house prices rose faster than inflation in 23 of 27 major Canadian cities between 1971 and 1994 — years when inflation was running rampant in this country.

Capital appreciation has always motivated people to invest in real estate, too. And with the principal residence exemption in the Income Tax Act being one of the last bastions of tax-free capital gains in Canada, there's no need to share with the government any increase in value on the sale of your home. No wonder the owner-occupied home is one of the most popular forms of investment for Canadians. By contrast, tenants pay their rent and other charges every month, without ever having anything to show for it.

Government incentive programs also exist which improve access to home ownership for potential first-time buyers (plus a limited number of other people). These include the First Home Loan program, which offers up to 95% mortgage financing (meaning a home can be bought with as little as 5% down), and the Home Buyers' Plan, the RRSP program that allows up to $20,000 to be borrowed tax-free and interest-free per person from an RRSP. Buying a home with only 5% down is examined in chapter 8, while the RRSP program (and a little-known strategy that will generate "free money" from the government) is discussed in more detail in chapter 9.

Too often the investment potential of home ownership is understated. Instead of calculating any increase in value against the purchase price, such gains should be compared to the down-payment — the initial investment in the house.

For example, suppose Steve, Jim, Tom and Keith each buy a house for $150,000. Five years later their homes are worth $157,500, an increase of $7,500. Steve has made $1,500 a year, or 1% per annum, tax-free. But that assumes Steve bought the house all-cash — something few people do. If Jim put $75,000 (50% of the purchase price) down on closing, five years later he has made $7,500 on his investment, or 2% a year tax-free. Tom put 25% of the purchase price down on closing, or $37,500. So Tom's $7,500 gain over those five years means he has earned 20% on his initial investment, or 4% per year tax-free. And if Keith put just 10% of the purchase price down on closing, his $15,000 investment has generated $7,500 during those five years — a tax-free return of 10% per year.

This example is not meant to encourage people to buy homes with small downpayments (actually, the reverse is recommended, to cut down on non-deductible carrying costs). Instead, it illustrates how even small gains in home prices are magnified into sizeable returns — tax-free gains, don't forget — especially for first-time buyers with modest downpayments.

The allure of home ownership, though, goes much deeper than just dollars and cents. Many of its benefits — the so-called intangibles — do not have a monetary value. Security, stability, privacy and a feeling of permanence are just some of the reasons why people strive so hard to own their own home. The back yard where the kids can play, the roominess in which to live, the community in which to plant roots, the pride of home ownership coupled with the fun of decorating a house as an expression of personal taste, all have inspired millions of Canadians towards the goal of home ownership. Almost two-thirds of Canadian households were home owners in the mid-1990s, up slightly from a decade earlier. As rapidly and dramatically as the world is changing, home ownership remains an old-fashioned virtue, one which will never die.

Choosing whether to rent or buy is not an easy decision. Developing a home-buying strategy early on will help potential buyers know what is involved in purchasing and owning a home, and whether home ownership is right for them.

3
Advantages of a Resale Home

A world of difference separates resale homes from brand-new homes being constructed by a builder. (Existing homes are generally called "resale" homes. Rarely are they dubbed a "used" or "pre-owned" home.) A resale home actually exists. Purchasers see what they get, and get what they see. They can touch it, inspect it and measure it. No need to speculate, visualize and imagine what the finished product will look like. In many respects builders don't sell homes; they market plans, an "architect's rendition" and a choice of color selections.

Buyers of newly built (or yet-to-be-constructed) homes must also be sold on the builder's reputation. Questions commonly asked are: How long has it been in business? What is its reputation? What is the quality of its work? How has it handled previous buyers? What if the builder becomes insolvent before or after closing? When buying a resale home, none of these issues is a concern. While a purchaser may want to know who was the builder, the focus of attention is the home, plain and simple.

As part of their sales brochure, builders include a detailed list of 30, 50 or even 100 features or "appointments" that accompany the house. These lists appeal to many potential buyers of brand-new homes, allowing them to easily compare what's being offered by different builders. Purchasers of resale homes who like this approach can prepare their own checklist of features and appointments based on the information in chapter 18. Each time a resale home is viewed, mark off those items in the house. Attach any promotional information or "feature sheet" highlighting the property, too. Make extra copies of the checklist, if necessary. After viewing a few homes, trying to remember which house contained which items is nearly impossible. With just a little effort, though, a detailed and organized inventory of the distinctive features of different homes can easily be prepared.

While newly built homes provide their owners with modern equipment that should last for many years to come, unfortunately the home-buying process parallels ordering dinner in a restaurant *à la carte*. Many of the items buyers want, from air conditioning to more electrical plugs, are only available as an extra, upgrade or option — at an additional charge. When a used car is bought, factory-installed extras may warrant a slightly higher sale price. Rarely, though, does the increase cover the initial cost of those items. The same is true with resale homes. Buyers view the house "as is" — as a package. Rarely are they prepared to pay considerably more for a house simply because it contains upgraded carpeting or better quality windows, or has a "premium lot." Sellers of resale homes know this, often lamenting how they will not get out of a house the money they put into it!

Most resale homes are sold in existing communities and neighborhoods that have a certain level of charm and maturity. By contrast, many buyers feel that new homes built in new subdivisions have a cold, stark look that will take many years to soften. Until grass is laid and roads are paved, mud is a major inconvenience for new-home buyers, especially after a rainstorm. Newly built homes in developing communities also may lack the support services, recreational facilities, transportation links, schools and shopping available in more established areas. This topic is discussed in more detail in chapter 10, "Know the Community and Neighborhood."

The offer to purchase a newly built home is a buyer's nightmare, too. Both lengthy and complex, it imposes onerous restrictions and responsibilities on buyers, far beyond what they anticipate. New-home contracts also contain a catalogue of hidden charges that builders expect a buyer to bear. Not so with resale offers. While they do exhibit a distinct pro-seller slant, offers for resale homes are not nearly as one-sided as those prepared for builders. Most real estate associations and boards have developed standard form resale offers, with which agents and lawyers in the area become familiar. Being much shorter contracts, they are much easier to read and understand. Unlike new-home contracts, few "termination" clauses or "hidden zingers" appear in resale offers. Any that do are quite noticeable, generally being specifically added to the printed form.

Probably the biggest problem and the most common complaint about buying a new home involves missed or delayed closing dates. When a new home is not completed on time, buyers must scurry about, making arrangements for alternative accommodations on very little notice. But not with a resale house. Since it already exists, the closing date in a resale transaction is meaningful. Virtually all resale deals close on time, allowing purchasers to take possession when scheduled. That provides resale buyers with a level of assurance sorely lacking in many new-home transactions.

Buyers of newly built homes must also anticipate coping with a certain level of aggravation after closing. Besides the unfinished work, defects and problems inevitably begin to surface. Rarely is the rectification work completed when buyers want and expect it done. Resolving these outstanding issues may mean spending considerable time on the phone with the builder's service department. Time off work may also be necessary, meeting with the service rep on site to address the problems face to face. These headaches are a non-monetary expense when buying from a builder.

Buyers of older resale homes are not immune from problems with the house after closing, either. They run a very considerable risk of inheriting the vendor's headaches — any hidden defects. But that hazard can be considerably reduced if a home inspector is hired to conduct a thorough investigation of the property *before* the offer becomes firm. Knowing more about its state of repair not only allows for a possible readjustment of the purchase price, but also helps buyers properly budget for the ongoing costs of maintenance and repairs after closing.

Buying a resale home actually can save buyers money. Just

because a property is brand new does not mean it is in move-in condition on closing. Windows must be covered (sheets on the windows are not very appealing!). A fence may have to be erected, a driveway may have to be laid, and some basic landscaping may be desired. By contrast, the older home Wayne and Sandra bought included many improvements and features as part of the purchase price. These items, which would not have accompanied a newly built house, included drapes and drapery tracks; blinds, sheers and other window coverings; upgraded electric light fixtures; an outdoor patio; landscaping; and five appliances (fridge, stove, washer, dryer and dishwasher). While not everyone is as fortunate as Wayne and Sandra, many of these chattels and fixtures are typically included in the sale of a resale home. Buyers operating on a tight budget always find a resale home in move-in condition very appealing; it's better value for their money.

Older homes have a certain charm associated with them, too. Fine woodwork, ornate brickwork, and leaded glass doors and windows are just some of the attractive features of older resale homes.

The GST is another major distinction between new and resale homes. Virtually all resale homes are GST exempt, as described in chapter 25. New homes, though, are subject to GST (although the GST New Housing Rebate reduces the tax rate from 7% to about 4.5%). Many new homes today are sold "GST included," the builder paying the GST and keeping the GST rebate. By purchasing a resale home, buyers "avoid" the GST.

Obviously the debate between resale and newly built homes will never end. A market exists for both; it is simply a matter of personal choice. Despite the immediate appeal of a brand-new home, a majority of buyers opt for a resale home for one simple reason. A known quantity is being acquired on a fixed, pre-arranged date. To many people, this factor outweighs all others.

4
When Is the Best Time to Buy?

The "seasons" of the real estate market closely parallel the cycles of nature. After hibernating in winter, the market blooms and blossoms in spring. After a summer hiatus, the market usually experiences a vibrant fall, slowing down with the first "staying" snow. HOBS — the development and application of a unique home-buying strategy — encourages buyers first to consider when they want to close the purchase and take possession of their home. Then they must work backwards, leaving ample time to find the property, negotiate the offer and close the transaction.

The quietest time for the real estate market is the beginning of December through the middle of February. With the onset of winter and the inconveniences that it brings, fewer buyers are prepared to go "house-hunting" or even view open houses. Moving in winter presents a special set of problems. Trekking through ice and snow with heavy furniture and boxes inevitably leads to blotches of dirt, grime and slush on carpets and floors. Extra care must be taken with weather-sensitive plants, to avoid damaging or even killing them. A severe snowstorm might even cause the move to be delayed. Christmas, of course, and mid-winter holidays also account for some of the softness of the market that time of year.

Like holiday package trips, many good deals are available for people prepared to buy "off-season." Although the supply of resale homes does decline over the summer and especially the winter months, many homes continue to be listed, for a variety of reasons. Sellers tend to be more flexible on both price and terms during these quiet times, too. After all, what vendor can afford to lose an interested buyer, simply because the price offered is marginally too low or the buyer insists on acquiring the appliances? In fact, many people feel the best time to buy a house is the week before Christmas! With most people preoccupied with the holiday season (meaning minimal demand), and earnest sellers being the only ones listing their homes at this time, serious buyers can often strike quite a bargain in the days leading up to Christmas.

Some buyers with winter contracts choose a "long closing," the actual completion date being well in the future. Eric and Lisa, with two children in school, are a perfect example. Changing schools in mid-year could cause considerable disruption. By signing an offer in March with a June closing, Eric and Lisa benefit from a winter contract while minimizing the effects of a winter closing. Winter sellers will often accept an offer with a long closing, as it brings them piece of mind. For those who have already bought another house (probably conditional on the sale of the current house), both deals can now proceed. Sellers who have not yet bought can now go house-hunting confidently, knowing their old home is sold. A long closing also allows them to negotiate the purchase from a position of strength, as they now can buy firm (not having to make it conditional on the sale of their current home). Anyone not buying another house can start looking for suitable rental accommodation with a precise occupancy date in mind.

First-time home buyers should remember that real estate agents are not overly busy during the winter. That sluggish winter market affords buyers an excellent opportunity to meet agents, learn about the market, and seek answers to their many questions in developing their home-buying strategy. Over the winter, agents have more time to solidify relationships for an immediate or not-too-distant purchase. Even if they are not ready to buy at this stage, buyers who use this time to formulate their HOBS will have a valuable head start when they finally decide to make their move.

Inspecting a home in the winter affords an opportunity not

available in summer, to check the effectiveness of the home insulation. A roof free of snow is a sure sign of poor insulation in the attic. A sizeable area free of ice and snow around the perimeter of the house at ground level is also a sign of heat loss from the walls due to inadequate insulation.

In late February, as the first good weather appears (if only occasionally), many people's thoughts turn to buying a home. With a long, cold winter behind them, people's interest in real estate grows like the buds on a tree. The number of prospective buyers attending open houses or just out looking on nice weekends in late winter and early spring is astounding. Homes show well in early spring, too. Lawns and trees are beginning to green. Flowers are starting to bloom. A fresh coat of paint on the exterior, coupled with some outside clean-up work, can make a tired house look young again and more marketable.

The delay between the offer being accepted and the actual closing date also explains why interest in the resale market resumes in February and March. Several weeks of exploring and negotiating may be necessary before a suitable house is found. More time will pass before the offer is accepted and any conditions are satisfied. Generally speaking, this interval between acceptance and closing lasts a minimum of 30 days, often much longer. Those out house-hunting in early March may finally strike a deal sometime in April. A 60-day closing makes it a June transaction. April showers may bring May flowers, but spring contracts spawn summer closings.

Having children attending school, more than any other factor, determines when buyers want to close their deals. Danny and Marilyn are like most young couples with school-age children. They decided to move in the summer, between the school years. While the week before Labor Day is a very busy time for real estate closings, the last week in June usually surpasses it. Danny and Marilyn opted for a June 29th closing. That way their children had more time to meet and make friends over the summer, instead of facing a new group of children the first day of school. That early summer closing also provided Danny and Marilyn with a great opportunity to freshen up the property during the warm weather.

Midsummer is a quiet time in the real estate market. Buyers, sellers and agents alike are on holidays. Beautiful weekends are spent resting and relaxing, rather than searching for new quarters. As in the winter months, agents selling resale homes will have more time to devote to first-time buyers. Sellers tend to be more flexible at this time, too, in response to the weaker demand.

After Labor Day, life returns to normal. The kids are back at school and "everyone" is back to work. But surprising as it may seem, autumn traditionally spawns a strong real estate market. Fall buyers of resale homes may wish to relocate before winter unleashes its fury, or before their children are too far along in school. Other purchasers are anxious to move before Christmas, the house itself being the ultimate Christmas gift for the family. Handymen often want to renovate, remodel or upgrade a property before inclement weather sets in.

When is the best time of year to buy a house? While individual circumstances will dictate the final decision, there are some basic rules of thumb. Spring and fall are generally more seller-market oriented, in response to the reduced supply of listings and the increased number of buyers. Prices have a tendency to spike upwards during the spring (and to a lesser extent during the fall) as a result. The reverse holds true — in terms of prices and sales — during summer and winter.

Remember, too, that real estate transactions do not just happen overnight. Even the most straightforward deal will take several months from start to finish. Purchasers preparing their home-buying strategy should ask, "When would we like to close the purchase and move?" Working backwards from that date, buyers should allow sufficient time to locate a property, negotiate the terms of the offer and close the transaction. That will help buyers determine the best time to start looking for a home.

5

Which Comes First —
The Purchase or the Sale?

This chapter is designed for existing home owners who will be
involved in "back-to-back" or "double-ender" transactions —
selling one home and buying another. First-time home buyers,
though, will find it helpful as a further application of the
HOBS, or home-buying strategy, that every buyer must develop
to effectively purchase a home.

The classic dilemma on the mind of every home owner planning to move is: "Do I buy first or sell first?" Good arguments
exist both ways, and there is no "right" answer. Buyers who do
their homework and devise a HOBS will know exactly where
they are going, when they are moving, what the purchase price
and other closing costs will be, and what price is needed on the
sale of their existing house to make the move economically
viable, *before* submitting any offer to purchase another home.
Cautious buyers applying HOBS will lean towards selling first,
although a "best-of-both-worlds" option also exists.

Many purchasers fear having two signed contracts in existence at the same time, one for the sale of their current home
and a second for the purchase of their new home. Logically,
they ask: What happens to the purchase if the sale does not
close? Where will they live if the sale closes but the purchase
does not? Despite these legitimate concerns, it should be re-
membered that the vast majority of residential resale deals do
close as and when scheduled. Any problems usually can be
detected and resolved well before closing, leaving people ample

time to make alternative arrangements if absolutely necessary.

Most home owners think about buying a new home before they consider the sale of their current home. The reason is obvious. Once the decision to move is made, first and foremost on most buyers' minds is the purchase — where to relocate, what type of house to buy, and what features it should include. Quite often, selling the existing house is assumed as a foregone conclusion. Once home owners have found the resale property they want to buy, all their attention is focused towards getting *that* house. Surely there is someone who will buy their present home, and at an acceptable price.

People who buy first like Stan and Karen must recognize they now have an interest in two properties. Selling their existing home within a short period of time then becomes their number-one priority. With the clock ticking, they lack the luxury of time to haggle over prices and other terms in a sale offer. The expression "vendor has bought" is a sure sign that prospective buyers can strike a harder bargain. Depending on how desperate and pressing the situation, sellers who have bought are often more flexible and accommodating on issues such as price, appliances and other personal property, and a new survey. No seller can afford to lose a willing buyer if the price is at the lower end of the range, even if it means sacrificing a fridge or stove. As the closing date for the purchase approaches, the pressure mounts for even more significant concessions, to end this self-imposed nightmare. The alternative is to be stuck with two homes!

By contrast, selling first and buying later gives buyers like Sam and Diane considerable piece of mind. Knowing their home is sold, they now can devote their time and energy to looking for another residence. Knowing how much money they will be receiving on the sale of that house helps in establishing a price range for their new home. With the existing home already sold, Sam and Diane also can avoid having to submit an Offer to Purchase that's conditional on selling that property.

Yet selling before buying has its own drawbacks. Buyers unable to locate a satisfactory replacement home before the sale closes could find themselves with no place to live. With time increasingly becoming an enemy, buyers who have sold first might have to compromise their position and negotiate the final purchase price less vigorously. They might even have to spend more than budgeted, literally to avoid becoming homeless. No buyer in this situation can afford to lose an acceptable property over a small difference in price, a survey, or a few used appliances that the seller will not include in the purchase price.

Timing and the state of the market are two important factors to consider when deciding whether to buy first or sell first. When prices are rising (generally a seller's market), buying first makes more sense. That fixes the price for the new home, and allows the existing home to be sold later at a higher price. George and Louise were "moving up," that is, buying a more expensive home. By buying first and selling later, George and Louise satisfied the first rule of real estate: buy low and sell high. Archie and Edith did the opposite during that rising market — they sold first and bought afterwards. While they received a good price for their home, they could have made more by waiting. That same rising market also worked to Archie and Edith's disadvantage, as the new home cost them more than had been the case just months earlier.

The reverse is true during a falling market (generally a buyer's market). Then the rule of thumb is: sell first, buy later. People like Mike and Gloria who buy first in a falling market and then sell, not only overpay for their new home, but earn less from the sale of their old home, too. The additional funds that must be borrowed to finance the purchase can wreak financial havoc with even the best-laid plans. Buying first in a rising market and selling first in a slumping market is good advice. But it makes one enormous assumption, a critical element of any HOBS: that people know the state of the market at the relevant time.

One solution to the sell first/buy first dilemma is to buy a home "conditional" on selling the current home. Michael and Susan's Offer to Purchase will only become firm and binding if they sign an offer to sell their present home within a short, specified period of time (usually 60 days or less). If no one buys their home during that time, Michael and Susan's Offer to Purchase is cancelled. If, however, they sell their home during the conditional period, both deals proceed. Conditional offers with a "subject-to-sale" clause go a long way in resolving the "chicken-and-egg" dilemma of whether to buy first or sell first. For more information about conditional offers, see chapter 26.

While a conditional-on-sale offer would appear at first glance to be "the answer," its usefulness also depends on the current state of the real estate market. In a seller's market, conditional-on-sale offers are virtually nonexistent, as vendors believe that it is only a matter of time before someone else presents an offer to purchase on equal, if not better, terms. But in a buyer's market, sellers are usually anxious to receive an offer, any offer. Making it conditional on the buyer selling his or her current house is less likely to be rejected for that reason alone.

Keep in mind, too, that unconditional offers carry more weight with a seller, because a firm and binding contract results from its acceptance. Acknowledging this, Jay and Beth submitted an unconditional Offer to Purchase even though they had yet to sell their existing home. The potential danger they faced was obvious: what if they could not sell their present house before the purchase transaction was scheduled to close?

If security and piece of mind are paramount, the most prudent home-buying strategy is to sell first, buy later. Inevitably, though, people tend to buy first, thinking that the existing home can always be sold later at a good price. While it's tough to fight human nature, in the right circumstances an Offer to Purchase made conditional on the buyer selling his or her current home can be an excellent compromise. Equally important, it helps ensure that the head, and not the heart, ultimately carries the day.

6
Know What's Out There

Talk about the luxury of choice. Home buyers today have many different types of homes, styles of homes and forms of legal ownership from which to choose! Let's look at them separately.

Types of Homes

a) Single-Family Detached Dwelling: The house is not attached to any other property. More expensive than other types of homes because detached homes occupy larger lots with sizeable "setbacks" between the houses. They offer the greatest amount of privacy, too.

b) Semi-Detached or "Side-by-Side" Dwelling: Two otherwise-separate houses are attached with a common wall between the houses, or a common wall between garages.

c) Link Houses: A variation of semi-detached. Two homes appear detached above ground, but are actually attached below ground.

d) Duplex (Triplex): Two (or three) units in one building, stacked one above the other. Often the owner lives in one unit and rents out the rest to generate income.

e) Row Housing: A number of homes similar in design are linked with common walls on both sides. Each home owner owns his or her own building, plus the land comprising the lot. Sometimes called "freehold townhouses."

f) Street Townhouses: A variation on row housing. While they visually resemble row housing, all the land for the complex is owned by a condominium corporation, not the individual owners. Buyers acquire the unit itself, and an interest in all the land in the project.

Styles of Homes

a) Bungalow: A one-storey house.

b) Two-Storey: The entire property is two stories high.

c) Split-Level: Sometimes called a one and one-half, part of the house is one level and part of the house is two levels. A side-split has the second level on the side of the house, while a back-split has the second level at the rear.

d) Condominium Apartment: Exactly the same as a rented apartment, except that the unit is owned, together with an interest in the common areas.

Forms of Legal Ownership

a) Freehold: The home owner owns the building, as well as the land on which it sits.

b) Leasehold: The home owner owns the building but leases the land (usually from the government or a government agency).

c) Condominium: (Usually in an apartment building or a townhouse complex.) The purchaser owns his or her individual residential unit, plus a proportionate interest in the common areas. Condominiums are examined further in chapter 20.

d) Co-Op: Instead of owning a specific unit, the home owner acquires a share in the corporation that owns the building, plus the exclusive right to occupy and use a particular unit. On a sale, the share and that exclusive right (but not the unit itself) are transferred to the purchaser. Restrictions on selling the share may exist, or approval from the board of directors may be needed.

Arranging financing is difficult, if not impossible, as the purchaser only has the share to pledge as security, not the unit. Not overly popular in Canada.

e) Co-Ownership: Instead of shares being held in a corporation, a percentage interest in the building is owned in common with everyone else. The exclusive right to occupy and use a specific unit accompany that interest. Often used to avoid formally registering the complex as a condominium when a rental apartment is converted. Lenders are also reluctant to grant mortgage financing here, as buyers technically do not own the unit they occupy. Even less popular than co-ops.

7

Preliminary Considerations —
Your Needs and Wants

Once the decision has been made to consider buying a house, the next step is for you, the purchaser, to look at yourself and your lifestyle and design your own HOBS or home-buying strategy. Start by asking: What are we looking for in a home? What do we expect it to provide? When fashioning this custom-made home-buying strategy, and before embarking on any house-hunting expeditions, buyers must do some careful self-analysis, examining their needs and wants, their ability to pay the closing costs, and what it will cost to "carry" that property each month. Answering the questions raised in this chapter will help buyers determine what type of property to buy, and what features the house should contain. The next chapter will help buyers with the necessary "number-crunching."

Most people, especially first-time buyers, want to buy the biggest and nicest property available. But that can mean financial disaster. To prevent that from happening, buyers must keep both feet firmly planted on the ground and their sights lowered. Since few people have the financial resources to make their first home their "dream" home, a "starter" home is often bought. Not only is it within their means, but it satisfies present needs and wants and those of the foreseeable future. Over time, families expand in size, tastes change and incomes increase. This house is traded in, to be replaced by another. Often the process is repeated at least one more time, until a "permanent" residence is acquired.

Buyers following the HOBS approach should prepare two separate, pre-determined "shopping lists" in the privacy of their own home or apartment, before they ever go into the market-place looking for a house, or even contact a real estate agent:

a) a list of "needs" or "must-haves" — those essential features the house must contain; and

b) a list of "wants" or "would-like-to-haves" — optional items people hope to get in a house, if available and affordable. Wants should be weighted according to personal preferences, the most important items appearing top-of-the-list.

And what is the "ideal" home? Very simply, *it's the one that satisfies all of a buyer's needs and as many wants as possible, the property they can afford to buy and carry each month.* One washroom in a house is a "need," but a second may be a "want." If a home can be bought in the right price range with two washrooms, satisfying a "want," it warrants extra consideration.

Why the emphasis on needs and wants? Real estate agents can't help buyers locate this ideal home if they haven't examined themselves first, if they don't know what a house should provide. Parents constantly caution their children: "To be successful in school, do your homework." Buying a home is no different. Crafting a home-buying strategy means doing the very same thing: homework. Learning, studying, examining. The more that buyers know about their own needs and wants, their financial ability to pay for a house, the state of the market and closing costs, the more successful they will be in the home-buying process.

When creating a HOBS, remember that any property bought will be sold again, eventually. While this may sound like a strange comment, considering that no house has even been selected yet, buyers drafting a HOBS will not overlook its importance. The more a house contains "traditional" features, the easier it will be to market in the future.

The basic features for any house are the bedrooms and bathroom, kitchen, living room, dining room and storage space. After that, individual taste takes over. Is a three-bedroom home needed, or will two bedrooms do? Not only are three-bedroom homes much more common, they are much more in demand. How many bathrooms are needed or wanted? What about a usable basement? What sized rooms are needed or wanted? To help answer this question, measure your furniture plus your present-sized rooms. Is air conditioning a need or a want? What about a garage? Or a car-port? Private drive or mutual drive? How much room do the children need to play without disturbing anyone? Is the increasingly popular "family room" desired? How large should the kitchen be? Should it be at the rear of the house so the youngsters can be seen while at play in the rear yard? Where should the laundry room be located? How many levels of stairs are acceptable? What about storage space? A garden? Must the house have handicap facilities? In short, what type of house is most appropriate for you and your family?

How large a house can be afforded? Starter homes in the 1,100 square foot to 1,400 square foot range should satisfy most of these needs and a number of wants by providing three fair-sized bedrooms plus other good-sized rooms.

The personal make-up of the buyer is another influence. A handyman may find an older home to his liking, one that is structurally sound but which sorely needs tender loving care. His willingness and ability to apply "sweat equity" means that the only cost of upgrading the house is in the materials. A condominium would be inappropriate. By contrast, childless couples and empty-nesters (whose children have grown up and moved away) can enjoy the lifestyle and convenience afforded by condominium townhouses and apartments. At their stage in life, paying for the maintenance of the property is probably easier and cheaper than doing it themselves. Young couples with children may find that a semi-detached or link house will give them most of the benefits of a detached home, at a lesser cost.

Subjective factors should not be downplayed either. People are attracted to end units of condominium townhouses or row houses because they produce a feeling of living in a semi-detached home. Other purchasers totally shun condominiums, street townhouses, semi-detached and link houses, fearing the damage that would be caused by a fire in an adjoining unit.

In the space below, continue developing your HOBS — your unique Home-Buying Strategy — by listing your needs and wants: those items which are essential in a house, and those which are greatly desired.

	NEEDS	WANTS
Size of House		
Bedroom		
Bathrooms		
Kitchen		
Living Room		
Dining Room		
Basement		
Storage Space		
Laundry Room		
Other Rooms		
(Family Room)		
Other Features		
(Air Conditioning)		
Garage		
Driveway		
Back Yard		

Never put your last cent into a home. A cushion of money is needed for personal emergencies or those unexpected home-ownership costs. For help in deciding whether you can afford to buy and carry a particular home, read on!

8
Preliminary Considerations —
Financial

Buying a house demands that purchasers be both practical and realistic. Sacrifices and a change in lifestyle are inevitable. Holidays may have to be shelved, with weekends spent entertaining at home rather than on the town. More disposable income may have to be applied towards the cost of shelter than had previously been the case, too.

A key element of HOBS is to look for a home in the appropriate price range. Potential buyers must ask themselves *and honestly answer* the following question: What can I afford to buy?

In determining a proper price range, buyers must consider *both* the amount of the downpayment and the ongoing costs of home ownership. Purchasers must set a *realistic maximum price range* for a house and stick to it. The upper end of the range is the maximum price a buyer can afford to pay. The bottom end is perhaps 5% lower. "Maximum price range" is a more important consideration than just maximum price. Invariably, the best attainable price for a property is several thousand dollars higher than the anticipated price. By looking for properties at the lower end of the range, buyers can use this approach to gain some leeway to negotiate.

As hard as it is to say no, setting and keeping to a fixed maximum price range will avoid numerous problems in the future. Overextending yourself financially will cause grief and anxiety, could jeopardize your continued ownership of the property, and may put irreparable strain on your marriage or relationship.

"Living within one's means" is an old virtue, but one that takes on added meaning in today's taxing world.

Sam and Helen calculated their maximum price range to be $145,000 to $150,000. Although they valiantly tried to hold to a price of $145,000, the property was ultimately sold to them for $147,500, a figure still within their maximum price range. Using this approach, Sam and Helen came within budget while buying their home.

How is the applicable maximum price range determined? Several rules of thumb exist, which are just that — rules of thumb. One says the maximum price to pay for a house is 2.5 times the buyer's gross income. (Both 3 times as well as 3.5 times gross income are also used as guidelines.) Usually, but not always, the combined gross incomes of both spouses are considered, if both have solid jobs with a strong likelihood of continued employment. But lenders generally exclude any income that may be generated from a basement apartment or other rented portion of the premises, unless the mortgage is specifically arranged and approved that way.

Purchasers of owner-occupied homes should pay as much money as possible towards the purchase price on closing, after taking into account the considerable closing costs. The more money down, the less being borrowed and the lower the mortgage payments (a non-deductible expense in Canada), no matter what the interest rate. After all, there are only two ways to pay for a house: with your own money or with somebody else's! Since a mortgage is needed when using somebody else's money, to make up the difference between purchase price and downpayment, the answer to the question "What can I afford to buy?" is squarely tied to the question "What can I afford to borrow?"

While the finer points of mortgage financing are considered in more detail in chapter 21, the importance of thinking about a mortgage at this early stage in the home-buying process cannot be overlooked. And things have changed considerably in the last few years.

Traditionally, like Richard and Bonnie, most people gave very little thought to the mortgage until the very end, after the offer was signed, conditional on their arranging satisfactory financing within a very short period of time. That forced

Richard and Bonnie to scramble for a mortgage and accept the first package obtained, regardless of the terms. Shopping around for a mortgage was impossible — they didn't have the time. And if Richard and Bonnie couldn't arrange a mortgage in time, they couldn't buy the house.

That was then, and this is now. Today, home buyers can learn whether they qualify for a mortgage, and for how much, *before they even buy a house.* Every major institutional lender, and many mortgage brokers, offer a "pre-approved" or "pre-arranged" mortgage, one of the most important developments in Canadian mortgage financing in a generation. By meeting with a lender and outlining both their incomes and downpayment, buyers like Ian and Linda can get preliminary approval for a mortgage — often on the spot, in the branch — before they go house-hunting. Aware of what they can afford to buy, based on what they can afford to borrow, Ian and Linda can negotiate a deal from a position of strength. While the offer to purchase likely will still be made "conditional on financing" (to allow the lender to give formal mortgage approval), the likelihood of Ian and Linda losing the deal is virtually eliminated, since the mortgage financing is in place once a house is found.

What's best about the pre-approved mortgage? It's available at no cost, and with no obligation. If Ian and Linda buy a house and use the mortgage funds, great. If not, they've lost nothing.

Not only that, but a pre-approved mortgage caps the interest rate for between 60 days and 90 days, depending on the lender. And most lenders will also give borrowers the benefit of a rate drop during that time, too. So if rates go up, the rate is fixed. And if rates fall, the borrower pays the lower rate on closing.

Some lenders really embellish the product, giving qualified applicants a pre-approval certificate or wallet-sized card, stating how large a mortgage can be arranged. Usually, only two conditions are attached to the pre-approval: a) that the credit information be verified; and b) that the lender receive a satisfactory appraisal of the property once it is bought. But even when borrowers are pre-approved for a mortgage, there's nothing to stop them from looking elsewhere for a mortgage, and getting pre-approved there if that lender offers better terms.

Pre-approved mortgages are a reflection of the highly

competitive mortgage market in Canada. And they are an important marketing tool lenders use to generate new business. But unlike most marketing concepts, this idea really benefits borrowers.

When buyers are shopping for a pre-approved mortgage, an important question to ask is: for how long is the quoted rate good? Pre-approved mortgages typically have very short rate-guarantee periods, the 60 to 90 days mentioned earlier. To keep that rate, Ian and Linda must find a home, sign a contract and close the deal all within that time, or else the committed rate is lost.

What do lenders consider, in pre-approving borrowers like Ian and Linda for a mortgage? The property and the borrowers.

"Conventional" mortgages are limited to 75% of the lesser of a) the sale price and b) the appraised value of the property. This "loan-to-value" ratio (what's being borrowed, compared to the value of the house) means that for a conventional first mortgage, Ian and Linda must have at least 25% equity (their own money) in the property. For a property purchased for $160,000, the largest conventional first mortgage possible will be 75% of that figure, or $120,000. The other 25%, or $40,000, must come from their own resources.

Calculating how large a conventional mortgage can be arranged is quite simple. Assuming that the purchase price is the appraised value, just multiply by three the money set aside as a downpayment. So a $35,000 downpayment will allow a conventional mortgage of $105,000 to be arranged, for a total purchase price of $140,000. If the mortgage needed to purchase the house does not exceed that figure, the property value test has been passed.

What if Ian and Linda can't pay 25% of the purchase price on closing? This doesn't mean they can't buy a house. Instead, something different must be done. They can either a) arrange one first mortgage for 75% of the purchase price and a second mortgage for the balance of the required loan, or b) arrange one large "high-ratio" mortgage for the total amount needed (even though it exceeds 75% of the appraised value), with mortgage payment insurance. (Bothered by the stigma associated with the term "high-ratio," some lenders now call these "low downpayment mortgages.") This mortgage insurance, which protects the lender if Ian and Linda default, is available from CMHC (Canada Mortgage and Housing Corporation), a government agency, or GE Capital Mortgage Insurance Canada, a private insurer. Both methods require Ian and Linda to bear extra costs — either the set-up charges and higher interest rate on the second mortgage, or the insurance premium on the high-ratio mortgage. And Ian and Linda must have good incomes, too, to compensate for the smaller-than-normal downpayment.

High-ratio mortgage payment insurance is available for up to 90% of the purchase price. But it doesn't come cheap. Where the loan-to-value ratio is between 75% and 80%, the insurance premium is 1.25% of the entire amount of the mortgage (not just the portion that exceeds 75% of the purchase price). From 80% to 85%, it's 2% of the total mortgage amount. And between 85% and 90%, the cost of the mortgage insurance premium is 2.5% of the total mortgage amount. In Ontario, this insurance premium is subject to 8% provincial sales tax, too. While borrowers can pay the insurance premium directly on closing, most choose to add it on to the amount borrowed, and pay it off gradually over time.

First-time buyers — or anyone who hasn't been a home owner the last five years — can qualify for a mortgage of up to 95% of the purchase price under CMHC's First Home Loan Insurance Program, better known as the "5% down" program. That means Ian and Linda could purchase their first home with just 5% down, and pay just one interest rate on the whole mortgage.

The maximum eligible house price for participants in the First Home Loan Insurance Program varies across Canada. For greater Toronto and Vancouver, it's $250,000. In many other areas with high house prices (plus northern Canada), the maximum is $175,000. Elsewhere the limit is $125,000. Banks, trust companies, credit unions and caisse populaires can inform prospective buyers/borrowers which price range applies in any particular area, together with any other relevant conditions.

Two or more people who buy a home together can qualify for 95% financing, even if one has owned a home during the last five years. Unlike other incentive programs, spousal status is irrelevant. Bill owned a house until last year, and sold it when he married Judy, who has never owned a house. Because she didn't own a house the last five years, she and Bill can together apply for 95% financing.

Discretionary exceptions to the five-year rule are possible, too, for former home owners in hardship situations. Examples are: marital breakup (including common-law relationships); job relocation; and loss of equity on the sale of a home. In all cases, though, the net equity from the home being sold must be re-invested in the new home.

Besides the property, lenders also need to know more about Ian and Linda, the prospective borrowers: their financial background, and if they have gross annual incomes large enough and sufficiently stable to repay the mortgage. As with any loan application, lenders want a personal net worth statement consisting of a detailed list of assets and liabilities (what is owned and what is owed), sources of income, employment particulars, income information (usually verified by a "salary letter" from an employer or an income tax return), and credit references. A credit check then follows, to verify the information provided. Most likely an "equity letter" from their bank will be needed, too, confirming that sufficient money is available to pay the balance of the purchase price on closing. Once that letter is available, a copy of the accepted Offer to Purchase must be forwarded to the bank, too. In back-to-back transactions, where a sale and a purchase are involved, copies of both accepted offers will be needed, plus a statement verifying the balance owing on the current mortgage, to help establish the equity in the existing home. This combination of proposed mortgage, net-sale proceeds and buyer's own resources will provide the needed funds to close the purchase.

In looking at borrowers like Ian and Linda, lenders first consider how much of their gross annual family income can be applied to "mortgage expenses" — the monthly mortgage payment (principal and interest), plus taxes and heating, and 50% of the monthly condominium maintenance fee (if applicable). The generally accepted rule is that these items should not exceed 30% of a borrower's gross annual income. Occasionally that number is up to 32%. This is the gross debt service, or GDS, ratio.

Another calculation, the total debt service, or TDS, ratio,

compares the percentage of gross annual family income needed to service all debt payments — GDS expenses plus items like credit card, personal loan, and car loan. Depending on the lender, TDS payments should not exceed 40% to 42% of gross annual income. Most lenders adhere quite strictly to these rules.

In 1997 CMHC tightened its mortgage insurance requirements. No more than 32% of gross family income can now be applied to principal, interest, taxes, heating and 50% of condo fees (if applicable). And total debt load can't exceed 40% of gross family income.

Any financial gifts (i.e., from family members) must be in hand at least 30 days *before* an offer is signed. And borrowers must be able to cover at least 1.5% of the purchase price as closing costs — either in cash or by including it in their total debt calculation, repayable in a year.

Finally, participants in the First Home Loan Insurance Program must be able to qualify for a mortgage at the current five-year rate, and choose a minimum term of three years.

Quite often, parents lend a financial hand to help adult children buy a home. How that "help" is structured can have significantly varied legal consequences.

Ross and wife Phoebe have decided to turn to Ross's parents, Joey and Monica, for help with their downpayment. That prompts the question, is that "help" a gift or a family loan? What's the difference? Loans must be repaid, but not gifts. If it's an outright gift, Ross and Phoebe won't have to pay back any money.

If Joey and Monica opt for a family loan, the next question is, how should it be arranged? As a promissory note or a mortgage? Both are legally binding agreements, but only a mortgage creates a lien against Ross and Phoebe's home, by being registered against the title to their property.

Whatever loan route is chosen, what will be the interest rate and term? Will they be fixed? Or will the note/mortgage be "non-interest-bearing demand"? "Non-interest-bearing" means the lender foregoes any interest on the loan. Effectively that is what Joey and Monica are gifting to Ross and Phoebe, the interest on the loan each year. However, the capital stays protected, with Ross and Phoebe legally on the hook to repay it at some future date.

And by making it "demand," Joey and Monica can call in the note/mortgage at any time and for any reason. That's important in case Ross and Phoebe separate or divorce, they have a falling out with Joey and Monica, or Joey and Monica need the money because of a death or illness. Ross and Phoebe must then repay the loan to Joey and Monica (or their estate).

All this assumes Joey and Monica have ready cash to help Ross and Phoebe buy that house. If not, can Ross's parents still help out?

Yes. One way is to guarantee Ross and Phoebe's mortgage (what most people call "co-signing" a mortgage). But that means more than just Joey and Monica covering the mortgage payments if Ross and Phoebe default. It's also a commitment by Joey and Monica to perform all other mortgage clauses, from insuring the property to paying the taxes.

The other alternative is for Joey and Monica to book a mortgage on their home and then re-loan the money to Ross and Phoebe to complete their purchase. Plain and simple, this option is very, very risky.

As Joey and Monica will derive no direct benefit from the mortgage, they will need independent legal advice before any funds are advanced. How can Joey and Monica protect themselves if they borrow and re-lend? By insisting on an identical mortgage against Ross and Phoebe's home as the mortgage on their home. Nothing else — not even a promissory note — will do. Why? Because only a mortgage provides security for the repayment of a loan. If Ross and Phoebe simply sign a note and later default on it or go bankrupt, Joey and Monica may have trouble recovering what's owing from Ross and Phoebe. Yet Joey and Monica would be stuck with the mortgage against their own home. With a mortgage (or lien) against Ross and Phoebe's home, Joey and Monica would be in a much better position to recover what's owing to them and use that money to repay what they borrowed from the bank.

When getting family help to buy a house, remember to put it all in writing. Usually that means involving your lawyer to do the necessary paperwork. Any misunderstanding could ruin a family — and not just financially.

Besides investigating the issue of mortgage financing, buyers keen on knowing early on how large a property they can afford to purchase, should follow this practical three-step approach.

1. Start by looking at your total available downpayment. A small portion of it will be paid as a deposit when an offer is signed, the rest being paid on closing. Remember to leave enough money — perhaps 2% of the anticipated purchase price — to cover the many closing costs described in Chapter 23. Then see how large a property can be bought with a conventional mortgage, simply by multiplying the available downpayment by four. Any higher purchase price will necessitate arranging a high-ratio mortgage or a second mortgage.

    Eric and Marla have $35,000 available for a downpayment. By arranging a conventional mortgage, they could afford to pay $140,000 for a home ($35,000 times 4). By comparison, if Eric and Marla decided to arrange a "high-ratio" mortgage for 80% of the purchase price, that $35,000 (i.e., 20% downpayment) would allow them to buy a house worth $175,000.

2. Next, carefully examine what it will cost to "carry" the house each month. Two types of operating costs exist: the debt service costs described earlier, and the ongoing "carrying" costs for a home — hydro, water, heating, telephone, cable TV, insurance and property taxes. While the cost of these items will vary in different areas of the country (and depending on actual usage, too), information is available by calling the utilities involved and your insurance agent. Or it can be obtained from friends and relatives who are home owners. Or from the vendor of a particular home. A phone call to the municipal tax department will reveal the realty taxes payable for a particular property, and how often they are due (semi-annually, quarterly, or in six or more instalments).

    The cost of maintenance and repairs varies widely for resale homes. Factors include a house's age, the current degree of wear and tear, and the desire to change the "look" of the house after closing. What's the best source of information about the cost of maintenance, repairs and upgrades? The home inspector discussed in chapter 14.

Don't forget about other ongoing costs: lawn and grounds care; snow removal; appliance repairs; and furnace and chimney cleaning. In condominium projects, some of these ongoing expenses are included in the monthly common expense (maintenance) fee.

Using the chart below as a guide, record the estimated annual operating costs for different properties you find appealing.

ADDRESS OF PROPERTY			
Hydro			
Water			
Heating			
Telephone			
Cable TV			
Insurance			
Property Taxes			
Maintenance/Repairs			

The link between the size of a mortgage and a borrower's gross annual income means that the same question can be asked two different ways. How large a mortgage can be supported by the borrower's gross annual income? How large must the borrower's gross annual income be, to support a certain-sized mortgage?

Eric and Marla have combined gross annual incomes totalling $50,000. They are not buying a condominium. To learn how much of that income can be applied each month towards GDS items — the monthly mortgage payment (principal and interest), taxes and heating — Eric and Marla divide their gross incomes by 40. That means up to $1,250 ($50,000 divided by 40) can be applied towards GDS charges. Assuming the tax component is $150 monthly and the heating is $75 a month, Eric and Marla still have $1,025 a month to pay towards the mortgage. How large a mortgage they can arrange now depends on the interest rate payable. The following chart shows the amount to be paid per month for each $1,000 borrowed, amortized over 25 years. (These are known as "interest factors.")

Interest Rate	$ per Thousand	Interest Rate	$ per Thousand
4.5	5.53	7.5	7.32
4.75	5.67	7.75	7.47
5	5.82	8	7.63
5.25	5.96	8.25	7.79
5.5	6.10	8.5	7.95
5.75	6.25	8.75	8.12
6	6.40	9	8.28
6.25	6.55	9.25	8.44
6.5	6.70	9.5	8.61
6.75	6.85	9.75	8.78
7	7.00	10	8.94
7.25	7.16	10.25	9.11

By dividing the amount available for the monthly mortgage payment ($1,025) by the figure for any given interest rate, Eric and Marla can immediately learn how large a mortgage they can afford to carry at that interest rate. For example, if the current mortgage rate for the term selected was 6.5%, dividing $1,025 by 6.7 shows that Eric and Marla could handle a mortgage of approximately $152,985. Repeating this approach for 6% and 7% indicates that mortgages of $160,155 and $146,425 respectively could be booked at those interest rates. As these examples illustrate, the lower the interest rate, the larger the possible mortgage.

With a $35,000 downpayment and gross incomes of $50,000, Eric and Marla could easily arrange a conventional mortgage of $105,000, allowing them to purchase a home for $140,000. If they decided to go "high-ratio," that downpayment and their gross incomes would allow Eric and Marla to purchase a home for a "maximum price" between $195,155 and $181,425, depending on where the interest rate was between 6% and 7%.

There's also a "quick and dirty" way for buyers to learn

early if their gross incomes will qualify to service a mortgage. This fast method involves doing the calculations backwards. Instead of considering how large a mortgage could be arranged, based on the borrower's gross income, ask the following question: how large a gross income is needed to carry a specific mortgage? To answer that question, first add together the monthly mortgage payment (principal and interest) amortized over 25 years, one-twelfth of the estimated taxes, the monthly heating cost and half the monthly condominium maintenance payment (if applicable). Then multiply the total by 40. If your gross income(s) exceed this figure, the GDS ratio is satisfied. It's that simple.

Once the appropriate rate is selected, Eric and Marla should multiply the figure by the amount of the mortgage to be arranged, in thousands of dollars. In Eric and Marla's case, they considered a $150,000 mortgage at 6.5%. By multiplying 6.7 by 150, they calculated the approximate monthly payment to be $1,005. The monthly taxes and heating, remember, were $150 and $75 respectively. Therefore the gross annual family income needed to qualify for a conventional mortgage, using the GDS ratio, was ($1,005 plus $150 plus $75) times 40, or $49,200. As their gross income was $50,000, Eric and Marla had pre-qualified themselves for a mortgage.

3.   After doing all this, Eric and Marla should reduce that maximum price by at least 5%, to establish the maximum price range mentioned earlier. The calculated "maximum price" becomes the upper end of the limit, while the "adjusted" figure becomes the lower end of the range and the target price. This gives Eric and Marla some room to manoeuvre and still stay within budget.

To carry a conventional mortgage, Eric and Marla would argue that the highest price they can afford to pay is the adjusted figure at the lower end of the range, namely $133,000 ($140,000 less 5%). Knowing (but concealing) that the true maximum price they can afford to pay is $140,000, Eric and Marla can negotiate with peace of mind, even if the purchase price begins creeping towards the $140,000 threshold. They also know that $140,000 figure can be exceeded, depending on the interest rate, while still qualifying for a mortgage, if they are prepared to book a high-ratio mortgage. By doing just a few minutes of homework, Eric and Marla have discovered the maximum price range that is appropriate for them.

To determine the maximum you can carry, complete the following chart. Eric and Marla's completed chart is given as an example.

WHAT CAN ERIC AND MARLA AFFORD TO BUY?

STEP 1   Maximum Downpayment Available $35,000

STEP 2   Determine the upper end of the range:

Gross Annual Income ÷ 40 =	Gross Monthly Payment *(GDS)*	
$50,000	÷ 40 =	$1,250
Less: 1/12th of annual taxes		$150
Less: monthly heating cost		$75
Maximum monthly amount available		
for principal and interest payments		$1,025

Divide this figure by the interest factor on pages 36–37 to calculate the Maximum Mortgage available at various interest rates, in thousands (e.g., at 6.5%, it's $1,025 ÷ 6.7, or $152,985).

Therefore, at x%, the Maximum Purchase Price (the upper end of the range) = Maximum Downpayment Available + Maximum Mortgage.

At 6%, the Maximum Mortgage is $1,025 ÷ 6.4, or $160,155; the Maximum Purchase Price is $35,000 + $160,155, or $195,155.

At 6.5%, the Maximum Mortgage is $1,025 ÷ 6.7, or $152,985; the Maximum Purchase Price is $35,000 + $152,985, or $187,985.

At 7%, the Maximum Mortgage is $1,025 ÷ 7.0, or $146,425; the Maximum Purchase Price is $35,000 + $146,425, or $181,425.

STEP 3   To determine the lower end of the range (the target price), reduce the Maximum Purchase Price for any given interest rate by 5%:

At x%, upper end of range is $_____		while lower end of range is $_____
At 6%	$195,155	$185,395
At 6.5%	$187,985	$178,585
At 7%	$181,425	$172,350

WHAT CAN I AFFORD TO BUY?

STEP 1   Maximum Downpayment Available $_____

STEP 2   Determine the upper end of the range:
Gross Annual Income ÷ 40 = Gross Monthly Payment
$_____   ÷ 40 = $_____
Less: 1/12th of annual taxes $_____
Less: monthly heating cost $_____
Maximum monthly amount available
for principal and interest payments $_____

Divide this figure by the interest factor on pages 36–37 to calculate the Maximum Mortgage available at various interest rates, in thousands (e.g., at 6.5%, it's $1,025 ÷ 6.7, or $152,985).

At _____%, the Maximum Mortgage is $_____
At _____%, the Maximum Mortgage is $_____
At _____%, the Maximum Mortgage is $_____

Therefore, the Maximum Purchase Price (the upper end of the range) = Maximum Downpayment Available + Maximum Mortgage.

At ____%, $_____ + $_____   = $_____
At ____%, $_____ + $_____   = $_____
At ____%, $_____ + $_____   = $_____

STEP 3   To determine the lower end of the range (the target price), reduce the Maximum Purchase Price for any given interest rate by 5%:

At x%, upper end of   while lower end
     range is $_____   of range is $_____
At ____% $_____ $_____
At ____% $_____ $_____
At ____% $_____ $_____

One final thought about mortgage financing. Smart purchasers will stay away from buying a principal residence with "nothing down," that is, financing the entire purchase price with a mortgage. Assuming the purchase price is $140,000, that sum must come from somewhere: cash, mortgage or a combination of both. The mix might be $100,000 mortgages and $40,000 cash, $125,000 mortgages and $15,000 cash, or $140,000 mortgages and $0 cash down. If they did not invest any of their own money on closing, what would keep a purchaser attached to the property? Some people argue that a purchaser who buys with nothing down has nothing to lose by abandoning the property. Not so. Walking away from a home when prices are falling is not all that easy in most provinces. And it doesn't solve the borrower's problems, either. Lenders have the right to sue the borrower for any shortfall if the balance owing on the mortgage exceeds the value of the property. (This right to sue for a shortfall of funds does not exist in Alberta.) Whatever may be the merit in buying investment property with no downpayment, it has no place when buying an owner-occupied home.

9
The Home Buyers' Plan

For years, the federal government has offered incentive programs to first-time buyers. In the 1970s and 1980s, it was the RHOSP — the Registered Home Ownership Savings Program.

In February 1992, to stimulate lethargic real estate markets across Canada, Ottawa introduced the Home Buyers' Plan, or HBP, the technical name for what many call the "RRSP program." It originally allowed everyone — first-time buyers and move-up buyers — to borrow up to $20,000 tax-free and interest-free from their registered retirement savings plans to help buy or build a home. After 35 years (RRSPs having first come to Canada in 1957), the federal government finally recognized a link between RRSPs and home ownership: that a home is the cornerstone of any retirement plan.

Originally just a one-year program, it was given a one-year reprieve in late 1992. The 1994 federal budget extended the HBP, but at the same time cleaned up some of its inconsistencies and limited the program to first-time home buyers only.

Knowing whether to use the program, and how, could be the difference between making a monthly payment to a lender or a landlord.

Who can participate in the HBP? Only first-time home buyers, which includes anyone who hasn't owned a home they occupied as a principal residence in the previous five years (including the year of withdrawal). So if Tom withdraws funds from his RRSP in 1997 under the HBP, he cannot have owned his owner-occupied home at any time in 1993, 1994, 1995 or 1996. In addition, you can only participate in the program once in your lifetime. And how much can be borrowed from your own RRSP this way? Up to $20,000 per person, with no collateral for the loan, and no withholding tax. Participating is easy; just complete a simple form with your RRSP carrier. But make sure the funds are being removed from your RRSP under the Home Buyers' Plan, and not as a normal RRSP withdrawal.

How that five-year waiting period and the rules on spouses mesh is very complex. Can one spouse participate in the HBP as a first-time buyer if the other spouse is or was a home owner? The answer depends on who lived in the home owned by the spouse the last five years. (By the way, the definition of "spouse" isn't limited to just legally married couples. It includes a person of the opposite sex who, at that particular time, is living with you in a common-law relationship and i) is your child's natural or adoptive parent, or ii) has lived together with you for at least 12 straight months.)

If your spouse owned a home in the last five years that both of you occupied while spouses, neither qualifies as a first-time buyer. Chandler and Rachel are spouses. Rachel owned a home within the last five years where both she and Chandler lived while spouses. Therefore, neither qualifies as a first-time buyer.

But if your spouse owned and occupied a home in the last five years that you didn't occupy, you are a first-time buyer, but not your spouse. Elaine owned and occupied a home during the last five years, but spouse Jerry never lived there. So Jerry qualifies as a first-time buyer for HBP purposes, but not Elaine.

If neither spouse has been a home owner within the last five years, the HBP effectively allows married couples and many common-law couples to borrow up to $40,000 from their RRSP, tax-free and interest-free, when buying or building a house.

What types of properties qualify under the HBP? What you expect: resale homes and brand-new homes; single-family homes, semi-detached homes, freehold townhomes, mobile homes and condominium units (apartments and townhouses); apartments in duplexes, triplexes and fourplexes; together with a share in an equity co-op and co-ownership, provided it also entitles you to possess a specific unit. With one proviso. It must be located in Canada. Condos in the U.S. don't qualify. In addition, you must be a Canadian resident when participating in the HBP.

Funds can only be withdrawn if you have entered into a written agreement to buy or build a qualifying home. That means RRSP funds won't likely be used as a deposit, although they could be used as a second deposit once the contract has been signed and accepted. In most cases money withdrawn under the HBP will be withdrawn and used for closing, reducing the amount needed on a mortgage.

Charlie bought a house for $150,000. Having paid a $5,000 deposit, he plans to pay another $10,000 on closing. To finance his purchase, Charlie will have to arrange a mortgage for $135,000. However, if Charlie borrows $7,000 from his RRSP, that will cut the size of his mortgage from $135,000 to $128,000, lowering his monthly carrying cost for the house, too.

For funds withdrawn in one year, the purchase transaction must close (or the new house be habitable) by September 30 the following year. That should not be too difficult to attain. Most participants will withdraw the funds in the days before closing, and not before, to maximize the time the funds earn tax-free interest within the RRSP. And the property must become your principal residence within a year after closing/it being habitable. Again, this is more of a technicality than an issue.

Money withdrawn under the HBP doesn't have to be used directly to buy or build the qualifying property. Provided all the criteria are satisfied, the funds can be used for other purposes. So if Joel withdraws $5,000 from his RRSP under the HBP, that money does not have to be paid directly towards his purchase price. Joel can use other funds for the closing and apply the withdrawn $5,000 towards his closing costs, or spend it on paint, wallpaper, appliances and home furnishings — if he meets all the HBP withdrawal criteria.

One of the key changes introduced in 1994 is that funds must be on deposit in your RRSP at least 90 days before they can be withdrawn under the HBP — a key restriction. However, this also provides a fantastic opportunity for first-time buyers to generate a hefty housewarming gift from the federal government, if they already have their downpayment funds in place, as described below.

Participants are given a lengthy period of time — 15 years — to repay funds withdrawn under the HBP. Since annual repayments of at least 1/15th of the amount borrowed must begin in the second calendar year after the funds are withdrawn, and continue until the loan is fully retired, effectively there is a two-year "grace period" before the first repayment is due. So if Liz withdraws $15,000 in 1997, her first repayment of $1,000 (1/15th of $15,000) is due in 1999. Just like with RRSP contributions, however, Ottawa will allow the HBP repayments to be made in the first 60 days of the following year. Therefore, Liz effectively has until March 1, 2000, to make her first $1,000 repayment, for the year 1999. Each year after that, Liz must pay a minimum of $1,000 towards the RRSP loan until the year 2013 (actually, March 1, 2014). Considering how long people are given to repay the RRSP loan, how it will help them get into a house sooner, and how it will cut their monthly carrying cost, most participants don't get too alarmed over such a long payback period.

What's the penalty for not repaying the required amount each year? The shortfall gets added onto your taxable income.

Provided that at least the required amount is repaid to the RRSP in any given year, normal contributions can also be made to your RRSP in that same year, even if a balance is still owing under the HBP. In other words, it's not necessary to fully retire the RRSP loan under the HBP before making further contributions to your RRSP. Norman's required annual payback is $800. If he contributes $2,800 to his RRSP this year (his authorized limit being well above that), $800 will go towards the HBP repayment for that year, with the other $2,000 being a normal RRSP contribution.

Of course, Norman could decide to repay more to his RRSP than the minimum amount. If he chooses that option, Norman should designate in his tax return for that year how much more money is going towards his RRSP loan than would otherwise be the case. That will reduce Norman's annual repayment for later years, too.

An interesting strategy is to use RRSP funds under the HBP

to cut the cost of CMHC/GE Capital mortgage insurance. Ernie is buying a home for $150,000 with $20,000 down. Because Ernie's loan-to-value ratio exceeds 85%, his mortgage insurance premium is 2.5% of the mortgage, or $3,250. However, if Ernie borrows $2,500 from his RRSP under the Home Buyers' Plan (leaving a mortgage of $127,500), his loan-to-value ratio drops to 85%, and the insurance premium drops to 2%, or $2,550. A net savings for Ernie of $700, simply by bringing his loan-to-value ratio into a lower threshold using RRSP funds under the HBP.

Many financial commentators have criticized the HBP for allowing funds to be removed from an RRSP for up to 17 years, losing the tax-free compounding of interest during that time. This is a very valid concern. But a way exists to generate "free money" from the federal government, without in any way affecting the money in your RRSP. The key to success is that 90-day waiting period discussed earlier.

How, and why? Cheryl is a first-time home buyer. Her $10,000 downpayment is sitting idle, languishing in a low-rate savings account until she buys a house. Cheryl also has more than $10,000 in "unused RRSP contribution room," not having contributed the maximum to her RRSP in past years. (To learn this, Cheryl called Revenue Canada's TIPS — Tax Information Phone Service — line.) And Cheryl plans to buy her first home within the next four to six months. So Cheryl will put that $10,000 of downpayment money into her RRSP now. Because she is taking advantage of unused contribution room, the money Cheryl already has on deposit in her RRSP won't be affected or removed. And her contribution limit for this year will remain intact, too.

Just before closing (at least 90 days after the money is deposited), Cheryl withdraws the $10,000 under the HBP and uses it on closing as her downpayment. To finance the home purchase, Cheryl books a $100,000 mortgage. Assume that her average interest rate over the 25-year amortization is 8% and her combined federal/provincial marginal tax rate (payable on the last dollar of earned income) is 40% — the rate for net incomes between roughly $30,000 and $50,000.

That $10,000 RRSP contribution means a $10,000 tax deduction against Cheryl's income this year, and a $4,000 tax refund on this year's tax return (to be filed next April). Not too bad, considering the downpayment money was already set aside for Cheryl's purchase.

If Cheryl prepays that $4,000 towards her mortgage on its first anniversary next year, her overall interest expense falls by $19,815. Fantastic.

However, interest on a mortgage arranged to finance the purchase of a home isn't tax-deductible in Canada. Therefore, Cheryl's real savings is the pre-tax income needed to pay that $19,815 interest. In her 40% tax bracket, Cheryl must earn $33,025 at work, and pay a whopping $13,210 in tax, to be left with the $19,815 for the interest expense. That, of course, is the real impact of Cheryl's following this program.

Imagine: Cheryl can save almost a year's salary simply by parking her $10,000 downpayment — her own money — in her RRSP for at least 90 days via unused RRSP room, withdrawing it under the HBP, and using it to buy her first home!

Of course, Cheryl will have to repay $666.67 annually for 15 years towards her RRSP loan under the HBP, starting the second calendar year after her purchase closes. But she finds that to be a pittance, compared to this savings.

Let's recap. By temporarily shuffling her $10,000 downpayment money from a bank account into her RRSP for a minimum of 90 days via unused contribution room, Cheryl a) got a $10,000 tax deduction, b) got a $4,000 tax refund, c) cut her mortgage-interest expense by $19,815, and d) effectively "earned" $33,025 income — all at absolutely no cost. And remember, Cheryl didn't touch any of her money already in her RRSP, silencing the critics of the HBP. A very powerful strategy indeed.

At one time, a number of financial commentators touted how first-time buyers could purchase a home with no downpayment, using the HBP. Essentially they would borrow $20,000 on an unsecured loan, contribute the money to their RRSP, buy a house with closing at least 90 days off, withdraw the funds just before closing, pay off the bank loan, and use the tax refund generated (usually between $6,000 and $8,000) as the downpayment. If the refund was unavailable on closing, it too would be loaned to the home buyer, unsecured.

Those days are over. In early 1997, Canada Mortgage and Housing Corporation (which insures the mortgage financing first-time buyers need, often up to 95% of the purchase price) decided to clamp down on this "flip" arrangement. And rightly so, since home buyers are unwittingly taking on $20,000 of additional debt — the $20,000 that must be repaid to the RRSP over 15 years — even though the $20,000 bank loan was retired on closing.

CMHC-insured mortgages will only be granted to first-time buyers using "tax refund downpayments" if i) the personal loan for the RRSP contribution that spawned that tax refund was secured (i.e., no more unsecured $20,000 loans), and ii) the tax refund is available in-hand on closing. (Bridge loans are allowed until the tax refund is received, if properly secured.) So don't try borrowing money, to contribute to an RRSP, that would spawn a tax refund which would become your downpayment. It's a no-no.

If you're a first-time home buyer, carefully read and re-read this chapter to see if you qualify to participate in the Home Buyers' Plan. Using RRSP funds under the program may help you buy a home. Parking downpayment funds in an RRSP short-term could help you begin paying off your mortgage financing with that "free money" from the federal government.

10
Know the Community and Neighborhood

By now, prospective purchasers developing their own unique HOBS will have clearly defined needs and wants, and a sound understanding of what is affordable. Yet it is still premature to contact a real estate agent to go house-hunting. Buyers must first decide which of the many communities and neighborhoods they find inviting, and "get a feel" for house prices and values in those neighborhoods. Keep in mind that often there is a trade-off between price and amenities, lower-priced homes having fewer of the positive amenities (or perhaps several of the negative ones).

In real estate, the most important factor in buying a house is location, location and location. Obviously, a major component of a home-buying strategy is to select a property in the best possible location. But each of the above references to "location" has a specific meaning: community — the overall area where a buyer wants to live; neighborhood — smaller areas within a community, each with its own distinctive look, characteristics and charm; and site — the particular house being bought.

"Location, location, location" also describes the selection process most people follow when buying a house. Generally a community is selected first. Then the choice is narrowed down to a particular neighborhood within that community, containing its most desirable features. And finally the actual home is chosen. Issues to consider in selecting a community and a neighborhood are explored in this chapter. Features that affect the house itself are examined in chapter 18.

A community and neighborhood must reflect a buyer's own unique lifestyle and status in life. If unacquainted with appropriate areas, buyers applying their HOBS should spend some time driving or walking in and through the communities and neighborhoods that are appealing. Before proceeding any further, ask yourself: What kind of "gut feeling" did they generate? Did you like what you saw? What does it offer, compared to other areas? Is it well maintained? Would you like to be part of it?

If possible, go back at a different time during the week, on both a weekday and the weekend, and travel through those communities and neighborhoods by both day and night. Areas tend to take on a different character in the dark, both visually and audibly. With noise travelling much further at night, what is considered acceptable by day could be intolerable at night. Do the streets appear adequately lit? Do they appear safe and serene at night? To learn more about those communities and neighborhoods, stop and talk with some local residents. Who better to tell you what an area is really like?

For those communities and neighborhoods that pass this preliminary hurdle, examine them more thoroughly against the following factors. How each is ranked and weighted will differ from buyer to buyer. Yet each feature should be considered from both an objective as well as a personal point of view. Resale potential and market appeal of a home should never be overlooked, as not everyone views the strengths and weaknesses of a location the same way. The fewer the negative factors, the greater its future marketability. And remember: a positive feature can often be a negative, if that amenity is located too close to the home you're considering buying.

Older vs. Newer Communities

It is amazing how people's opinions are polarized in the ongoing debate between older and newer communities. Well-kept established areas exhibit a certain maturity, charm and character. The impression generated is laid-back and relaxed. By contrast, a newly developed community projects a feeling and image of freshness, vitality and youthfulness in its outward appearance. Older communities have a complete list of the facilities most residents need — schools, community centres, transportation links (transit and roads), support services (from libraries to day-care centres, youth and sports organizations), hospitals and, of course, shopping. Because their development takes time, these facilities may be lacking when residents in newer or outlying areas first move in. It's part of the non-monetary "price" associated with living in a developing area. Community and neighborhood services are like the trees that line the street. Both take many years to develop and mature.

While most resale homes are located in older areas, they aren't sold there exclusively. Resale homes appear in newer communities, too, as brand-new homes start to change hands just years after being built.

Proximity to Work and Conveniences

Access to and within a community is of crucial importance to most people. Not everyone wants to be a commuter. The difference between a half-hour trip and a one-hour trip (one-way) to work every day is over 10 whole days each year. Less time spent commuting to work means more time to spend with family and friends or enjoying the other pleasures of life. Commuter communities, though, are generally more reasonably priced, being somewhat distant from the hub of activity.

Before deciding to move to a suburban community, George and Pauline did a "test run" to see how long would be needed to travel to work in peak rush hour. They also learned how long a trip to the city centre would take off-hours. By checking this out ahead of time, George and Pauline did not face any surprises the first day they headed to work after moving.

Transportation

Public transportation is much more readily available in built-up areas than in newer communities. This is an important consideration for families with one car. Nonexistent, irregular or limited transit service can be very inconvenient. Residents in newer areas should never rely too heavily on the projected date for new transit routes to begin or existing lines to be extended in terms of distances and frequency of service. Even rush-hour service is only inaugurated when warranted. If public transit is available, check out how often it runs, especially at night and on weekends. Is an extra fare payable?

Given our harsh Canadian climate, consider how far is the walk to the nearest transit or commuter stop. One kilometre is probably the farthest anyone would want to walk in the worst winter storm! Also look at the network of roads in the general area. How close is the nearest highway or expressway? While many people want to be close to a major thoroughfare, they don't want to live "that close." Will noise and pollution be a factor? Is an interchange located nearby or planned? Is an expansion of the road system projected for the immediate future?

Schools

Education is a high priority for almost every home buyer. That means investigating the availability and proximity of schools — primary and secondary, public and separate. With the construction of schools lagging behind the development of newer communities, busing children to school often is a necessity. This is rarely a concern when buying a resale home, since the schools by then are well established. The school system itself should not be ignored, either, as it varies considerably from area to area. Different types of programs are offered (e.g., French immersion or services for the disabled) depending on the local board of education. As part of your HOBS, check out all aspects of a community's educational system early, to see if it can accommodate any special needs

Schools are another one of those concurrent positives/ negatives. Being close to a school is a real advantage. But do you want to live right next door to a school?

Shopping

Different classes of commercial development exist within a community. Large regional malls and plazas, generally commuter-oriented, are built to service the entire community. Intermediate-sized plazas, which are both commuter- and pedestrian-oriented, have smaller trading areas. Neighborhood or convenience shopping also exists, to satisfy local shopping needs.

Just a short trip through both an older and a newer community will illustrate how commercial development lags behind the growth of residential areas. Which comes first, the stores or the people? Until enough residents live in an area to make it economically viable for business to operate, commercial development is virtually nonexistent. That means purchasers of resale homes in newer communities and neighborhoods must travel much further to the types of shops they are accustomed to. When travelling through a community and neighborhood, learn where the different classes of commercial development are located.

Buyers of homes in a smaller community should also learn ahead of time where they can shop. Reflecting the nature of the area, smaller shopping centres predominate. If a large regional mall has been built in the area, learn where, and how long it will take to travel there.

Shopping is one of those features that be both a positive and a negative at the same time. Being close to shopping has its advantages, but being *too* close to shopping is a disadvantage. Traffic congestion, noise and visual pollution (such as loose garbage) may be a problem. Living adjacent to or just near a commercial development, whether large or small, may not bother some people, but it could deter others from buying a specific home. When considering these factors, remember to look at them from two different points of view: in terms of *buying* the property now, and in terms of *selling* it to someone else at a later date.

Support Services

One of the most marked contrasts between established and growing communities exists in the area of support services. Everyone needs a doctor, dentist, druggist, perhaps even a pediatrician. While buyers in older areas know exactly where these services are located, rarely are they in the vanguard of development. Usually these support services are part of the "in-fill" which follows significant residential development.

Adequate police protection, fire stations, day-care centres, ambulance service, nearby hospitals and frequent garbage pick-ups also follow in the wake of residential growth. Residents in newer developments constantly complain about inadequacies in these services, compared to the levels in more established areas. So before making any commitment, check this point out carefully!

Religious Facilities

Being close to religious facilities such as churches, synagogues, temples, mosques and religious schools is important to some people. Religiously oriented neighborhoods sometimes develop in an area, often centred around a religious facility.

Recreational Facilities

Older communities far surpass newer ones in the number of parks, playgrounds, community centres, skating rinks, swimming pools, tennis courts, baseball diamonds, soccer fields, libraries, theatres and museums they have to offer. Residents of newer areas are constantly demanding that high-quality recreational facilities be established in the early years of community growth. The key question, of course, is how to pay for them without overly taxing either the existing residents or new home buyers.

Besides having the above facilities, more established areas offer a full range of clubs and organizations: Cubs and Scouts, Brownies and Girl Guides; baseball clubs; hockey leagues;

soccer clubs; Neighborhood Watch; Block Parents; Parent-Teacher Associations. It's easy to simply "plug in" to these groups. Residents in newer areas become modern-day pioneers, having to form and nurture these associations from scratch.

Other Factors

Many other factors must be examined and considered now, as part of a home-buying strategy, before deciding on a community and neighborhood. These include:

a) Telephone Service — Local calling areas are surprisingly small outside major metropolitan areas. Many people are shocked to learn, following a move, that former local calls are now subject to long-distance tolls.

b) Potential Deterrents — Many homes are located on or near gas stations, railway tracks, apartment buildings, airports, cemeteries or industrial parks. Although these may seem insignificant, do not simply dismiss them as frivolous concerns. Not everyone thinks the same way. What one person chooses to ignore when buying a house could totally dissuade another when making that same decision. Remember that the property being bought now eventually will be sold again. When considering these factors, look at them *objectively* to maximize the resale potential of the property.

Peer Pressure

This is probably the greatest factor which motivates people to consider moving to a specific community and neighborhood. "All our friends are moving there" is a commonly heard cry. People also move to particular areas to have neighbors with similar ethnic, cultural, religious and socio-economic backgrounds, or to live in a "young area" alive with young children. Sometimes the composition of a community is an overwhelming priority.

Be realistic when considering a proposed move. Ask yourself if it makes sense for the right reasons in terms of your needs, wants and ability to pay. Has the proper home-buying strategy been devised first? Will you be buying with your head, rather than your heart? Living with friends and peers in a community or neighborhood may be a pleasant thought, but resist the temptation if it truly cannot be justified.

Before venturing into the marketplace, potential home buyers must become better acquainted with the real estate market in those communities and neighborhoods. Check the ads for homes in the weekend edition of the local newspaper. Call several real estate agents whose phone numbers were noted in those ads, or on "For Sale" signs in front of appealing properties. Ask those agents about the listing price, key features of the property, and what's included in the purchase price. Try to visit several open houses too, not necessarily with a view to buying, but to learn more about prices and values in the area.

Finding the most suitable community and neighborhood will take time. The more you ask, the more you will learn. And that will generate even more questions, helping to refine your decision. With a properly planned HOBS, home buyers will realize when they have located the area that is most appropriate for them. Like love, it may be difficult to describe in words. But when it has been found, you just know it.

To help rate the factors involved in selecting a community and neighborhood, jot down some notes, using the chart below as a guide.

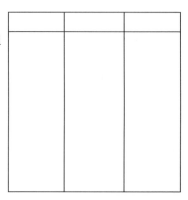

Community/Neighborhood			
Type of community — new or old			
Proximity to work			
Transportation			
Schools			
Shopping			
Support services			
Religious facilities			
Recreational facilities			
Other factors			

With so many decisions already having been made, buyers may think they are ready to rush right in and submit an Offer to Purchase. But not just yet, it's still premature! There's still much more work to be done! The next stage in formulating a HOBS involves contacting the real estate professionals with whom you will work. These are the people who will transform your ideas and your wishes into reality.

11
The Three Real Estate Professionals

The process of selecting and buying a home has become increasingly complex over the years. No one can know all the details and technicalities involved, from the pre-offer stage until the transaction is closed and the deed registered. A key component of the HOBS approach to buying a home includes using the services of three well-qualified real estate professionals, specialists in whom the buyer has total and unqualified trust: a real estate agent, a home inspector, and a lawyer. Simply put, buyers cannot afford to ignore any of these experts. Otherwise, once the money, deed and key change hands on closing, a buyer will have acquired not only the property but also any concealed problems.

The experience and expertise these professionals bring to a real estate transaction cannot be overlooked. Each has an important yet distinct role to play. Real estate agents help locate the right house at the right price for a buyer. Home inspectors carefully examine it, to advise whether it is sound or in need of repair, beyond cosmetics. (Much of real estate is still governed by the law of *caveat emptor*, or "buyer beware." This concept, and the trend away from it, are described in more detail in chapter 18.) Real estate lawyers process the transaction, ensuring that title to the property is transferred properly on closing. Together, these real estate experts can be expected to professionally and objectively guide buyers through a nervous yet extremely exciting time in their lives. The professionals' mandate should be to provide ideas and support where needed, to make the transaction and the transition as smooth and worry-free as possible.

Where do home buyers find a well-qualified real estate agent? Home inspector? Real estate lawyer? These questions will be answered separately in later chapters. While it's the real estate agent who is needed first, remember to contact and choose all three real estate professionals early on, *before* an offer to purchase is signed. Have each available "on standby," ready to move quickly once "the right house" — both suitable and affordable — has been found.

12

Real Estate Agents/Buyer Brokerage

Few people buy a home without using a real estate agent. Choosing the right agent is almost as important as, and is a prerequisite to, selecting the right property. A knowledgeable, sincere agent in whom a buyer has complete confidence will save him or her valuable time and effort while also reducing the headaches that accompany any home purchase.

Real estate agents are licensed salespeople who are paid a commission for being a "matchmaker"; they bring buyers, sellers and homes together. The "seller's" or "listing" agent lists the property for sale on the seller's behalf. It's their sign that appears on the front yard. Helping the buyer find the home, draft and submit the offer and negotiate on the purchaser's behalf is the "buyer's" or "selling" agent. Real estate brokers, on the other hand, are agents who have taken further educational courses and who are licensed to own and operate real estate offices where agents work.

For years, buyers of resale homes automatically assumed that if they and the seller each had their own separate agent, the buyer's agent was "their" agent, legally representing the buyers' interests. Not so. By law, both the seller's agent and the buyer's agent were viewed as representing just the vendor, the buyer's agent being a "sub-agent" to the seller's agent. Why? Because of the archaic conception (misconception, to buyers) that loyalty could only be owed to the person paying the commission, usually the seller. That left real estate purchasers legally exposed and totally confused.

In the late 1980s, "buyer brokerage" (also known as "agency disclosure") swept across the United States. Its premise was simple. Agency relationships should be established by conduct, not payment arrangements. Real estate agents representing a purchaser should be able to pledge their sole allegiance to that party in a transaction.

As of January 1, 1995, buyer brokerage came to Canada, an industry move introduced by the Canadian Real Estate Association, not one legislated by government. Now agents must disclose to buyers, sellers and other agents at the outset exactly who they represent, and get a written acknowledgment of disclosure. Finally, everyone will know exactly who an agent works for. And buyers who opt for buyer brokerage will be owed the same "fiduciary duties" by their agents as sellers have long enjoyed: loyalty, confidentiality, full disclosure and accountability.

What are the three types of agency relationships buyers could face today?

Buyer brokerage.
The new kid on the block. Two different real estate brokers (and therefore two different agents) are involved in a transactions, "one for one." One agent exclusively representing the buyer, another agent exclusively representing the seller. Buyers and sellers sign separate agreements with their agents, outlining the agents' duties and obligations. Buyer brokerage parallels the separate representation that real estate lawyers provide buyers and sellers. Buyer brokerage obviously eliminates the nagging problem of conflict of interest, the well-established principle that "no man can serve two masters."

Carefully review a purchaser agency agreement form before signing it. Unlike the "old" days when buyers could work with more than one agent at the same time, buyers agree to work exclusively with just one agent while the agreement is in effect. In that respect, a purchaser agency agreement is like a listing agreement, which ties the seller to only one agent.

How are buyer brokers paid? Directly by the buyer? Or by the seller's agent from the sale proceeds, as was formerly done? Although both options are acceptable, in most residential transactions the buyer broker is compensated by the listing broker. So despite the introduction of buyer brokerage, the payment of commission is still "business as usual." (If a buyer agrees to pay his or her own agent directly, remember that GST must also be paid on top of the agent's commission.)

Dual agency.
"One for two." Just one real estate broker is involved, representing both buyer and seller. Each party, though, may be working with their own agent in that firm. This situation generally arises when a broker's "office listing" is sold to a buyer, or when two different offices of a large, non-franchised real estate firm are involved in the same transaction. (Agents love selling office listings; they get both sides of the commission, a major reason why many agents are vehemently opposed to the elimination of dual agency.) Because dual agency represents the classic conflict-of-interest situation, the usual duties of confidentiality, full disclosure and total loyalty are impossible.

Dual agency is only allowed when properly disclosed and if a party provides its prior written consent. Often, a preprinted paragraph on the purchaser agency consent form permits dual agency. Whether dual agency should exist is an ongoing debate within the real estate industry. To some agents, the interests of buyers and sellers are so diametrically opposed, no form of disclosure can adequately resolve the problems inherent with conflict of interest. Buyers unwilling to accept dual agency must delete that clause from the purchaser agency consent form.

Sub-agency.
"Two for one." This is the way it was until January 1, 1995. Like with buyer brokerage, two different real estate brokers (and therefore two different agents) are involved in a transaction. But both work for just one party, the seller, the buyer's agent technically being only a sub-agent of the seller's agent. With sub-agency, buyers can do little more than expect their own agent to disclose all relevant information about a property, not misrepresent the facts, and honestly answer questions about a property. That's not much protection for a purchaser. Now that buyer brokerage is here, sub-agency's usefulness — if it ever

had any — is long gone. In some areas of North America, sub-agency has already been outlawed. The sooner it is relegated to the scrap heap of history, the better.

Often the term "co-operating broker" is used. It's a wishy-washy generic term appearing in many offers, broadly referring to the buyer's agent without spelling out its exact legal status (as buyer broker, dual agent or sub-agent).

Where can buyers find a "good" real estate agent? How do buyers new to the market meet agents?

Real estate agents are a service industry. Satisfied customers and the referral business they generate are the cornerstones of every real estate agent's success. Asking friends, family, neighbors and co-workers for the names and phone numbers of agents they have dealt with in the past is an excellent way of finding an agent. Open houses are another route. Agents hold open houses to display the features of a property to other agents and purchasers. Equally important for buyers is the opportunity an open house presents to meet the listing agent for that property. By attending several open houses, prospective buyers can kill two birds with one stone: view the features and learn the values of properties, and at the same time meet and talk with a number of different agents. One of those contacts could well become the buyer's agent on another property.

Another way to meet an agent is by checking the newspaper ads. List the names and phone numbers of agents active in the area where you are looking. Other purchasers will walk or drive through that area and call an agent whose number appears on a number of "For Sale" signs.

Once you have the names of several prospective agents, interview them before choosing one. As with any other type of personal relationship, the "right chemistry" must exist. Ask yourself, does the agent instil confidence in you? Do you have a good rapport with the agent? Do you feel comfortable and at ease with the agent, satisfied that he or she will work in your best interests? Does the agent demonstrate the level of professionalism you expect? What is his or her approach to buying real estate, and is it compatible with yours? Is the agent insistent on your allowing dual agency, or is a buyer brokerage arrangement satisfactory?

Spend time talking with the agent before ever going out to look at properties. Give the agent a copy of your shopping list. The more familiar the agent is with your needs, wants, personal tastes and financial position, the easier it will be for the agent to locate the right house at the right price with the right financing. Once you have selected your agent, you should expect them to:

- Know the market thoroughly, both in general as well as in the proposed neighborhood. Knowing what homes are worth is an agent's job.
- Assist you in selecting a neighborhood and community, if you are new to the area (due to a company transfer, for example).
- Provide you with a market analysis for communities and neighborhoods that interest you, including full details on the price at which comparable properties have sold.
- Know you as thoroughly as the market — to be a good listener who understands your needs and wants, who will help you modify them where necessary, and who appreciates the limitations of your price range. (Remember: the "ideal" house is the one that satisfies all of your needs and as many wants as possible, the property you can best afford to buy and carry each month.)
- Pre-screen properties, so that only those which are both appealing and affordable are viewed.
- Help inspect prospective homes at mutually convenient hours (but not at a mere beck and call).
- Be aware of the constant stream of new listings.
- Be up-to-date on changes taking place in the marketplace.
- Know about and advise on the various methods of financing the purchase, and any applicable government incentive programs.
- Know how the asking price of a property compares with current resale values.
- Learn as much as possible about the vendor as the house itself, including the background to the listing, and why the vendor is selling, before submitting any Offer to Purchase. How long has the property been on the market? Has the price been reduced? Has the vendor already signed an Offer

to Purchase, firm? Is the vendor being relocated? Is the property a "distress sale," arising from death, marital split or job loss? Sellers fall into three categories: willing, anxious and desperate. The more desperate the seller, the less likely that he or she will hold out for a higher price or haggle over picayune points — especially if a "quick closing" is offered. The more the buyer knows about the seller at the outset, the more vigorously the buyer can negotiate.

- Prepare promptly the Offer to Purchase in accordance with your instructions, and suggest that it be reviewed by a real estate lawyer before signing.
- Be candid in setting a realistic price when submitting the offer.
- Negotiate skilfully and vigorously the price and other terms in the offer.
- Assist you in objectively making the difficult decisions every buyer faces.
- Move quickly, yet efficiently, to be both a mother hen and a catalyst, both a confidant and a devil's advocate.

In short, a real estate agent should be an agent in the truest sense of the word, a person employed to act on behalf of another.

Once an agent has been selected, be candid and honest with him or her, and stick with the agent. (As noted earlier, many purchaser agency agreements now require this.) Because the agent's job involves considerable legwork, for which no money is received until the transaction has closed, agents have the right to expect the same degree of loyalty from buyers as buyers expect from their agent.

Do not visit an open house without "your agent." It could cost him or her a lot of money. Marty and Karen had been house-hunting with a real estate agent, Terri, for weeks. But Terri did not accompany them to one open house where Maureen, the listing agent, was on duty. So Maureen became their agent for this property. When Marty and Karen submitted an offer on it, Terri could not be shown as the buyer's agent, because she did not introduce them to the property. As both listing and selling agent, Maureen made double what she would have made if Terri had been involved. Poor Terri did not earn any commission on the sale of that house, although she had spent considerable time before with Marty and Karen.

Occasionally, problems arise in the period "from contract to closing," between signing the offer and completion — anything from delays in the delivery of mortgage documents to your lawyer, to a seller not co-operating in providing access to the property. These are the times when a real estate agent must go to bat for you. After all, the agent's commission is in jeopardy if the deal doesn't close! Despite what may be said elsewhere, an agent's work is never done simply when the offer is signed and accepted. Where necessary, they must be prepared to help out until the deal has closed and the purchasers are in possession of their house. So don't be afraid to call on your agent before closing, if need be.

The importance of working with an agent is best illustrated by comparing the problems that often arise in private sales. Without an agent, buyers and sellers are constantly in direct contact. Emotions may run high, frustration may turn to anger, and face-to-face discussions may develop into confrontations — which could jeopardize the transaction. Real estate agents, on the other hand, are impartial, objective intermediaries whose role as a "go-between" may be the difference between a deal and a wasted effort.

In today's high-tech world, many real estate listings can be viewed on the Internet. Simply answer a few questions, and properties that satisfy those criteria will appear on-screen, with both pictures and written descriptions. This is an exciting and effective way to eliminate much of the dreary manual work involved in finding the ideal property. Once you have viewed the listing on-line, your agent can take you to view the actual property.

Sometimes circumstances determine the selection of an agent. Brian recently bought a home, conditional on selling his existing home. As part of that deal, Victoria, the agent who sold Brian the new home, also became the listing agent for Brian's present home. While Victoria made two commissions this way, Brian could not retain his nephew Dennis to sell his current home. Detailed information on these "back-to-back" transactions appears in chapter 26 on conditional offers.

Finally, let your real estate agent know at the outset how much you are relying on his or her experience and expertise to find your ideal home. The confidence you instil in your agent won't soon be forgotten. As professionals, most agents will rise to the challenge — to your mutual benefit.

13

Private Listings, Exclusive Listings and MLS Listings

Houses are like toothpaste. Neither can be sold effectively without proper marketing. The more exposure a house receives, the greater the likelihood interested buyers will be attracted to it.

Real estate commissions are sizeable. On even the most inexpensive properties, commissions run into the thousands of dollars. Before listing a property with a real estate agent, some sellers will try to sell it privately, if only to test the waters. Often this involves little more than putting a "For Sale — Private" sign on the front lawn and an ad in the newspaper. Because no one in the real estate industry is actively "flogging" the house, the amount of exposure this private listing will get is very limited. No purchaser will be introduced to a private listing by a real estate agent, since there is no commission for the agent in the event of a sale. The real estate industry has an interesting term for private home sellers: FSBOs (pronounced fisbos) — "For Sale By Owner."

Once a real estate agent is hired, the property may be listed in one of two ways: "exclusively" or "MLS" (Multiple Listing Service). With an exclusive listing, the property is listed and advertised for sale only within the listing broker's office and other branches of the same company. Exclusive listings are sold most often where a large broker has a network of offices to give them wide exposure, or where the listing agent's firm concentrates its activities in a narrow area. With an exclusive listing, details of the house and its features are not distributed to all of the members of the local real estate board or association, as would be the case with an MLS listing.

Multiple listings give detailed information on the lot, building, items included in the sale price (such as chattels and fixtures), any available financing of the property, plus a photo. Listings of 90 days are the norm, which should provide an agent with ample time to generate interest in a property, market it and sell it. In an attempt to save money, some sellers will list their property exclusively for a limited period of time (30 days), following which the property "goes MLS" for another 60 days if still unsold. Far and away, most properties are listed on the Multiple Listing Service. And those are the properties which can be viewed in cyberspace via the Internet. So buyers seeking the greatest selection of homes should consult the MLS listings first.

While the seller pays the commission to the agent(s) on closing (plus GST), indirectly it's the buyer who foots the bill, because the amount of commission is built into the sale price. (Of course, this is not the case if a buyer chooses buyer brokerage and then opts to pay his or her agent directly.) Despite what many people think, commission charges are not etched in stone. Commission rates are negotiable, although generally accepted standard charges do exist in each area. Virtually unheard of until the early 1990s, cost-cutting and discounting has now become a fact of life among realtors.

Exclusive listings carry a lower commission charge than MLS listings, which are distributed much more widely. In urban centres, the usual commission payable on an exclusive listing traditionally has been 5% of the sale price (plus GST). Six percent (plus GST) has been the norm for properties listed on MLS. Cottage or rural properties may bear a commission as high as 10% of the sale price (plus GST). Sometimes the commission is payable on a split scale — e.g., 7% on the first $100,000 of sale price and 3% on the balance (both plus GST). But in recent years, many agents have begun to accept lower commissions — perhaps 5% (plus GST) in urban areas. And discount brokers have been operating for a fee as low as 3.5% (plus GST), too.

14
Home Inspectors

When buying a used car, it's what's under the hood that counts. In recent years, a whole new industry, the diagnostic centre, has developed, where used-car buyers can get an independent evaluation of a car's condition before buying it. Isn't there even more need for such information when purchasing a resale (used) house, where the financial commitment often is 10 times as large? You would think so! Yet too often people make only a brief, cursory inspection of the key operating features of a house before buying it, being sold instead on its cosmetic condition. Even when inquiries are directed to items like the roof, the electrical and plumbing systems, the furnace and insulation, the answers provided by a seller are too often accepted strictly at face value.

Most buyers feel that the obvious flaws can be dealt with in subsequent negotiations with the seller, before an offer is finally accepted. Unfortunately, it's the not-so-obvious flaws, the maintenance deficiencies and structural defects, that will cost buyers huge sums of money in the future, after the property has changed hands. How can a buyer know what it will cost to bring a house up to standards, in addition to the purchase price, without first having the property inspected?

Unlike some brand-new homes, existing properties do not carry any kind of warranty. Instead, the age-old rule of *caveat emptor* — "let the buyer beware" — is still applicable when buying a resale home. But how can a buyer beware, if he or she does not know the defects to look for and beware of?

Understandably, not all purchasers feel comfortable or confident inspecting the "guts" of a resale house. To help buyers make an educated decision that a home is "sound," a new industry, the home inspection industry, has been developing in Canada since the mid-1980s. Home inspectors are not new; they have operated in the United States and the United Kingdom for years. The cost of having a home inspected is minimal, compared to the expense and agony of unforeseen repairs, hidden defects and unpleasant surprises. For buyers developing and applying their own unique home-buying strategy, an impartial home inspection when buying a resale property is a must. Otherwise, it's like blindly buying a used car.

Home inspectors visually inspect the structure and the systems of a property, both internally and externally, and provide a detailed and itemized written evaluation report on the present condition of the house. Estimated life expectancies should be provided for items like the roof, furnace and driveway. Some reports will even include recommendations for preventative maintenance and cost estimates for major repairs and improvements. This way, home buyers can budget for these anticipated costs in the future.

Don't expect a home inspector to comment on value or price, or even recommend whether you should buy the house. Because the home inspector doesn't know all the factors involved in the transaction, the ultimate decision whether to proceed must rest with the purchaser.

Rarely is a home inspection conducted before an offer is submitted. If the offer is not accepted, the cost of the report would be money thrown away. Instead, when a suitable property has been found and all other terms successfully negotiated, the Offer to Purchase is made "conditional on," or subject to, the purchaser obtaining a satisfactory home inspection report within a specified number of days after acceptance. Otherwise, the deal is off.

"Conditional on home inspection" clauses are no longer a novelty in an Agreement of Purchase and Sale. Most sellers won't object to them appearing in an offer, because the "conditional" period is usually quite short — just a few days.

Sellers who are confident their property will stand up to scrutiny have nothing to fear from this type of clause. On the other hand, sellers who strenuously object to a home inspection are bound to raise suspicions. But not every agent will automatically recommend that a home inspection clause appear in the Offer to Purchase. It's something that prudent home buyers will insist be included, as part of their HOBS.

Home inspectors are usually given very little time in an offer — perhaps as little as two or three days — to conduct an examination and prepare their written report, a fact well appreciated by members of the industry. Yet buyers can easily maximize the amount of time available for the inspection. Instead of contacting an inspector for the first time once an offer is signed, buyers should do so, as part of their HOBS, *before* submitting an offer. Find out their charges. Shop around and get at least three different price quotes. Learn how extensive a written report is provided. What is excluded? How much time will be needed to conduct the inspection? Once a home inspector has been selected, ask him or her to be "on standby" until an offer is accepted. With the necessary preliminary work done early, little time will be lost during that precious but condensed "conditional" period immediately after acceptance.

When compared to the cost of the house itself, the charge for a home inspection is small. Although fees vary, many inspections run in the $250-to-$350 range (plus GST).

Like real estate agents, home inspectors are a service industry. Referrals and references from satisfied customers are critical to their success. So if you are unsure which home inspector to use, check with friends, family, neighbors, your real estate agent and your lawyer. See if they are familiar with any of the home inspection companies in your area and the quality of their work.

A home inspection should cover all the major areas of a house. For starters, the structure itself will be inspected. Features that should be examined include the electrical, plumbing, wiring, heating and air-conditioning systems; fireplace; walls (for fresh plaster and wallpaper placed over cracks); floors, ceilings and the state of kitchen and bathroom fixtures; waterproofing and signs of water infiltration or dampness;

foundation structure; insulation and ventilation; signs of ter-
mite infestation and wood rot; condition of doors and windows;
and condition of the basement. External evaluations should be
made of the roof and gutters; siding, eavestroughs and downspouts; soffits and fascias; garage; foundation; porches;
chimney; driveway; masonry and brickwork. In short, a home
inspection report should give buyers a realistic, objective and
experienced assessment of items which too often in the past
were overlooked or taken for granted.

Despite what many people think, home inspectors are
unable to guarantee with absolute certainty that a house does
not have urea formaldehyde foam insulation (UFFI). That can
only be done by opening up every wall cavity, an impractical
task. Home inspectors can, however, conduct tests (by removing
electrical outlet faceplates or examining exterior walls, where
UFFI would have been injected into the wall cavities) to see
if UFFI likely exists in some or all of the walls.

A home inspection is not an appraisal of the property for
financing purposes. That is a separate inquiry, conducted to
determine its fair market value. Buyers arranging a new mortgage will end up paying for both the cost of a home inspection
report and the cost of a property appraisal.

Usually a verbal report is given following the inspection, the
written report following within a day or so. Sometimes the report
is available at the end of the inspection, having been prepared
from a "checklist" while the home was being examined.

Home inspectors strongly recommend that purchasers
accompany them on the inspection whenever possible. That
way, the inspector can point out defects and problem areas in
person, the written report providing the detailed commentary.
This also provides home buyers with an excellent opportunity
to familiarize themselves with the house (e.g., the location of the
main water shut-off and the fuse box/circuit breaker), ask questions and raise issues while they are fresh in everyone's minds.

Armed with a home inspection report and depending on its
contents, buyers may do one of the following:

1. Proceed with the offer as is.
2. Walk away from the transaction, if serious defects or

deficiencies are found, by giving the proper notice. Of course, this assumes that the offer was made conditional on obtaining a satisfactory report.

3. Renegotiate the purchase price downwards (in a conditional-offer situation), if major problems need to be rectified.

Mark and Rhonda found themselves in this situation recently. Although the house being bought was only five years old, the home inspection report disclosed serious electrical problems that would cost $1,500 to correct. After lengthy negotiations, the purchase price was reduced by $1,000, with Mark and Rhonda agreeing to repair the problem themselves after closing.

When Harold and Roberta learned that their prospective house had a leaky roof, they were able to knock $1,000 off the purchase price.

What is the biggest problem with home inspections in Canada today? It's a totally unlicensed and unregulated industry, with no standards or criteria governing its members. Because anyone, with limited (or no) qualifications, can call himself or herself a "home inspector," the risk exists that some home inspectors operating in Canada today are unqualified. Not very reassuring for the public.

Everyone else involved in the purchase and financing of a house is licensed: the lawyer, real estate agent, mortgage broker, and insurance agent. But not the home inspector, on whom the buyer places almost total reliance when making the final decision whether to proceed with the purchase. All the more reason to hire an inspector (or to avoid one, if necessary) whom others have dealt with previously. And all the more reason to check out the home inspector — including his or her credentials — as carefully as he or she will check out the property.

How do shady home inspectors bullet-proof themselves? Here are just three ways; be on the lookout for these types of situations:

• By setting up a limited company and then operating without liability (or negligence) insurance. If the home inspector makes a mistake, the poor unsuspecting buyer will never recover anything from a court judgment. Solution: make sure your home inspector carries liability insurance.

- By inserting very broad "exculpatory" clauses into their contracts, which severely restrict the scope of the inspector's work, and their opinion, too. So make sure you carefully read the home inspection contract before signing it, looking out for these exculpatory clauses. If in doubt, have your lawyer review it, too.

- By limiting their liability to the cost of the inspection report. If something is missed, the inspector returns the fee paid to the buyer, says "I'm sorry," and is off the hook. This equates botching a home inspection with ruining a roll of film during processing. Again, make sure this type of clause is not in the home inspector's contract. If it is, tell the inspector to take a hike.

Granted, there are a number of very good home inspectors in Canada, with excellent backgrounds and qualifications (sometimes as professional engineers). And several industry organizations, including the Canadian Association of Home Inspectors, or CAHI, with branches in several provinces, have been established in recent years to set standards, oversee their membership, and impose mandatory insurance requirements. Nevertheless, anyone can be a home inspector in Canada at any time, without being affiliated with one of these organizations. That leave unsuspecting home buyers prey to unscrupulous and fly-by-night operators. In many respects, the home inspection industry is a disaster waiting to happen.

By the way, never let a home renovator be your home inspector. He or she may overemphasize deficiencies and defects in the hope of drumming up business repairing or improving the property. To ensure objectivity, stick with an independent home inspector.

Using the chart below as a guide, list those home inspectors you contact, the price they will charge for a home inspection, the nature of their report, and other pertinent information:

Name
Phone Number
Price of Report
How Long to Complete
Does Report Include:
1) Present Condition of Property?
2) Anticipated Life Expectancies?
3) Preventive Maintenance Program?

Now let's turn our attention to the third member of the real estate trio, the lawyer. He or she is the party who will complete the work on the house which the agent found, and which the home inspector found to be sound!

15
Selecting a Lawyer

Too often, choosing a lawyer to process a home purchase is left until the offer is signed and accepted. Not only is that too bad, it's backwards, as a good real estate lawyer can provide invaluable assistance to buyers of resale homes *if he or she is contacted early, before the offer is signed.* Just as with a home inspector, buyers as part of their home-buying strategy should make inquiries, have preliminary discussions and choose a lawyer (or a notary, in those provinces where notaries are allowed to handle real estate transactions) *well before an offer is ever submitted.* In designing a HOBS (home-buying strategy), the selection of a lawyer should be one of the first decisions made, never the last.

Many people feel intimidated dealing with lawyers. First-time home buyers have often never required their services. Quite a few years may have passed since "seasoned veterans" who already own a house have used a lawyer. Yet developing a working relationship with a lawyer early will greatly benefit the home buyer. How, then, to select a real estate lawyer?

Like the real estate and home inspection professions, the legal profession is a service industry. Personal contacts are the cornerstone of any law firm's clientele. Despite its being able to advertise, satisfied clients and referral business are the lifeblood of a legal practice.

In hiring a lawyer, the client should be concerned firstly with his or her level of experience and expertise, and secondly with the degree of comfort he or she provides. Buyers who are "lawyerless" should start compiling a list of three or four recommended lawyers by seeking names from friends, relatives, neighbors and co-workers. What type of dealings did they have and what was their opinion of the lawyer? Have other people such as real estate agents, mortgage brokers and mortgage lenders heard of or dealt with the lawyer? Do they have any suggestions? What is the lawyer's reputation, both professionally and in the community at large? Does he or she have a particular degree of expertise that other people have recognized? While some provincial law societies downplay use of the term "specialist," it is a fact of life that some lawyers carry on a more extensive real estate and mortgage practice than others. With real estate law being so complex today, make sure your lawyer doesn't just "dabble" in real estate, doing the odd deal.

Yet it is equally important for buyers to feel at ease and have a good rapport with their lawyer. Since a home purchase is an extremely important event in most people's lives, the lawyer selected must demonstrate a genuine, sincere interest in the client. The lawyer's role is part advisor, part conscience, and part nursemaid. The lawyer and his or her staff must be prepared to answer the routine questions that all buyers consider of vital importance. But beyond that, a lawyer should be expected to provide invaluable information, insight and guidance on topics as diverse as the contents of an offer, mortgage financing, basic tax and family law issues, government incentive programs, and closing costs. He or she must be able to reassure buyers when minor problems arise that they are not insurmountable. He or she must be prepared to explain all aspects of the transaction to the client so they are clearly understood. Lawyers, effectively, are the "hub of the wheel," interacting with a multitude of people: realtors, other lawyers, mortgage lenders and brokers, home inspectors, insurance agents, surveyors, and utility companies.

Compile your list of lawyers' names well ahead of time, preferably pre-contract. Waiting until the deal is struck before picking a lawyer adds unnecessary pressure to a buyer who likely already is nervous and anxious. If a lawyer isn't selected in advance, how can the lawyer provide input into the transaction before it becomes etched in stone?

Carefully analyze the names on the list. Perhaps one or two keep reappearing from different sources. If so, that's as good a place to start as any! Take several minutes and call the lawyers, to learn about them and their experience and to discuss both the proposed transaction plus their acting for you, as well as their fees.

Fees are a very sensitive issue in the legal profession. Some lawyers will not discuss fees on the telephone, while many others will. But legal fees (plus GST) are only one of the overall costs that buyers will incur in a real estate transaction. So it is important to know early on not just the lawyer's fees but more importantly the total closing costs (i.e., how much money will be needed, in addition to the downpayment). These charges, which are constant no matter which lawyer is used, include disbursements (plus GST), provincial transfer tax, adjustments with the vendor, and costs associated with arranging a mortgage. See chapter 23 for more details on these hidden closing costs. And learn what the lawyer will charge to review the draft, unsigned Agreement of Purchase and Sale. Often there's no extra fee if a lawyer quickly peruses and comments on the offer. But if major changes are needed, or complex clauses drafted, a further fee is usually collected.

When contacted for an estimate of their fees, very few lawyers actually volunteer the all-important budgeting number purchasers need: how much money should be set aside to close the transaction, a.k.a. the hidden closing costs, including disbursements (plus GST). This reticence is most unfortunate, as it leaves buyers totally in the dark on properly calculating the total amount of money needed to close. For lawyers simply to quote a figure for fees, and not advise buyers of this "all-inclusive" budgeting number, borders on misrepresentation.

Experienced real estate lawyers have a good idea what these hidden costs will be, even at the pre-offer stage. Any lawyer who voluntarily provides this information when asked for a price quote should be given serious consideration as your lawyer for that reason alone. Obviously that lawyer is prepared to give you a straight bill of goods at the outset, a fair and reasonable estimate of the true and total cost of closing the transaction. Surprises are for birthdays, not real estate transactions. Most last-minute surprises can be eliminated if that "all-in" figure is learned early, and planned for. If none of the lawyers contacted offer this information, it's up to you, as part of your home-buying strategy, to ask for details about the lawyer's fees *and* overall closing costs.

Most of these closing charges are fixed and non-negotiable. Yet occasionally a lawyer will quote a substantially lower figure. When that happens, the lawyer is simply baiting the hook. What you may be quoted is a half-truth — his or her fee for the purchase (as asked) — without being told about the additional fee payable for completing the mortgage component of your deal. Unfortunately, you are only being told what you want to hear now, with the unpleasant news to be sprung later. The same is true with disbursements. Why penalize a lawyer who has been honest and candid in disclosing what those closing disbursements will total, by choosing instead someone who is deliberately "lowballing" you just to get the business?

The lawyer Rod and Micki retained was the only one who was prepared to discuss both fees and closing costs at the outset. Were they ever glad he did! Although the legal fees totalled $900 (plus GST), the complete amount needed to close was nearly $3,000 when the other charges were added in. Armed with this information before signing their offer, Rod and Micki could accurately budget their finances for closing, enabling them to apply for a mortgage that was just the right size.

To advise Rod and Micki accurately about the overall closing costs, their lawyer first asked many questions about the proposed transaction: what type of property is being bought (freehold or condominium); what the purchase price is; how it is being financed (one mortgage or two; assumed, vendor-take-back or new mortgage); how it is heated (oil, gas or electric); if a survey exists; and when the deal will close. The answers to these and other questions helped Rod and Micki's lawyer gauge the amount of "hidden" costs.

While lawyers normally charge for their time on an hourly basis, block fees are the norm in a real estate transaction, based on the amount of work to be done. A cash transaction (no mortgage) involves less work than one with a new mortgage. That, in turn, is easier to process and cheaper than a purchase where two new mortgages are being arranged. A vendor-take-back mortgage, where the vendor holds the mortgage on closing, involves less work than a new mortgage with a third-party lender. Even easier than both is a transaction where the purchaser assumes an existing mortgage. The quoted fee should be broken down this way, so the purchaser knows the amount being charged for each component of the transaction. Only by knowing more about the deal can a lawyer can set his or her fee appropriately. Of course, the quoted fee assumes that the transaction proceeds without any unexpected or unusual problems. If glitches arise, a fee adjustment may be necessary.

The value of the property should not alone determine what a lawyer charges, although it may be a factor. In terms of actual work, a purchase transaction with one new mortgage is the same whether the purchase price is $100,000 and the mortgage is $75,000 or the purchase price is $500,000 financed by a $375,000 mortgage. But the more expensive the property, the greater the lawyer's exposure and the greater the need for professional liability insurance.

Where the same lawyer handles both the buying and the mortgaging of the property (which usually is the case), it would be unfair to charge a buyer double the purchase fee. While additional time must be spent processing the mortgage side of the transaction, much of the work from the purchase applies equally to the mortgage. The additional fee charged for the mortgage component should reflect this.

The legal profession is a competitive business. In most areas of Canada, legal fees in real estate transactions vary from lawyer to lawyer. Although local law associations publish suggested fee schedules, or "tariffs," for real estate deals, many lawyers honor them in the breach, charging less than tariff as their fee. But be wary of cut-rate fees. Too often that means the lawyer is cutting corners in the quality of the work being done — a problem that may not rear its head for years.

Purchasers should shop around and compare various price quotes for legal fees. There is, however, more to selecting a lawyer than just fees. *Never let price be the sole determining factor in choosing a lawyer.* When dealing with professional services, quality, not price, is the key. Like all professionals, lawyers specializing in real estate work, proficient and experienced in their field, charge more for their services than a rookie. But it's worth the extra expense. In the long run, buyers get what they pay for. A savings of $25 or $50 is nominal compared to the overall amount a buyer will pay to close a transaction. Rejecting a highly recommended and qualified lawyer, just to save a small amount of money, is being penny-wise and pound-foolish.

Once you have selected a lawyer, make an appointment to meet with him or her. Often this is done when the Offer to Purchase has been prepared but is still unsigned. At that time, finalize the question of fees and discuss when and how they are to be paid. In most real estate transactions, the lawyer's fees are paid in full on closing. On request, some lawyers will make other arrangements, if settled early. More and more lawyers are asking clients for retainers of several hundred dollars at the outset, to offset some of the initial disbursements. Be prepared for this out-of-pocket outlay as well.

At that meeting, learn the name of the secretary or law clerk assisting with the file. While delegating responsibility is essential for any legal office to operate efficiently, no one should be dealing with a lawyer's office but never see or talk to a lawyer! Some lawyers operate high-volume real estate "factories" where the fees charged are nominally lower. For good reason: client/ lawyer contact is often nonexistent. Regardless of the promise of any savings, avoid dealing with this type of law firm. The ultimate responsibility to the client rests with the lawyer, not his or her staff. As a purchaser, you are paying your hard-earned money to retain that lawyer. You have a right to communicate and meet with that lawyer, especially when meeting to sign the closing papers.

As with home inspectors, have the lawyer available "on standby" before ever putting pen to paper. This way, the lawyer can be contacted *to review the draft offer before it is signed*. This critical issue is discussed in chapter 27.

One final word about lawyers acting in real estate transactions. It is acceptable for one lawyer to represent both the buyer and a lender in a purchase transaction, their interests being compatible at this stage. However, one lawyer should never represent both the buyer and the seller in the same transaction.

This is the classic conflict-of-interest situation, where each side should have separate representation.

Now that the three real estate professionals have been assembled, it's time to examine in greater detail the particular property you're thinking of buying.

16
Home Sites

Home buyers who have developed a HOBS (home-buying strategy) will now have narrowed down their choices of location (community) and location (neighborhood). The next stage is to zero in on a specific location, a particular resale property within that neighborhood. As with the selection of a community and neighborhood, every buyer as part of their HOBS will view and rank the features raised in this chapter differently. Yet each point should be carefully considered with both the purchase and a subsequent sale in mind. To maximize the potential resale value of a property, buyers should always remember the need for objectivity. Factors unimportant to one person could be paramount to another.

Lot Sizes

Lot sizes are usually quoted in terms of street frontage: a 25-foot lot, a 40-foot lot, and so on. Too often, though, depth is overlooked. Yet the deeper the lot, the deeper the front and back yards. Years ago, lots 120 feet deep were prevalent in older areas. This meant two cars could easily be accommodated in a driveway. In newer subdivisions, lots are only 100 feet deep, resulting in shorter front yards and driveways. Coupled with the trend to narrower (and therefore cheaper) lots, this leads to serious on-street parking problems. Just try to find a parking spot when the distance between two driveways is half a car length!

With the increased use of metric measurements in real estate, lot sizes have shrunk even further. The "metric" 35-foot x 100-foot lot often turns out to be 10.5 m x 30 m. In actual fact, this is equivalent to 34.45 feet x 98.43 feet!

Lot size is important for another reason. It determines how large a house can be built on the lot, a major consideration for people planning to enlarge the premises. Most municipalities base the maximum permitted size of a house on the size of the lot itself, a factor called "coverage." Sixty percent coverage means the size of the house (in square feet) on a lot cannot exceed 60% of the size of the lot itself. Eddie and Ellen bought a property recently with a lot size of 35 feet x 100 feet. The house itself was 1,400 square feet in size. With a maximum allowable coverage of 60%, the largest house permitted on the lot was 2,100 square feet (60% of the total lot size of 3,500 square feet). Obviously, the deeper the lot, the larger the house it can support. *When examining lot sizes, don't forget about depth!*

Parking

Parking is a very important consideration to most people. While the "suburban dream" is a two-car garage, obviously that is not always available. So be practical. Ask yourself, is a house with a one-car garage adequate? Will a longer driveway compensate for the lack of a second garage? If no garage is available, see if a mutual drive exists, or if a parking "pad" can be built in the front yard. (Usually that requires municipal approval, since part of that land belongs to the city or town.) In some older areas, the only type of available parking may be on-street parking. If so, check with the local municipality ahead of time about any restrictions that may exist as to overnight or permit parking. If private parking is an absolute necessity, find out now, before an offer is submitted, whether it is available.

Mutual Drives and Rights-of-Way

Home owners are entitled to privacy. Anyone coming onto their property without consent is a trespasser, unless a legal right of access exists. Mutual drives or walkways, found in many older areas of urban communities, are typical examples of that right. The term "mutual drive" is an everyday expression explaining a legal concept — the right-of-way.

Alan and Jack are next-door neighbors who share a mutual drive. Alan's deed says that Jack has the right to use the south four feet of Alan's property, 75 feet in from the street. Jack's deed says Alan has the right to use the north four feet of Jack's property, 75 feet in from the street. Although each owns his own 4-foot x 75-foot strip of land, both Alan and Jack have an equal right to use this 8-foot x 75-foot right-of-way, without any interruption by the other. Due to the dual rights of ownership and usage, Alan and Jack must agree on the proper use of the right-of-way. That includes parking on it, since neither Alan nor Jack can use the right-of-way alone, to the exclusion of the other. Snow removal, maintenance and repairs must also be agreed upon. Owning a house with a mutual drive or mutual walkway is a surefire way of gaining an early introduction to a next-door neighbor. As co-existence is the key, surprisingly few problems normally arise with mutual drives.

Municipal Easements

Mike and Leah own a house where a "service corridor" of telephone and hydro wires runs the width of their property, underground, across the rear five feet of their lot. Although Mike and Leah own this land, the municipality has the right to maintain its equipment in its present location and to send representatives onto that area, without being considered a trespasser. This five-foot strip of land is called a municipal easement, and is usually granted to a municipality or other utility supplier such as the telephone, cable television, hydro, natural gas or water company.

Municipal easements in older areas run across the rear of the lot, the wires usually being placed above ground. In newer areas those services have been relocated to the fronts of properties. Often the wires are located overhead, though they have gone underground in the newest of subdivisions. (As part of a local improvement project in older areas, those overhead wires may be buried underground, adjacent to the street at the front of the lot.)

Not all municipal easements are visible to the naked eye. Imagine how surprised Len and Gail were to learn that a 10-foot-wide sewer easement ran across the back yard of a property they were thinking of buying, completely undetectable above ground. Another type of easement that still runs across the rear of many properties, both old and new, is a drainage pipe and "catch basin," described more fully below.

Detailed agreements registered on title state how the area affected by the easement can be used. Obviously, rights of access are given to the municipality or utility company. Usually they have the right to trim and even remove trees and shrubs if they interfere with the operation of the utility service. No permanent structures such as extensions to the house or a swimming pool are permitted on the easement, either.

Buyers who have specific future plans to use any portion of the rear or front yards should advise their real estate agent and lawyer before an offer is signed. Proper steps can then be taken to determine if a municipal easement exists, and if so, where. A properly drawn, up-to-date survey will disclose the existence of these easements, as should the deed. Since many offers say that buyers agree to take title subject to "minor" municipal easements for utility purposes, the time to raise these concerns is now, at the pre-contract stage.

Party Walls

Lorne and Miriam live in a semi-detached house. Greg and Marilyn live in a unit of row housing. In both cases the "common wall" between their property and the adjoining property is known as a party wall.

The boundary line between the properties runs directly

through the middle of the party wall. Because structural support is required from both sides of the wall, neither owner can remove his side of the wall without the consent of its co-owner. Owners of homes with party walls face another concern: noise from next door. To learn if this might be a problem, ask the home inspector to check the level of sound insulation in the common wall. Inadequate soundproofing could lead to hearing much of what the neighbors do in their home! Party walls, and the level of sound they transmit, could bother some buyers but not others.

Road Allowance

Like most home owners, Bernie and Hilary were shocked to learn they do not own most of their front yard! In Ontario, for example, municipally owned road allowances are 66 feet wide. While the actual paved roadway may be only 26 feet wide, the total area of land owned by the local municipality is 66 feet in width. That means the municipality owns another 20 feet on either side of the asphalt. Included in this 20-foot strip of land are the boulevard, sidewalk and utility services. The remainder is land which appears to be part of Bernie and Hilary's front yard, and which they use as part of their front yard, but which is really owned by the city or town.

While Bernie and Hilary are responsible for maintaining that portion of their front yard, the trees and bushes growing on it legally belong to the municipality. Before removing or even trimming the trees or bushes on their front yard, Bernie and Hilary should check with the local municipality. Otherwise, they could face a charge of damaging or destroying municipal property!

Similarly, municipalities are responsible for their trees and bushes. One of its trees could cause damage to a house or its occupants, by its roots growing into the sewer system, for example, or by housing a hornet's nest. The municipality then would have to correct the problem at its own expense, and compensate the home owner for damages.

In newer residential subdivisions, the municipality also owns triangular pieces of property at all four corners of a street intersection, called "sight" or "daylighting" triangles, in addition to the road allowance. This way, municipalities can ensure that the line of vision for motorists at an intersection won't be obstructed. Many owners of corner lots have planted shrubs or trees, only to find out later that they were placed on a municipally owned sight triangle.

To learn where the municipally owned road allowance or sight triangle begins, examine the survey for the property. Measure the distance from the building to the property/municipal boundary line. If the exact location of the lot line is extremely important, do this before submitting an offer. If no survey is available, the offer could be made conditional on determining and being satisfied with the exact location of the boundary line, based on a new survey, within a set number of days after the offer is accepted.

Zero Lot Lines

Municipal zoning by-laws require that houses be located a certain distance from the property line. Often this "setback" was four feet, meaning the area between the houses was eight feet wide. As land prices skyrocketed in the 1960s and 1970s, a new planning concept, the zero lot line, was developed. To keep the cost of housing affordable, developers were allowed in some areas to build more houses per acre by reducing the gap between houses. One home is still located four feet from the boundary line, while the other is built virtually right up to it. Hence the "zero" lot line, with the gap between the houses reduced to slightly more than four feet. With almost four feet saved per lot, developers were able to increase densities this way, and keep house prices reasonable. Zero lot lines, in effect, are a way of manufacturing land!

All the houses on the following survey sketch have a zero lot line on their southern boundary. Just over four feet exists between the houses to permit roof overhangs, eavestroughs and downspouts to extend from the walls. The segments between the houses (marked as Parts 5, 6, 7 and 8) are all "maintenance easements," areas of common usage that are a necessity with zero lot line properties. Maintenance easements are similar to the mutual drives and rights-of-way discussed earlier.

Felix is the owner of Lot A on the survey. Oscar owns Lot B, which includes the area marked Part 5 between the two lots. In his deed, Felix is permitted access onto Part 5 only of Oscar's property without interference from Oscar, in order for Felix to maintain his property. Oscar's deed confirms that Felix has this right. Practically speaking, Felix can use the area between the two homes as if he owned it, and without being considered a trespasser, to paint his house, clean the eavestroughs and downspouts, gain access to the roof, and otherwise repair and maintain his property. Oscar, in turn, has a similar right over Part 6 of Lot C that Henry owns.

Much concern has been expressed over zero lot lines in recent years. With the houses so close together, owners complain about the resulting claustrophobic feeling. And the smaller separation between the houses makes zero lot line pro-perties somewhat of a fire hazard, too. A fire in one home

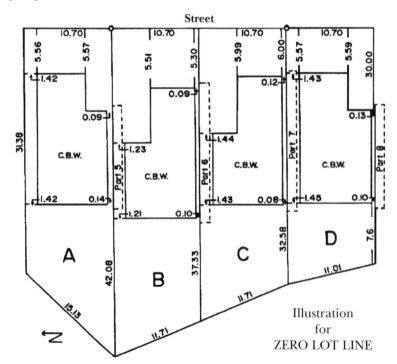

Illustration
for
ZERO LOT LINE

could easily spread to its adjoining properties, especially on a windy day. Maintenance easements are greatly shielded from the sun, too, making it impossible for grass to properly grow there. Unless they are covered with crushed stones, patio stones or bricks, maintenance easements are ugly at the best of times and muddy at the worst.

Corner Lots

Some people love them and some people hate them! Fans of corner lots adore the feeling and look of roominess they provide, since portions of not one but two road allowances can be used by the home owner. All that extra land, though, means additional grass to cut, more sidewalk to clear of snow, and more fencing to erect with no neighbor on the other side to split the cost. Privacy considerations and security threats are probably the greatest deterrents to owning a corner lot. Unless the back yard is totally enclosed with a fence, anyone on the street can easily peer in. That makes it easy for unwanted visitors to remove personal items like patio furniture, lawn equipment and barbecues.

On the Sunny Side of the Street

A popular song decades ago still has relevance today. When selecting a house, decide whether you want to receive morning or afternoon sun. Houses on the west side of the street get morning sun at the front of the house and afternoon sun at the back. Elliott and Mandy, with two young children, chose a house on the west side of the street. The afternoon and evening sunlight provides additional time for outdoor play. Across the street, of course, the reverse holds true. Home buyers should also consider on which side of the house the master bedroom is located. People who dislike waking to bright morning sun may not want their bedroom facing east or south.

Darryl and Michelle bought a house on the north side of the street. After one winter they discovered that the snow on their front yard and driveway melted faster than Rita's across the road. Yet Rita, with the kitchen in the rear, received the nice rays of the morning sun while she ate breakfast. Those who like to sunbathe will have much more exposure from the sun in the back yard of a house on the south side of the street. Windows facing south also get more light, resulting in lower heating bills.

In choosing a side of the street, carefully consider the effect of the sun on the house (both inside and outside), plus your personal lifestyle.

Zoning By-laws

Few buyers address their minds to the question of zoning. They automatically assume that a residential neighborhood is zoned just that — residential. Yet learning more about the zoning for a particular house, its neighborhood and its community, is absolutely crucial.

Home ownership is affected by zoning by-laws in three ways:

a)   The use that can be made of the property;
b)   The restrictions imposed on the height of the building and the distance that must exist between the house and the front, side and rear yard property lines ("setbacks"); and
c)   The density permitted (in other words, how much house can exist on the lot).

Most zoning by-laws dealing with permitted uses are phrased in the negative: "no uses are permitted, except . . ." If a property is to be used in a particular way — be it to operate a home office, rent out the basement or carry on a home business — check it out with the local zoning department early. Alternatively, make the offer conditional on the zoning allowing the property to be used that way. To check afterwards for the first time is too late.

Terry and Evelyn wanted to erect a satellite dish in their back yard. When they learned that the zoning in the area of their proposed purchase prohibited a dish, they decided to buy elsewhere. Larry and Lynn planned to buy what appeared to be a triplex. Revenue from the basement apartment was needed to offset the monthly expenses. Upon inquiring at the municipal offices, they learned that the property was zoned for a duplex only and that the basement was being used illegally. They didn't even submit an offer.

For an excluded use to become a permitted use, the property must be rezoned, which usually involves an application to the local municipal council.

Yard setbacks are dealt with somewhat differently. Often a proposed addition or extension to the building would violate the zoning requirements, but only slightly. When the general intent and purpose of the zoning will not be violated, exceptions to the by-law, called "minor variances," are granted.

Ross and Pam wanted to build an addition onto their home that would result in the west wall being only four feet six inches from the property line instead of the required five feet. Before building, Ross and Pam had to obtain a minor variance from the zoning by-law.

In Ontario, the body that grants minor variances is the Committee of Adjustment. If the proposed alteration would significantly depart from the requirements of the zoning by-law, a formal rezoning of the property becomes necessary. Anyone planning changes to the external structure of a building after closing (whether outwards or upwards, since height requirements exist in most areas, too), should inquire further about these requirements early, before proceeding too far with a draft offer.

Municipal by-laws also regulate many other aspects of home ownership. Fences, hedges and patios are just some of the areas regulated in terms of height, setbacks and coverage.

Zoning by-laws impose various different density levels, which in turn permit many different types of possible dwellings, all under the umbrella of "residential" zoning. Don and Wendy were shocked to learn that the medium-density zoning in a neighborhood they investigated would allow single or semi-detached dwellings, townhouses, multiple-family dwellings, condominiums, and apartment buildings. Think about it — there isn't much else!

Zoning by-laws are not retroactive. Just because zoning standards are tightened over time does not automatically render a legal use of a property illegal. Otherwise, houses would have to be torn down and businesses would have to close every time a zoning by-law was changed. The question becomes, which came first, the cart or the horse, the by-law or the building? When a zoning by-law is passed or amended, it exempts buildings that were lawfully erected and legally used before that time. In other words, only future uses are prohibited, not prior legal uses. Even though the requirements of the current zoning by-law may be violated, these "non-conforming uses" are still "legal" provided they continue uninterrupted in the future.

The concept of legal non-conforming uses can lead to some strange results. Craig erected a satellite dish in May, when the installation of dishes was not prohibited. Although Nick, his next-door neighbor, thought about installing a dish, he did nothing. In June the municipality passed a by-law prohibiting satellite dishes. Now Nick cannot install a satellite dish without violating the by-law. But Craig's dish can stay in place forever as a legal non-conforming use, because his dish was in place before the by-law was passed.

Knowing whether a property is a legal non-conforming use is very important, especially in older areas. Years ago properties were built and used with little regard for planning and zoning standards. How else could the following appear in one block of a downtown neighborhood: a corner grocery, two houses, an auto repair shop, three more houses and a corner restaurant? How else could detached homes have only 15 inches separating them? These are perfect examples of uses and standards that could not be duplicated today. Yet these violations of the current zoning by-laws are permitted for as long as the land is used that way, since the use preceded the by-laws. Any discontinuance of that use, however, will permanently destroy the protection of it being legally non-conforming. So Craig can keep his satellite dish in its present location forever. But if he ever removes it for an extended period of time, the dish will lose the status of being a legal non-conforming use.

Buying a home means investing a substantial sum of hard-earned money in a property. Buyers should do everything they can *before submitting an offer* to ensure that an attractive residential community and neighborhood will retain that character in the future. To do this, call or visit the municipal offices. Discover how the immediate area is zoned and what the zoning permits. Also, check on the "official plan" for the area, a general statement of land use policy for a community/neighborhood and a guide for future development. Ask if any rezoning or specific site development applications are pending which might affect its character. Unless the proper inquiries are made *early*, a future unexpected high-density development could be an unwelcome surprise.

Other Factors

Different people view fire hydrants, streetlights, hydro boxes, supermailboxes, stop signs and catch basins (grated outlets, usually at the rear of a property, where water travelling over land can enter the storm sewer system) differently. Fire hydrants do not add to the esthetics of a house and make parking in front of a house impossible. On the other hand, they are handy to have nearby in case of a fire. A streetlamp in front of a home makes it a less inviting target for night prowlers. Yet that bright light may make it more difficult to fall asleep in those bedrooms at the front of the house. Green hydro transformer boxes appear above ground in many newer areas. Few people like them; they are clumsy looking and are an allure for dogs. Besides being unsightly, supermailboxes attract daily pedestrian traffic — the neighbors picking up their mail. Being close to a stop sign is important to some people. Traffic should be travelling slower than normal when approaching or leaving an intersection with a stop sign. Catch basins are unsightly, the terrain around them always sloping downwards. Because a catch basin is the external outlet for a sewer easement, its surrounding area must be kept clear of buildings, structures, improvements or expensive landscaping. Having a catch basin at the rear of a property substantially affects the use and enjoyment of that area.

A checklist dealing with the factors raised in this chapter appears at the end of chapter 18, "The Home Itself."

17
Be Patient!

It's time! Yes, prospective home buyers are now ready to start looking at specific homes in earnest. The time has come to go house-hunting with your real estate agent, to locate that dream home. But before you do, stand back and consider what you've accomplished so far.

By now you have your own, tailor-made home-buying strategy. Both your needs and wants have been carefully considered. Your financial ability to pay for and carry a home has been examined, and a pre-approved mortgage arranged. Decisions have been made on both a community and a neighborhood, plus the factors affecting specific home sites. Preliminary discussions have been held with the three key real estate professionals — real estate agent, home inspector and lawyer — and all are awaiting your next move. Having done your homework, you know what will be the ideal home, and should be able to capitalize on a good opportunity quickly if it comes your way. Not only is your adrenalin level likely quite high, but you are finding it difficult to contain your enthusiasm. At this stage you are fully prepared to move forward, totally aware of where you are going. Without question, you are ready to act.

Still, finding that ideal house — *the one that satisfies all of your needs and as many wants as possible, the property you can best afford to buy and carry each month* — will take time. It will also involve more research, and may even necessitate modifications to your home-buying strategy. Many homes that could satisfy the needs and wants on your shopping list will be shown by your real estate agent. You may be asked to view some properties at open houses held by listing agents. Yet there is no simple answer as to how long it will take, and how many houses must be examined, before the house you *really* want is found. *So be patient!* The careful analysis you have applied to date in developing and applying that HOBS, in deciding what and where to buy, must now be focused on particular properties. This is the only way a proper, educated decision to buy a home can be made.

On the other hand, *do not procrastinate.* Well-priced homes do not remain available forever. Too often, purchasers who dawdle learn to their regret that a property has already been sold. Your home-buying strategy, though, will save you valuable time and enable you to move quickly when the right opportunity arises. It could be the difference between buying the house and missing the boat. Soon after seeing a house, buyers with a HOBS in place will know whether that house adequately fills the bill.

Determining what is included in a house is very straightforward. Learning what will not accompany it is much harder. To solve this problem, Don and Aline applied another HOBS idea before submitting an offer. They attended several open houses for properties outside their price range, inquiring about the features that accompanied each home. By preparing a chart listing those items, Don and Aline established a yardstick against which to compare houses in their price range. Immediately they knew when an affordable property offered good value for the money, as it included features normally found only in higher-priced houses. That turned out to be the home Don and Aline bought.

But don't rush into things! Don't be swayed by the argument, too often raised, that someone else is waiting to buy the property. If that's the case, let them! Once an Offer to Purchase is accepted, it is too late to change your mind. Better to lose a property you're not 100% sold on, than purchase a property that doesn't fit the bill. Be absolutely certain the property being bought matches that definition of the ideal house. Make sure your home inspector and lawyer play their important roles before the contract becomes firm and binding. Because of the amount of money involved, buyers cannot afford to be overwhelmed, intimidated, or caught up in the emotion of the moment. Keep your composure and only make decisions with your head, not your heart.

Children learning how to ride a bicycle get better with each outing. Practice makes perfect. So, too, with buying a house. *Don't get discouraged.* Each house viewed is an opportunity to learn a little more about the home-buying process, to gain a little more experience and confidence, and to redefine (or confirm) what you are seeking in a house.

Several points should be kept in mind when inspecting properties:

1. Keep your comments, criticisms and reactions to a particular property to a minimum. You are there to inquire about a property, not to denigrate it. Analysis of a home should be done in a private conversation with your agent as soon as possible after the appointment.

2. Consider a home from your own point of view, bearing in mind your own lifestyle. Ignore how it is presently used or maintained. Don't let fancy decor or superficial features such as paint, wallpaper and a few accessories influence you. How a room or even a whole house is finished and furnished will not reflect how it will look when you move in. Instead, try to visualize the potential in a property. Imagine how it would appear if painted or wallpapered differently, with your own furniture placed in the rooms. If you like what you see, then examine the house even more closely.

3. Be courteous to both the home owner and yourself. Make each visit as easy as possible. Keep distractions to a minimum, by keeping children and pets at home when out viewing houses, if possible.

18
The Home Itself

Now that specific homes are going to be examined and compared, keep in mind the following questions. What makes one particular house more suitable than other houses? What factors distinguish one home from another? What features should buyers be looking for in a particular property?

When looking at prospective homes, keep your shopping list of needs and wants handy. As part of the HOBS approach, compare how many needs and wants are satisfied by each particular home. Remember: the ideal house, the property ultimately chosen, should satisfy all of your needs and as many wants as possible, while remaining affordable. Constantly refer back to your checklist to refresh your memory on what is a need and what is a want.

As in the selection of a community and neighborhood, prepare a personalized ranking system, separating key features from unimportant items. Again, be sure to consider each feature carefully, in terms of both buying the property and selling it to someone else in the future.

The printed form of most offers says a buyer has inspected the property before signing the contract. Although a home inspector should examine the property once the offer is accepted, buyers must still thoroughly investigate a property even before putting pen to paper. Noticing that the paint is peeling, the plaster is cracked and the floors and carpeting are worn does not require any expertise. Yet those flaws may dissuade you from even submitting an offer. Remember, too, that a home inspector is hired to examine the structure of and the systems in a property. As the purchaser, you must examine the nonstructural items and esthetics in the house — the items listed in this chapter. Of course, you should not be afraid to bring any concerns to the attention of the home inspector, for him to investigate further.

Spend as much time in the house as you reasonably need. It's a shame, but true, that people spend more time researching and investigating the purchase of a VCR or computer equipment than a house. A proper perusal of a house just isn't possible during a single visit of a half-hour or less, after dark one evening.

Remember to view homes both in the daytime and at night. Certain features may only be noticeable after the sun has set — e.g., the exterior lighting of the house and the effect of street-lights. When seriously considering a property, bring a friend or relative along, too. It never hurts to get an unbiased, reliable and objective opinion.

And remember: when buying a resale home, the doctrine of *caveat emptor*, or "buyer beware," is still relevant. But what exactly does "buyer beware" mean?

Although sellers have an intimate knowledge of their home, they only have a narrow duty to disclose "defects in quality" (i.e., problems with its physical condition). Those property defects fall into two categories, patent defects and latent defects.

Patent defects are obvious flaws, visible to the naked eye, which buyers should detect when inspecting a property with ordinary care. Example: a crumbling chimney. Latent defects are not as apparent; they would not be revealed by any inquiry a buyer could make before striking a deal with the vendor.

The law imposes different disclosure rules on sellers for each type of defect. Sellers do not have to draw a buyer's attention to patent defects; *caveat emptor* prevails. The onus is on buyers to inspect, inquire and discover, to ascertain the physical condition of what they are buying.

The law on latent defects is much more complex. Vendors have a duty to disclose latent defects which render the premises dangerous (e.g., the presence of radioactive contamination). Similarly, any latent defects which sellers know (or ought to know) would render the premises unfit for habitation must be disclosed.

However, sellers have no legal obligation to volunteer information about latent defects which only affect the value of a property, provided they do not pose a health or safety risk. Once again *caveat emptor* applies, even though the latent defect might be a material factor that negatively affects a property's value. In one case, the presence of methane gas in well water was a latent defect which the vendor did not have to disclose. The court said it was not a health or safety risk; it only affected what the property was worth.

All this assumes that the vendor makes no attempt to deliberately conceal or cover up a patent or latent defect. Fraud, mistake and misrepresentation are exceptions to the rule of *caveat emptor.*

To protect themselves fully, home buyers must ask pertinent questions about specific areas of concern, add the appropriate clauses to their Agreement of Purchase and Sale based on the answers received, and conduct a proper property inspection before the deal becomes firm and binding (usually involving a home inspector).

Thankfully for buyers, a discernible move away from *caveat emptor* is underway. In many American states, either "seller disclosure" laws have been passed that force sellers to reveal property defects to prospective buyers, or the real estate industry itself has made completion of a standardized disclosure form mandatory when listing a property.

What must be divulged? The U.S. test is relatively clear-cut: "known hidden defects" — i.e., latent defects. Sellers must reveal conditions they know, or ought to know, exist in a house that could affect a purchaser's decision to buy — everything from the structure to the systems.

Unfortunately, the Canadian real estate industry has been much slower to embrace the concept of seller disclosure. The B.C. Real Estate Association was the first to make completion of its Property Condition Disclosure Statement mandatory for all MLS listings, in 1993. Not all provinces or real estate boards across Canada have followed suit, although some boards and realtors voluntarily use a similar form.

Seller disclosure is not meant to replace home inspections. The disclosure forms emphasize how purchasers must make their own enquiries. And rightly so, since purchasers still assume any patent defects with a resale home, unless clauses to the contrary appear in the offer.

Before submitting an Offer to Purchase, learn whether seller disclosure exists in the area where you want to buy. If so, get a copy of the property disclosure statement in advance, and thoroughly review it. If not, be extra careful, since with *caveat emptor* "what you see is what you get."

YOUR CHECKLIST

Type of House
  Single-family detached_____   Duplex (triplex)_____
  Semi-detached_____   Townhouse_____
  Link_____   Row house_____
  (freehold or condominium?)_____

Style of House
  Bungalow_____   Back-split_____
  Two-storey_____   Condominium apartment_____
  Side-split_____   Square feet_____

Rooms

How many rooms are in the house? What are their types and sizes (bedrooms, bathrooms, kitchen, living room, dining room, other rooms such as a family room or laundry room)? What is the overall layout of the house? Is it a centre hall plan? Does the layout of the rooms suit your lifestyle? Will traffic flow be difficult from room to room? Is the kitchen also a hallway? Is there adequate cupboard and counter space in the kitchen? Is there adequate space in the kitchen for a fridge, stove and dishwasher? Is the dining room near the kitchen? Are the dining room and living room adjoining? Is the kitchen at the rear of the house? Are there visible "high-traffic areas"? Is the laundry room on the main floor or in the basement? Is a bedroom located on the main floor, or in the basement? Does the master bedroom have an ensuite bathroom? How many levels of stairs are in the house?

As part of their HOBS, purchasers should prepare a rough sketch of all levels of the house, and then measure their furniture and appliances to ensure they will fit in the various rooms.

Basement

Is there a basement? Is it finished? Is it high enough to be used, or is it little more than a crawl space? Are there signs of water damage? Termites? With a little work, could it be converted to additional living space?

Storage

No house ever seems to have enough storage space. Is there ample closet space? Where is it located? Is a closet located in each bedroom? Is there a linen closet? Is there a broom closet, where cleaning materials and a vacuum cleaner can be stored? Can any changes be made inexpensively to create more storage space? Is there a pantry in the kitchen? Are there sufficient kitchen cupboards? Is the front closet large enough to hold your winter outerwear and that of your guests?

Heating and Cooling

How is the house heated — oil, gas, or electric? Natural gas is today the cheapest means of heating a home. Is it heated by forced air or by hot-water radiators (the older style of heating)? Is there supplementary heating, such as a wood stove? What about a heat pump? How old is the furnace? What type of furnace is it? Is it covered by a warranty plan? Is the house air conditioned? Is there a humidifier attached to the furnace? Does it have an electronic air cleaner? When were these items last serviced? Have permanent electric baseboards been built onto the floor (a sure sign of a cold or drafty area or room)? Ask for the furnace and air conditioner to be operated, depending on the season, to be sure both work properly.

Water Heater

Is it owner-owned or a rental? How is it heated? How old is it? Does it need replacing or repair?

Plumbing

Do the toilets flush properly? Are there any leaks? Does hot water flow from the faucets and shower heads properly? How high is the tub enclosure tiled?

Is the flow of cold water adequate? Flush the toilets, run the showers and try the faucets. Don't be dissuaded by an embarrassed agent or seller who has "never heard of such a thing." After all, it is the buyer who acknowledges that he or she has inspected the property, not the agent or the seller.

Check the location of the laundry taps for the washing machine. Do the same for the main water shut-off. Check the tub, toilet and sinks for scratches, dents and marks. Are they white or colored? Test the outside hose bibs. Note how many there are and where they are located.

See if there are any water stains on the floors, ceilings or walls or under sinks — a sure sign of water leaks, past or present.

Is there a dishwasher? Has the plumbing for a dishwasher even been installed or "roughed in"?

Electrical

Does the house have a fuse box or a set of circuit breakers? Where is it located? What is the amperage? (The standard is 100 amps, but 200 amps may be needed for a home office.) How many different circuits are run into the fuse box or circuit breakers? Is there room for expansion?

Is the wiring aluminum, copper or the old-fashioned "knob-and-tube"? Are there sufficient electrical outlets throughout the house? Are there sufficient electrical outlets in "high-volume" rooms (bedrooms, kitchens)? Are they adequately located? Are there any outside outlets? Where? Will all the electrical light fixtures accompany the house, or will any be excluded? Are they adequately located? Is there a heavy-duty plug for a stove and dryer? Check the light switches and outlets to make sure they work. Learn the location of the main electrical shut-off switch.

Garage and Driveway

Is there an enclosed garage? For one or two cars? Carport? Is it a private or mutual drive? Is it wide enough for two cars? Is it long enough for two cars? Is it paved or gravelled? What is the condition of the driveway? Does the garage door open properly? Is it a pull-out or roll-up door? Has an automatic garage-door opener been installed? Has a parking pad been installed at the front of the house, with municipal approval?

Landscaping

Is the grass in good condition or will it have to be replaced? Do the trees and shrubs look healthy? Will diseased ones have to be removed? Is there room for a garden to be created?

General Condition of the Interior

Walls — Are they painted? Wallpapered? Are they badly chipped or cracked? Can they be "lived with"? Are they plaster or drywall?

Floors — Are they cracked, badly scuffed, marked, or scratched? Are they linoleum, tile, vinyl, ceramic or wood?

Ceilings — Are they cracked or broken? Are there any signs of water stains?

Carpeting — Where is it located? Is it totally worn out? Is it worn out in places? Does it need cleaning? How good is the underpadding?

Windows — Are they single-pane or thermopane? Are they broken? Do they open properly and easily without excessive force? Try to open one or two windows to see. Have they been adequately caulked and weather-stripped?

Storms and Screens — Do they exist? Are they broken? Are any missing?

Doors — Do the doors open and close properly? Do the locks work properly? Do any of the locks have deadbolts? Have the doors been adequately weather-stripped?

Outside Items

What is the visible condition of the brick and mortar? The aluminum siding? The wood panels? The stucco? The chimney? Eavestroughs and downspouts? The steps and stairs? Outside painted areas? Do they need a fresh painting? How does the roof look? Have any shingles lifted? Are any missing? What about the porch? Is there a television antenna or TV tower? Test the reception. Does the ground around the perimeter of the house slope away to permit proper drainage and prevent water accumulation around foundation walls?

Rear Yard

How large is the back yard? Is there sufficient room for children to play? Is there a patio or deck? Do they need repair? Is the back yard fenced? Is the fencing solidly erected? Wood or chain link?

Type of Construction

Is the house solid brick or brick front? There is an important difference.

Solid-brick homes are supposed to represent a more solidly built house, the bricks being part of the inherent construction of the property. A solid-brick house has alternating rows of bricks facing side-out and end-out, with five rows of bricks facing side-out followed by one row facing end-out.

Newer homes are often brick front. All rows of brick face side-out. Here the brick is simply a veneer, just like aluminum siding or wood, surrounding a wood-frame construction. Brick front is very popular, to convey the impression of the house being a "brick" home.

Is the house wood frame, with stucco or aluminum siding attached to it? Is it a combination of the above?

Additional Items and Special Features

Is there a fireplace? Where is it? Is it a ceiling-to-floor fireplace, or only mantle height? Does it work properly? When was the chimney last swept? Does it have its own separate flue?

Will any appliances and fixtures accompany the house (fridge, stove, washer, dryer, dishwasher)? Are they in good working order? When were they last serviced?

How well insulated is the house? With what type of insulation? Has any insulation been added recently? Does the house have a programmable thermostat, which allows the temperature to be lowered automatically for times when the house is not occupied?

Does the property include drapes, drapery tracks, valances and window blinds? Do the bathrooms have mirrors? Do they need repair? Is there a smoke and carbon monoxide detector? Test the door chime. Walk on the floors and up and down the stairs, testing for squeaks and stability. Are the handrail and pickets made of wood, or just the rail? Is there a kitchen hood fan? Is it ducted to the outside?

In the space below, list the features and overall impressions about specific properties of interest. Record the information on this scorecard immediately after viewing the houses. Otherwise, one property will very quickly be confused with the others. Many real estate agents prepare information or data sheets, highlighting the features of properties for sale. Other agents will provide a copy of the listing to prospective buyers. Attach those sheets here as well. Don't forget to rank the properties viewed on how well they satisfy your shopping list of needs and wants and meet that definition of the ideal house.

	HOUSE #1	HOUSE #2	HOUSE #3
Address			
Price			
Mortgage Arrangements			
Taxes			
Type of House			
Style of House			
Size of House			
Lot Size			
Parking			
Mutual Drive & Right-of-Way			
Municipal Easements			
Party Walls			
Road Allowance			
Zero Lot Line			
Corner Lots			
Side of the Street			
Zoning By-laws			
Other Factors			
House Layout and Rooms			
Living Room			
Dining Room			
Bedrooms			
Kitchen			
Family Room			
Bathrooms			
Basement			
Layout of Rooms			

Have you seen a property you like? What does it have to offer compared with other homes you have seen? Would you like to own it? If so, the time may be right to consider making an offer.

19
Purchasing Rural Property

Anyone buying property in a rural area must investigate a number of additional topics as part of their home-buying strategy. All inquiries must be made before the offer is signed, so that the necessary clauses, drafted appropriately, can appear in it.

Permit for the Sewage Disposal System

Rural properties rely on septic tank systems consisting of holding tanks and tile drainage fields to dispose of sewage. Compare this with the municipal sanitary sewer system available in most urban areas. Knowing the condition of the septic tank system at the outset is essential.

Find out where the septic tank and tile bed are located. Ensure they are far enough away from any well so that the quality of the drinking water will not be affected. Ask to see any maintenance records the seller has for the septic tank system, and check them carefully. Learn when the tank was last cleaned out. Most importantly, have the condition of the septic tank and tile drainage field checked to ensure they function properly and are not undersized. While it is difficult to open up the tile bed itself and dig test holes, any wet or boggy areas are a sign that problems may exist with the septic system.

Jack and Rhonda made their offer to buy a country home conditional on having the septic tank system inspected and approved within a set number of days. During that conditional period, they also insisted on receiving a copy of the certificate of approval and use permit issued by the health department for the septic system; otherwise, their offer was null and void. While this was no guarantee that the sewage disposal system would continue to function in the future, Jack and Rhonda at least knew that it had been installed properly and that there were no apparent problems when they waived the condition.

Mac and Rena took a slightly less elaborate route when they bought rural property. They simply inserted several conditions into the offer. One required that there be no work orders, deficiency notices or complaints on file with either the provincial environment ministry or the local health unit. Another required that any certificate of approval or use permit issued for the construction, enlargement or alteration of the sewage disposal system be delivered to them before closing. With this information, Mac and Rena were satisfied with the state of the septic system when they closed their purchase.

Well Record

Ask the seller for a copy of the report prepared by the contractor when the well was dug. It should show when that was done, the location of the well on the property, the method of drilling and the bedrock materials encountered, casing and open hole information, details of the plugging and sealing, plus data on the rate of water flow from the well at that time. Because information on the water flow may be many years old, the pumping rate should be tested again, the offer being made conditional on a certain rate being achieved. Many institutional lenders require that an up-to-date pump test be conducted, meeting certain criteria, before they will advance funds on a mortgage secured by rural property. If that's the case, why not insert a similar clause into the Offer to Purchase?

Water Quality

Purchasers want to be sure the water is safe for drinking, or potable. In urban areas this is easy. Everyone assumes that the water flowing from a tap connected to a municipal water supply system is safe. On a rural property, however, where water is drawn from a well, or directly from a body of water like a lake or river, the property owner must constantly ensure the water is safe for drinking.

A sample of water taken from the well on the property, or from the lake or river, can be tested to determine its potability. A bacteriological examination of that sample is conducted, often by a provincial public health laboratory, to determine the total coliform count as well as the fecal count. Total coliform bacteria are located in animal wastes, sewage, soil and vegetation. Fecal coliform bacteria are a much greater concern, as they are more likely to represent sewage contamination, their source being the intestines of warm-blooded animals like humans. Less than 2 total coliforms per 100 ml and zero fecal coliforms per 100 ml are the acceptable limits, rendering the water safe for drinking. These bacteriological tests have nothing to do with the chemical quality of the water (the presence of sodium, fluoride and nitrates), which is also important.

When Stan and Tammy bought a rural property, they inserted a detailed condition into the offer dealing with the potability of the water supplied by the well. The offer was made conditional on a sample taken immediately before the offer was signed, indicating that the well water was potable. A second examination was to be conducted one week before closing, requiring that the water again be tested to ensure it was bacteriologically safe for drinking. If not, the seller would be obligated to install whatever chlorination system was necessary to continuously treat the water. Both tests indicated that the water was potable, and Stan and Tammy's purchase closed smoothly.

Utility Easements

An easement is right-of-way granted by the owner of the property to another party. Some provincial hydro-electric commissions have rights-of-way across rural properties that are not registered on title. The right-of-way can consist of a major transmission tower, or simply poles, wires and anchors running across the property. In either case, a visual inspection of the property should reveal if any such rights-of-way exist. If it's important that no hydro right-of-way traverse the property, insert a condition to that effect into the offer.

Access to Provincial Highways

Entrance or access points onto provincial highways may require a permit issued by the provincial highways ministry. While David and Lynne might own a property abutting a provincial highway, no access would be permitted until the government granted its approval. This reverses the normal rule, that access onto a property from a roadway is permitted at whatever location the owner wishes. This way, the government can prevent driveways from being placed in locations where the line of vision is poor, e.g., on hills or a curve. When they purchased their property, David and Lynne added a condition to the offer, that the required permit from the department of highways be delivered on closing.

Seeing a lawyer before signing an offer is a key component of everybody's HOBS. When a rural property is involved, there is all the more reason to see a lawyer early in the process — to ensure that these key conditions not only appear in the offer but are properly worded to protect you, the purchaser.

20
Condominiums

As small, independent communities, condominiums represent a different type of lifestyle, where community interests often take precedence over individual rights. Anyone contemplating a condominium purchase, especially existing home owners, must thoroughly understand how they work and how they differ from conventional property ownership. Only in this way can purchasers be absolutely certain their personal lifestyle and the condominium way of life are compatible.

Condominiums, also known as Strata Titles in British Columbia and Co-ownership of Immoveables in Quebec, have been very popular over the years in Europe and in parts of the United States as a form of middle- and upper-class housing. Although condominiums by their nature impose limitations on personal freedoms, their owners emphasize how condominiums give them the best of both worlds: home ownership, plus convenience and a more independent lifestyle. The condominium ensures that many of the traditional responsibilities associated with home ownership (such as cutting the grass and shovelling the snow) are provided — for a fee, of course, the payment of a monthly maintenance charge.

When condominiums were first introduced to Canada in the late 1960s, their historical foundation was ignored. Condominiums were promoted as a means of providing "affordable" housing. In their formative years, condominiums developed a black eye arising from the excruciating problems selling and maintaining them as a form of low-income housing. The abuses of some builders developing early condo projects did not help their initial reputation either. Only in the mid-1970s, when condominiums returned to their historical roots, housing for middle- and upper-income Canadians (the so-called "luxury condominium"), did the boom in condominium development really begin.

Today, condominiums have a special appeal for people entering retirement — the so-called "empty nesters" — a phenomenon that is expected to continue with the greying of the baby boomers. Condominiums are also attractive to young couples anxious to live in the city core at a reasonable price, owning their own home instead of renting it.

Condominiums are creatures of provincial statutes. While minor variations exist from province to province, the following commentary applies to most condominiums across the country.

Only the purchase of a resale condominium unit will be examined here. Just as acquiring a newly constructed home differs considerably from buying a resale property, so too with condominiums. Purchasing a unit in a new, unregistered condominium complex subjects buyers to a set of rules and situations no other purchasers face.

What Is a Condominium?

While the term "condominium" is often used as an adjective for a type of building, it really describes a unique system of land ownership. The purchaser of a unit in a condominium, whether townhouse or apartment, acquires

a)   a specific residential dwelling unit where title is registered in the buyer's name. Many of the expenses usually associated with home ownership (e.g., realty taxes, mortgage payments, maintenance and repairs to the unit, and sometimes even utility charges) remain the buyer's responsibility.

b)   a percentage interest in the remainder of the condominium property and the common areas, properly called the "common elements," which are owned by all unit owners. Included here are the hallways, stairwells, lobbies, driveways, elevators, walkways, parking garage, recreational facilities, grounds and playground, as well as the land itself upon which the building is situated.

c) some parts of the common elements fall into a third category, exclusive-use common elements. Although owned and maintained by the condo corporation, their use is restricted to just one owner. Typical examples are balconies, parking spaces and storage lockers in condominium apartments, and lawns (front and back) in townhouse developments. More on exclusive-use common elements appears below.

Like single-family homes, condominium units are bought, sold and mortgaged separately. Any unit owner who does not pay his or her mortgage or property taxes will not jeopardize anyone else's unit in the complex.

Since all unit owners own the common elements, they are all responsible for paying their proportionate share to maintain it. A monthly maintenance (common expense) fee is levied against all unit owners for the expenses incurred operating the condominium corporation. An owner's share of the total common area expenses should correspond to his or her interest in the common elements. By owning a three-bedroom unit, Carey and Sharon would own a larger percentage of the common elements and therefore would pay a higher monthly common expense or maintenance charge than William and Samantha, owners of a two-bedroom unit.

All unit owners also become members in the condominium corporation, which handles the project's business affairs.

Types of Condominiums

Most condominium developments are either high-rise apartments or low-rise townhouses. Important differences do exist between the two. Apartment condominiums generally have higher monthly common expense payments, due to the very nature of living in an apartment building. Maintaining, repairing and cleaning a bank of elevators, interior common elements, and an underground garage are costs only high-rise condominium owners incur.

Townhouse condominiums usually treat utility charges differently, too. Hydro, water, gas and cable television charges are often excluded from the monthly maintenance fee, being separately billed to individual townhouse units. With condominium apartments, these charges are often bulk-metered to the condominium complex as a whole, and included in the maintenance fee (although this situation is starting to change). That means energy-efficient condo townhouse owners (e.g., people who always turn off the light when not in a room) don't end up subsidizing their more extravagant co-owners, allowing them to control their own costs.

Advantages of Condominium Ownership

Convenience — that is the biggest advantage of condominium ownership. It's the best of both worlds: home ownership without its mundane burdens and tasks. Unit owners don't have to do any maintenance outside the unit. As part of the monthly charge, the grass is cut, snow removed, grounds landscaped and exterior maintained. Obviously, condominiums won't appeal to the home handyman, people who want a backyard garden, or anyone who hates paying for a service they can provide themselves. Although that convenience comes at a cost, it is a major reason for the increased popularity of luxury condominiums amongst older people, empty-nesters, childless couples and some career-conscious individuals.

Other people are attracted to condominiums by the recreational facilities they include. Swimming pools, squash and racquetball courts and fitness/exercise equipment are just some of the recreational features that magnify the appeal of condominium ownership. And condominiums provide an enhanced level of security, too. Access is restricted, depending on the project, sometimes to the building alone (like a rental apartment building), but often to the entire complex, with a security guard monitoring who enters the grounds.

Disadvantages of Condominium Ownership

By their very nature, condominiums place severe restrictions on the personal freedoms traditionally associated with single-family ownership. Individual rights must yield to the common good. After all, a condominium unit owner is a hybrid — a cross between a home owner and a tenant — whether the condominium is a townhouse or an apartment complex. Because anything done by one unit owner could affect others in the complex, restrictions are imposed to regulate how the condominium *and its individual units* are used. Condominium unit owners effectively face another level of government — federal, provincial and municipal, plus the laws, rules and regulations of the condominium corporation, enacted to control activities within its boundaries and ensure peace and harmony.

How acceptable those restrictions are, often depends on the background of the buyer. Unlike former owners of single-family homes, former tenants will be familiar with having rules and regulations for the complex. Doug recently bought a unit in a high-rise condominium after years of owning his own home. Like a conventional home owner, Doug has control over many aspects of property ownership: how to finance his purchase, how to decorate his unit, when to sell his property and for what price. However, many other rights are shared in common with other unit owners, and can only be decided by committee. Some Doug recognizes and accepts, such as the use of the common elements and the operation of the condominium corporation as a small business. What Doug is having a difficult time accepting are the regulations imposed by the condominium corporation on *the use of his own unit.* More information on condominium rules and regulations appears later in this chapter.

Factors to Consider When Buying a Condominium

As with any other real estate purchase, purchasers of a resale condominium unit must develop and apply their own unique, tailor-made home-buying strategy, or HOBS. The same considerations described earlier about community, neighborhood and specific site location obviously apply here as well. But a number of other issues, unique to condominiums but similar to those encountered living in an apartment building, must also be considered. These include:

- adequacy and location of parking spaces, for both owners and visitors (parking spaces are explored in more detail below)
- adequacy, location and accessibility of locker and storage space (is it inside or outside the unit?)
- proximity to the elevator and the garbage chute
- how well the unit is lit by natural light (a great concern for people wanting to grow indoor plants)
- floor level in an apartment condominium (often a premium is paid for upper floors)
- the maintenance fee: How much is it? What does it include and exclude? Who pays the utility charges (hydro, water, gas), heating and cable television?
- the type of complex: Adult only? Are there adequate facilities for children? (While the concept of an adult-only complex has been criticized for violating the Canadian Charter of Rights and Freedoms, some are designed and built to discourage families with young children from purchasing a unit)
- recreational and other amenities: Swimming pool (indoor or outdoor)? Sauna? Tennis/squash/racquetball courts? Meeting/multi-purpose room? Health club?
- security: Is 24-hour security provided for the residents?
- noise level: Is there adequate sound insulation to ensure proper sound-proofing? (Unlike with a brand-new condominium, buyers of resale units have the advantage of being able to hear the level of sound being transmitted through walls, ceilings and floors. If noise is a concern, make sure the unit is distant from garage doors, saunas, laundry rooms, elevators, garbage chutes, and heating and electrical plants.)
- rules and regulations: what you can and cannot do, both with your unit and within the complex.

What Do I Own and What Can I Use?

The documents establishing the condominium, called the "Declaration" and the "Description," state precisely what is acquired when a condominium is purchased. While the boundaries are the same for the most part, some differences do exist from project to project. In layman's terms, a dwelling unit generally consists of the area from wall to wall, ceiling to floor — "a box in the sky." Legally speaking, the boundaries of a unit are generally defined to be the upper surface of the concrete floor slab, the lower surface of the concrete ceiling, and the interior surface of the unfinished walls. Everything else, including the space between the floors and the units, are common elements.

Knowing the precise boundaries of a dwelling unit is very important, as it determines who is responsible for repairing damage. Individual unit owners like Arnold and Hyla must repair and maintain their unit, while the condominium corporation is responsible for maintaining and repairing the common elements. Recently, a leaky pipe damaged the walls in Arnold and Hyla's fourth-floor unit, as well as the hallway outside their apartment. While the condominium corporation will have to repair the wall itself and repaint its surface in the hallway (common elements), Arnold and Hyla are responsible for repainting or wallpapering the surface of the walls within their unit, since they own it.

Parking spaces provide an interesting lesson on how a condominium purchaser acquires an interest in the property. Parking (and often locker) units can be acquired in one of four different ways, depending on the specific project: a) freehold; b) leasehold; c) exclusive-use; and d) allocated. A freehold unit is best for a buyer, the allocation method being the least advantageous. While all give a unit owner rights to a specific parking space, the legal interest acquired varies greatly.

Norma bought a freehold parking unit. She owns it outright, just like her dwelling unit, a deed to the parking unit being registered in her name. Since she also bought a second parking unit, she can use it, lease it or sell it to anyone else in the condominium complex, depending on her particular situation.

If a freehold unit is not available, a leasehold parking unit is the next best choice. They are owned by the condominium corporation as part of the common elements, but are leased to people like John, the owner of a specific dwelling unit, on a long-term basis, perhaps as long as 99 years. The dwelling unit and the leased parking unit go hand in hand for the term of the lease. When John sells his dwelling unit, the lease is automatically transferred to the new owner of the dwelling unit.

Exclusive-use common element parking spaces are the most common types distributed among unit owners. Like with leasing, the condominium corporation owns the parking spaces as part of the common elements. But instead of leasing them to individual unit owners, the condominium Declaration specifies who has the exclusive right to use which parking space, in perpetuity. Julie, the owner of dwelling unit 4, level 11, has the exclusive use to use parking space 160. If she sells her dwelling unit to Alex, he automatically acquires the exclusive right to use parking space 160. This exclusive right of usage, which links the parking and dwelling units together, is nontransferable unless the dwelling itself unit is conveyed. With exclusive-use parking spaces, a specific parking unit is guaranteed to a specific unit owner forever, without a deed ever being registered.

The worst way for a purchaser to "acquire" a parking unit is the allocation method. Although each unit is entitled to a parking space, the directors of the condominium corporation determine its precise location. Who gets what parking space then becomes a political issue. As properties are sold, "prime" parking spaces, closer to the elevator, can be re-allocated to long-term residents and those on the board of directors. Newer occupants wind up with parking spaces in less advantageous locations.

Most condominium owners are surprised to learn they do not own the backyard patio or front and rear yards of townhouses, or the balconies of apartment condominiums adjacent to their dwelling units. All of these are part of the common elements owned by the condominium corporation. What unit owners have, though, is the exclusive right to use those parts of the common elements, to the exclusion of other people, identical to the exclusive-use common element parking space. Often the condominium corporation will repair and maintain those areas, although occasionally the responsibility rests with the unit owner.

Before signing any offer for a condominium unit, purchasers applying their HOBS will learn exactly what the unit includes, the nature of the parking and locker unit, and those areas which are exclusive-use common areas. The best way to do this is by making the Agreement of Purchase and Sale conditional on reviewing and approving the condominium documents, an approach described in more detail below.

Rules and Regulations

As a mini-community, every condominium imposes restrictions on certain activities of its residents. Usually (but not always), they are incorporated in the Rules and Regulations passed by the directors of the condominium corporation. Many are practical and make good sense. Similar to house rules in apartment buildings, they promote the safety, security and welfare of the unit owners. Condominium rules must strike a balance among the unit owners, to prevent unreasonable interference with the owners' use and enjoyment of their property.

Some Rules and Regulations, though, do not simply deal with the use of the common elements. *They also affect a unit owner's use and enjoyment of his or her property, by regulating and restricting the way individual units are used.* Obviously, that annoys some unit owners. Yet that is the very nature of condominium ownership — the different lifestyle discussed earlier — where restrictions are placed on some personal freedoms, to provide the greatest protection for the greatest number of residents. Typical Rules and Regulations affecting units deal with pets, or require that certain areas in an apartment unit be carpeted to keep noise levels low for the floor below.

Owners of condo units in townhouse projects often question the need for Rules and Regulations. In reality, a townhouse complex resembles a small subdivision. Builders often impose restrictions in a new subdivision to control how it is developed and maintained. For example, the prohibition of clotheslines and TV antennas adds to the esthetic beauty of a subdivision.

So too with the Rules and Regulations in a townhouse complex.

Only in the rarest of cases can owners of single-family homes be forced to spend money against their will. Not so in a condominium. Consider the situation a unit owner like Joey faces, where a major expenditure such as the refurbishing of recreational facilities is approved by an overwhelming vote of the unit owners. Everyone, even those owners like Joey opposed to the project, is then obligated to pay their proportionate share of the expense. Many condominium owners, especially former owners of traditional homes, are uncomfortable with this arrangement.

Like landlords in apartment buildings, representatives of most condominium corporations are allowed to enter a unit without notice at any time in an emergency, to repair the unit or to correct any condition which could cause damage or loss to the unit or the common elements. To ensure proper access, the condominium corporation is entitled to retain a key to all locks for each unit. While this type of emergency access can be justified to protect the overall interests of unit owners, it greatly differs from the privacy and security of a single-family home. While former tenants may feel quite comfortable with this arrangement, the idea may be foreign to long-time traditional home owners.

Before signing any Offer to Purchase, learn more about *all* the restrictions and house rules imposed by that condominium corporation. Are any of them unacceptable, or inconsistent with your intended use of the unit? The question of pets is a classic example. Different condominiums have different Rules and Regulations on the keeping of pets, varying from one extreme to the other. Some prohibit pets altogether. Others restrict the type of pets (dogs, cats, birds and tropical fish) allowed, and where they are permitted. Still others impose weight restrictions on pets, or numerical limits, while others will allow any pet to live there, provided it is not a "nuisance" (as determined by the condo board of directors at its absolute discretion). And occasionally, a condo project will tighten up its pet rule. Those pets that currently reside in a condo unit can continue to live there, but they cannot be replaced after they die.

Learning more about the condominium's Rules and

Regulations in the pre-contract stage is very important. Knowing where to find all those restrictions is much more difficult. To the surprise of many people, not all rules and regulations appear in the Rules and Regulations! Often they are buried in the condominium constitution, the Declaration. This way the rule is virtually unalterable, requiring unanimous consent of both owners and lenders before it can be changed. Rules and Regulations, on the other hand, can be easily amended by the directors of the condominium corporation. So it's not enough simply to examine the Rules and Regulations of a condominium project in order to discover all its rules and regulations.

Aaron and Sharon wanted to keep their French poodle when they moved to a condominium apartment. When they asked the real estate agent (before the offer was signed) about pets, he pointed out that the Rules and Regulations were silent on the point, implying that pets were permitted. However, Aaron and Sharon wisely made their Offer to Purchase conditional on their lawyer reviewing the condominium documents and approving them. From that perusal, they learned of the no-pets clause in the Declaration. Aaron and Sharon decided not to purchase that unit.

If keeping a pet such as a dog is important, buyers in Aaron and Sharon's situation can do one of three things:

a) Add a condition (not a warranty — see chapter 25 for the difference) to the offer, that a dog is permitted in the unit and on the common elements. This way, if no dogs are allowed, buyers like Aaron and Sharon can cancel the contract, as the condition had been breached.

b) Ask the seller for the Rules and Regulations and the other condominium documents before signing any Offer to Purchase, and review them. To avoid future problems, never simply rely on the information provided by the seller or either agent. Ask questions about areas of specific concerns, and independently verify the answers given before signing anything. And remember, not all rules and regulations appear in the Rules and Regulations.

c) Make the Offer to Purchase conditional on your lawyer reviewing and approving the condominium documents.

Otherwise, the deal is null and void. Usually, seven to ten days will be needed to obtain these items and examine them. For more information on making an offer conditional this way, see chapter 26.

Points to Know About Owning a Condominium

1. The Condominium Corporation

Once the Declaration and Description are registered, the condominium is born, together with a "non-share capital" corporation. All unit owners are members of the condominium corporation, and each unit has one vote, no matter how large a percentage interest in the common elements accompanies that unit.

Like any other business corporation, the condominium corporation has officers and a board of directors elected by the condominium owners to manage its affairs. By-laws are enacted and rules are passed, provided that the proper corporate procedures are followed. Because running the condominium corporation on a day-to-day basis can be very time-consuming, most corporations retain the services of a management company, its fees being added to the common expenses. Smaller projects are often self-managed.

The management company attends to the upkeep, maintenance and repair of the common elements and other assets of the condominium corporation; keeps the corporation's records up to date; collects and disburses the common expense funds; enters into contracts and other agreements on behalf of the corporation, often with dollar limits; and prepares the annual budget, which forms the basis of the monthly common expense charge. Policy decisions continue to rest with the board of directors.

A common complaint of many unit owners is that decisions are made without their input. But who makes those decisions? The board of directors. Directors are almost always residents in the complex who take the time to get involved in the management and operation of the condominium corporation. So instead of complaining, participate! Become part of the decision-making process. Seek election to the board of directors. Learn firsthand about condominium ownership, with the best possible "on-the-job" training. Don't leave it up to someone else; get involved yourself. As a member of the board of directors, you will know what is happening, as it happens, since you are making it happen. Finally your voice will be heard and your ideas considered. And it's an excellent way to meet your neighbors, make new friends and gain valuable experience.

2. Common Expenses (Commonly Called Maintenance)

The common expenses are monthly fees paid by unit owners for the upkeep, maintenance and repair of the common elements as well as the operation of the condominium corporation. While these expenses can vary from project to project (especially in townhouse vs. apartment condos), the following are typically included in the monthly maintenance payment: utilities (if not individually metered); operating costs such as snow removal and lawn maintenance; the cost of repairs and maintenance of common elements; service contracts; personnel; supplies; insurance on the common elements; fees paid to the management company; administrative charges; and contributions to the reserve fund (discussed below). To see exactly what the common expenses cover, refer to the condominium's Declaration. Many condominium owners are rightly upset when garbage disposal fees are included. In a sense, they are paying double for garbage pick-up, once to the condominium corporation and once to the municipality.

Like with unpaid realty taxes, if one unit owner does not pay his or her share of the common expenses promptly, all unit owners must bear the burden. To ensure that everyone pays his or her due when due, the condominium corporation can place a lien against a unit when common expenses are unpaid. If registered in time, that lien can also have priority over any previously registered mortgages. The condominium corporation can, if necessary, sell a unit to recoup outstanding maintenance charges. While this may prevent a particular unit owner from getting out of hand, widespread default could endanger a condo corporation's economic health.

To learn more about what's being purchased, and avoid

inheriting the seller's financial headaches, the buyer gets his or her lawyer to order an "Estoppel Certificate" from the condominium corporation before closing. "Estoppel" is a legal term whereby a party is bound by the contents of a statement, if that statement is relied upon by its recipient. An Estoppel Certificate provides a status update on the unit and its current owner, plus information about any maintenance arrears for the unit. But an Estoppel Certificate also contains valuable information about the condominium corporation itself, such as the amount of the reserve fund, pending or contemplated lawsuits, and alterations and improvements to the common elements. Accompanying the certificate are pertinent condominium documents such as the Rules and Regulations, Declaration, By-laws, Certificate of Insurance, most recent financial statements and current budget for the corporation. The budget is a key item to review, as large outlays of money on common elements over the next year is an indication that a project is starting to show its age, meaning higher maintenance fees down the road.

3. Selling/Leasing Units

According to the provincial condominium acts, dwelling units can be freely sold, subject to any restrictions in the Declaration. Whether such restrictions on sales are enforceable is another question. Like co-op units in Canada, boards of directors in the United States often must approve any subsequent purchaser of a condo unit. In effect, this gives the board a veto over who can own a unit in the complex. Though permitted by condominium legislation in some areas of Canada, such restrictions are rare in this country.

The right of unit owners to rent their property is clear, though, provided that they comply with the provisions of the condominium Declaration. While condominium corporations may have the right to place restrictions on the leasing of units, rarely is this done in Canada. Quite common, however, is the requirement that specific information about the tenant be given to the condominium corporation. The tenant in turn must agree in writing to comply with the Rules and Regulations, Declaration and By-laws of the condominium corporation during his or her tenancy.

4. Insurance

The distinction between individual units and common elements is most noticeable when dealing with insurance. Insurance coverage is arranged by the condominium corporation through a master policy on the common elements only. It provides protection against loss by fire, water, smoke and other major perils on a replacement cost basis. The premium paid for this insurance coverage is included in the monthly maintenance payment. Liability coverage for the common elements also must be maintained by the corporation.

However, this coverage does not protect the unit owners, their units, "improvements and betterments" made to their units or the contents of their units. Public liability coverage for units is also not provided by the condominium corporation's insurance. These items remain the responsibility of the unit owners.

The insurance industry has developed "condominium unit owner's package insurance" to provide the insurance coverage unit owners need. Coverage of this type is a hybrid, recognizing that a condominium itself is a hybrid between conventional home ownership and a tenancy. In some respects this insurance coverage resembles a home owner's package, as the unit itself is owned, while in other areas this coverage parallels a tenant's package, because the unit is only one in a larger complex. When arranging insurance coverage before closing, inform your insurance agent that a condominium unit is being bought. The appropriate condominium unit owner's package insurance coverage can then be booked.

Options to consider in addition to the basic unit owner's insurance and contents coverage include: insuring all improvements and betterments made to the unit; insuring on an all-risks basis (it provides much broader coverage than the standard named perils); plus replacement cost coverage. Personal liability coverage, which protects unit owners if they are sued by someone injured in the unit, should also be included. Some insurance companies will even provide coverage at nominal cost for any loss suffered by a unit owner arising from a deficiency in the condominium corporation's insurance coverage. This could arise if the common elements are damaged and the condominium corporation's insurance coverage is inadequate to fully repair the damage. All unit owners would then have to make up the shortfall by way of a special assessment. With this additional coverage (called loss assessment coverage), owners are reimbursed with the amount of the special assessment.

Two incidents at a party held in Donald's condo apartment illustrate the different types of insurance that must be arranged. Mickey, a guest at the party, broke his ankle when he tripped on the rug in the hallway of the apartment building. Because his accident happened on a common element, Mickey must make a claim against the condominium corporation's personal liability insurance coverage. Minnie, on the other hand, tripped on a rug inside Donald's suite, breaking her ankle. So Minnie will have to look to Donald's personal liability insurance coverage. The same is true with a fire. Depending on whether it occurred on a common element or within a unit, the different insurance policies would be responsible for bearing the cost of repairing the damage.

5. The Reserve Fund

One of the problems early condominiums faced was a shortage of money for major repairs. As an inducement to sell units, developers pegged the amount of the monthly common expenses (maintenance) artificially low. No money was being set aside for a "rainy day." When costly repairs were needed or major assets had to be replaced, condominium corporations lacked the necessary funds to do the work. Special assessments had to be levied against units to generate the needed cash. If unit owners refused or were unable to pay, liens were registered against their units, followed by proceedings to sell them. This pitted neighboring owners against one another in their own complexes. Yet who was the real author of the problem? The developer.

Reserve funds, the money for a "rainy day," now exist to solve this dilemma. Each condominium corporation must maintain a reserve fund to provide sufficient money to cover the cost of major repairs and the replacement of major assets which wear out, such as roofs, sidewalks, heating, electrical and plumbing systems, elevators, laundry machines, carpeting, and recreational and parking facilities. A portion of each monthly maintenance payment must be set aside to be paid into the reserve fund. The exact amount of the reserve fund contribution is based on the expected repair, replacement cost and life expectancy of the common elements and corporate assets. In Ontario it must be at least 10% of the maintenance otherwise payable. Older condominiums should have larger reserve funds, as the likelihood of needing to repair and replace major assets and equipment is considerably greater.

A unit's proportionate interest in the reserve fund is easy to determine. Simply multiply the total amount in the reserve fund by the unit owner's share of the common elements. (To learn the amount of money being held in the reserve fund, see the Estoppel Certificate.) Per unit, the amount of money involved could be in the hundreds, even thousands, of dollars.

According to the Estoppel Certificate issued when Irv and Ethel purchased their condominium unit, the corporation's reserve fund amounted to $177,960. Because they owned .550514% of the common elements, their proportionate interest in the reserve fund totalled $979.69.

Does the seller get a credit for this amount from the purchaser when the unit is sold? Obviously, sellers feel they are entitled to be reimbursed for this money, as it represents prepaid funds, comparable to prepaid realty taxes. Buyers argue that no adjustment of the reserve fund should be made, as provincial condominium acts prevent the money from being paid out to its owners. Money in the reserve fund should be viewed as an asset of the corporation by law, just like the bricks and mortar of the building. By acquiring a unit, the buyer should also acquire the vendor's interest in the reserve fund, without adjustment.

Many offers deal with the issue, specifically stating that no adjustment of the reserve fund will be made on closing. Even if an offer is silent on the point, this is the generally accepted point of view. Of course, an offer could be drawn specifically requiring the amount in the reserve fund to be credited to the vendor. In that case, the buyer should be prepared to pay a sizeable additional sum of money on closing. As with much of real estate, buyer beware.

A serious problem would exist if the reserve fund had insufficient money to cover the cost of unexpected major repairs.

While the Estoppel Certificate provides information about the size of the reserve fund, normally this information is obtained shortly before closing, too late to permit a buyer to withdraw from the transaction. All the more reason purchasers should make the Offer to Purchase a resale condo unit conditional on reviewing and approving the condominium documents — including the Estoppel Certificate, which contains information about the reserve fund. For details, see chapter 26.

More and more older condominiums are conducting "reserve fund studies" today. Here, an engineering company surveys the state of the common elements and their life expectancies, and determines if there will be sufficient money available in the reserve fund to replace those items as they wear out. If not, a special assessment may be necessary to "top up" the reserve fund. Or an increase in the monthly maintenance fee may be needed. Information about whether a reserve fund study has been conducted, when, and the results of the investigation, will accompany the Estoppel Certificate. A move is underway to make reserve fund studies mandatory for all condominiums across Canada.

6. Mortgage Clauses

Most mortgages secured against condominiums include specially tailored clauses. Some examples:

- Lenders are given the right to exercise the borrower's vote at any meeting of the condominium corporation. Although it is usually not exercised, lenders want this right to protect their investment, which often is larger than the owner's.
- Copies of all relevant notices and documents must be sent to the lender, so that it knows what is happening in the condominium.
- The borrower must agree to punctually pay all common expenses to the condominium corporation. When a borrower defaults, the lender can pay the arrears and add it to the mortgage debt. Many lenders will do this, as up to three months' unpaid maintenance fees have priority over and rank higher than a first mortgage.
- Borrowers must agree to comply with, observe and perform

all duties and obligations imposed by the provincial condominium act, the Declaration, By-laws, Rules and Regulations of the condominium corporation. Noncompliance gives the lender the right, *at its option*, to demand repayment of the mortgage in full. Taking this to the extreme, possession of a pet in violation of the condominium's Rules and Regulations could be grounds for a lender to terminate the mortgage!

The days of lenders treating mortgages on owner-occupied condominium units differently than those on single-family homes are over. No longer are higher interest rates charged or mortgages granted with a lower loan-to-value ratio.

What a Condominium Offer Should Contain

To reflect the uniqueness of condominium ownership, several additional clauses must appear in the offer submitted. Purchasers of resale condominiums should ask the following questions and ensure that the offer addresses the following issues:

- Find out the condominium unit and level number, plus the condominium corporation number. Note that the unit number does not have to correspond with the apartment number. So Cheryl's suite 717 could be Unit 14, Level 7. Many high-rise buildings lack a 13th floor for post-office purposes, but do not ignore it as part of the legal description. Skipping the 13th floor on the address board throws the numbering for the upper floors totally out of whack. So Linda's suite 1802 might be known legally as Unit 5, Level 17.
- Make the Offer to Purchase conditional on your receiving the relevant condominium documents from the condo corporation and approving them.
- Make sure the reserve fund is not to be adjusted in the seller's favor.
- Learn whether the parking space (and locker) is freehold, leasehold, exclusive-use or allocated. And learn if any additional fee is payable for parking.

- Does the unit owner have an exclusive right to use any other area: patio/balcony; front yard/side yard?
- How much is the monthly maintenance (common expense) payment? Does it include hydro rates? Water rates? Heating charges? Cable television fee? When was it last raised? If a year has passed since the last increase, expect it to be raised imminently.
- Have any special assessments been made against the unit which have not been fully paid? If so, make sure the seller pays them before closing. Are any special assessments contemplated or proposed? A unit owner should know this, since special assessments can only be levied if approved at a meeting of the condominium corporation. Has such a meeting been held recently, or is one scheduled?
- Are any substantial alterations or improvements to the common elements planned?
- Has the seller already assigned his or her voting rights to a mortgagee? If so, the buyer or the buyer's new lender can only exercise that vote if the seller's mortgage is dis-charged.
- Are any legal actions pending by or against the condo-minium corporation? This is very important, since a judgment against the condominium corporation also is a judgment against each unit owner *at the time of judgment.* No one wants to buy a lawsuit, or someone else's headache.

Perhaps someone slipped on some ice outside the build-ing, and is suing the condominium corporation. By closing the transaction, the seller dumps his or her potential liabil-ity onto the buyer. That's why learning this information now, not later, is so important. With sufficient advance notice, arrangements can be made to ensure that the seller satisfies his or her proportionate interest in any judgment against the condominium pertaining to the time the seller owned the unit.

Too often, clauses like these are drafted in offers as war-ranties. As is noted in chapter 25, buyers cannot refuse to close a transaction if a warranty is breached. They must proceed with the closing and sue the seller for damages afterwards. If these issues are important, to the point that you as a purchaser would want the right to cancel the contract immediately if the information provided was incorrect, then these clauses should be framed as conditions, not warranties.

- Are there any restrictions in the Declaration or the By-laws on the sale of the unit? Learn this now, before submitting an offer. According to the fine print in some standard form resale offers, if the written consent of the condominium corporation or its board of directors is required, the offer is made conditional on obtaining that consent before closing. This is small consolation to buyers like Neil and Jane, who only learned about the approval requirement a week after their offer was accepted, and just three weeks before closing. Imagine how they felt seven days later upon learning that their application for consent was rejected. Here were Neil, Jane and family, two weeks before closing, with no place to live, no Offer to Purchase and no recourse against the seller for damages. That's right! The contract was conditional on obtaining that consent. And as the condition was never satisfied, it never became firm and binding. This was disastrous for Neil and Jane, who had made numerous plans based on the anticipated purchase of this property, including the sale of their present home.

  As a member of the condominium corporation, the seller should have known whether any restriction on sale existed. The real estate agent also should have verified this information independently before preparing an offer, the same as the particulars of a mortgage to be assumed must be verified.

- To safeguard against this happening, all buyers of resale units should do the following:
  a) Ask the agent and the seller whether any restrictions exist on the transfer of the unit.
  b) Based on their reply, insert a *condition* into the offer that no restrictions exist in the condominium documents on the sale of the unit. Don and Pat did this, and were they ever glad they did! Two weeks after the offer was signed, they learned that approval to the transfer was required despite the assurances given

by the agent and the seller, Peter. This meant the condition in the contract had been breached. Don and Pat then had to decide whether or not to make the necessary application for consent, something they were not legally obligated to do. While saying yes, Don and Pat did so only on clearly spelled-out terms. If the required consent was not available three weeks before closing, then Don and Pat could withdraw from the transaction and Peter the seller would have to compensate them for *all* expenses incurred in finding alternative accommodations. Thankfully the consent was granted on time and the deal closed as scheduled.

With more than a generation of history and experience in this country, condominiums are no longer foreign to most people. However, as part of your home-buying strategy, recognize what condominiums are and how they work, before considering if your personal lifestyle is compatible with the condominium world.

21
Mortgage Financing

Few Canadians are fortunate enough to buy a home without having to arrange a mortgage. Because it plays a pivotal role in the purchase transaction, buyers should shop as prudently for a mortgage as they do for a house. While the legal concept of a mortgage —security for the repayment of a loan —is the same everywhere, packages of terms and features vary considerably from lender to lender, making the choice of a mortgage all the more difficult. In this chapter, some of the key elements of mortgage financing for resale homes will be explored. Further detailed information on mortgages —what they are, how to arrange the best possible mortgage, and then how to pay them off as quickly as possible —is available from two other books, *Hidden Profits in Your Mortgage* and *The Perfect Mortgage*, both from Stoddart Publishing.

As noted in chapter 8, devotees of the HOBS approach to buying a house will not leave the question of arranging a mortgage to the very end, after the offer is signed, almost as an afterthought. Instead, they will go mortgage shopping and get pre-approved well *before* any Offer to Purchase is submitted. This will allow them to learn in advance what is available in the marketplace, and decide which features are most appealing, free from the time pressures that other purchasers face. The alternative is to submit an offer conditional on arranging satisfactory financing within a very short period of time after acceptance. Purchasers then inevitably accept the first mortgage offer presented, whatever the terms, lacking the luxury of time to pursue any better deal. Leaving the need for a mortgage to that late in the process is never in a purchaser's best interests.

By following this key element of a home-buying strategy, borrowers can approach the question of mortgage financing from a position of strength. All the necessary questions will have been asked, and the right mortgage package and lender selected, all at the pre-offer stage. Instead of *whether* a mortgage will be granted, the question now concerns *who* will grant that mortgage. Then, once the offer is signed, there's little more to be done than file the formal application.

A key element of a HOBS encourages purchasers to take the draft, unsigned offer to their lawyer for review and comment. More and more purchasers are doing this with unsigned mortgage commitments, too, to ensure that the commitment contains what it is supposed to contain. Nothing unexpected is added in, and nothing important is missing. Most mortgage commitments can be reviewed in a very short period of time, making the cost to the purchaser nominal (assuming there's any charge at all).

To arrange a mortgage loan, buyers/borrowers must know more about the nature of the beast. Expressions that will be encountered include:

> **Equity:** The owner's interest in the property; the difference between the fair market value of a property and the outstanding mortgages. Howard and Sheila own a house worth $180,000 and owe $110,000 on their mortgage. Therefore, their equity is $70,000.
> **Term:** The life of the mortgage —anywhere from six months to 10 years, sometimes even more. It is *not* the same as the amortization.
> **Amortization:** The period of time that it would take for the mortgage to be fully paid off, if all payments were made on time, with no prepayments and no late payments. Only at the end of the amortization period is the mortgage fully paid off. Shorter amortizations mean higher mortgage payments but lower overall interest costs. A typical mortgage has a three-year term, 25-year amortization. That means the

mortgage matures in three years' time, while the payments are calculated as if it would take 25 years for the loan to be retired in full.

Blended payments: The same amount of money is paid to the lender each payment during the term of the loan, whether those payments be monthly, weekly, bi-weekly (every two weeks) or semi-monthly (twice a month). However, the mix between principal and interest changes with each payment. Over time, the principal component increases, while the interest component decreases.

When buying a resale property, buyers can "get" a mortgage in one of three ways: by assuming an existing mortgage; by having the seller take back a mortgage for the unpaid balance of the purchase price; or by arranging their own mortgage.

Assuming an Existing Mortgage

Maynard is selling his home, which already has a mortgage registered against it. If Dobie, the purchaser, assumes or takes it over on closing, he will assume all of Maynard's rights and obligations under the mortgage. When calculating the amount payable by Maynard on closing, the amount of the assumed mortgage is deducted from the purchase price. Thus Dobie is buying the house "cash to the mortgage," the cash payment to Maynard plus the amount of the assumed mortgage totalling the purchase price.

Why assume an existing mortgage? It is an easy, quick and inexpensive way to find a mortgage. Because it is already on title, there are no appraisal or legal fees. When the interest rate on the mortgage is less than the current rate for the remaining term, the buyer will save money, too. A mortgage with a below-market rate can be a selling feature of the house, if assumable.

However, because the mortgage is already outstanding, its terms are non-negotiable. If the principal outstanding is too small or too large, the rate too high, or the term too short or too long, the mortgage may not be acceptable for a purchaser to assume. Knowing all these details about a mortgage that might be assumed, before an offer is submitted, is critical.

By law, mortgages are automatically assumable by a purchaser of a property unless any restrictions appear in the mortgage itself. Many mortgages today contain "due-on-sale" clauses, meaning they become due at the lender's option if the property is sold. That also means the mortgage is assumable if a purchaser like Ed applies to assume it, qualifies for the mortgage, and is allowed by the lender to assume it. Obviously this last point is very important.

Anyone who plans to assume an existing mortgage on closing must learn early on whether it is assumable, and on what terms. The listing agent should have verified this and other particulars of the mortgage (including outstanding principal, interest rate, payment, maturity date and prepayment privileges) when the listing was obtained. Otherwise, a buyer could be planning to take over a mortgage which has restrictions on it being assumed.

Granting a Vendor-Take-Back Mortgage

Here the seller agrees to hold a mortgage for the unpaid balance of the purchase price (a "vendor-take-back" or VTB mortgage), to help the purchaser acquire the property. This defers the payment of part of the purchase price for a number of years after closing.

Arranging a VTB mortgage parallels assuming an existing mortgage in a number of ways. It is an easy, quick and cheap mortgage to arrange. Once the offer is accepted, the buyer has been approved for the mortgage. There are no credit checks, application or appraisal fees, or legal expenses for the purchaser.

The wording of the clause in the offer dealing with the VTB mortgage dictates the terms of the actual mortgage. That means the terms of the VTB mortgage must be settled *before* the offer is accepted. Key points to consider include the amount of principal being borrowed with the VTB mortgage, the interest rate, the payment (or the amortization period for the loan), and its term. Special clauses such as prepayment privileges and assumability on sale must appear in the offer, too, to be picked up in the mortgage. The same with postdated cheques. The absence of a clause in the offer requiring the delivery of post-dated cheques means a borrower is not obligated to deliver them to the vendor/lender.

The way most offers are drafted, VTB mortgages are both fully open (meaning they can be prepaid at any time, in whole or in part, without any penalty) and fully assumable. Since a VTB mortgage represents unpaid purchase money, most sellers would like the mortgage to be prepaid as quickly as possible. But to the chagrin of many sellers, VTB mortgages are often automatically assumable, as the seller's agent forgot to include a due-on-sale clause in the offer.

VTB mortgages are often used by home owners to sell their property. With a VTB mortgage, the offer does not have to be made conditional on financing. Upon acceptance, the offer becomes firm and binding and the mortgage is committed, just like that. The interest rate likely will be .5% to 1.5% below the market rate for a comparable institutional mortgage, too, the purchaser receiving that rate break as an inducement to buy the house. Despite that, the rate paid to the seller is also higher than he or she would receive simply by investing the funds in a term deposit or Guaranteed Investment Certificate. That makes a VTB mortgage a win-win situation often for both seller and buyer. If the seller needs the money before the mortgage matures, it always can be sold, too. That why it's important for buyers to know more about the background to the sale. It could indicate whether a VTB mortgage is possible.

Several points about VTB mortgages should be kept in mind. First, most are for a short term only, one to three years. Second, a VTB mortgage should never be considered as permanent financing. Few VTB mortgages are renewed at maturity, the vendor already having waited years to receive this unpaid balance of the purchase price. Because sellers are under no obligation to renew a VTB mortgage unless such a clause appears in it (which is rare), refinancing costs will have to be incurred in the near future. They could have been avoided if a longer-term institutional mortgage had been arranged when the property was purchased.

Arranging a New Mortgage

Far and away, this is the most common type of mortgage financing. Purchasers negotiate their own mortgage, arrange a cash transaction with the seller, and pay the mortgage proceeds together with their own funds to the seller on closing.

Where can purchasers get a mortgage? A number of traditional sources exist: banks, trust companies, insurance companies, credit unions and caisse populaires. Mortgage brokers also bring lenders and borrowers together, often today at no cost to the buyer/borrower, the lender paying a fee to the mortgage broker. Before using a mortgage broker, ask whether any fee will be charged (and if so, in what amount), and what services will be provided. Many lawyers and accountants also have lender clients who invest in mortgages. Private lenders will often offer more liberal prepayment privileges, or slightly better interest rates, to be competitive. Mortgages can even be arranged in a high-tech way today, with a number of lending companies now on the Internet to help arrange mortgage financing.

Lenders consider both the property and the borrower when deciding whether to grant a mortgage loan and how much to advance. To determine the value of a property, institutional lenders will have it appraised at a cost to the purchaser of $150 to $200 (plus GST). Private lenders may not require an appraisal when mortgage funds are advanced to finance a purchase, as the purchase price helps determine what the property is worth. For more information on the rules of property qualification, and whether borrowers have the financial ability to repay the mortgage, see chapter 8.

Mortgage options available at institutional lenders differ considerably. No two lenders offer the exact same package of features. While rate should be a factor when shopping for a mortgage, it should never be the *only* factor in choosing a lender. Proper application of your home-buying strategy requires that you inquire about and analyze these features at the pre-contract stage, and learn which lender's mortgage is most appropriate for you.

a) Interest Rate

The rate of interest charged on a mortgage is closely tied to its term. Generally, the shorter the term, the lower the rate. That means a premium is paid each month during the entire term of a long-term mortgage (three to five years), that higher rate being the cost of the security provided by the longer, fixed-rate commitment. While short-term mortgages of six months and a year carry lower interest rates, they also subject borrowers more frequently to the volatility of the interest rate market.

A quick perusal of the newspaper or Internet will indicate how most lenders charge the same interest rate for the same mortgage term. So what distinguishes one lender from another? Its package of mortgage features.

Keep in mind that the posted rate is not necessarily the only rate for a mortgage. Banks and trust companies will often give rate breaks of .25% (short-term) to .5% (long-term), the more business you bring them (or you've done with them), ranging from RRSPs to GICs, term deposits, car loans and credit card accounts. This is an unadvertised feature called "relationship pricing."

When obtaining quotes for interest rates, also see for how long the rate is guaranteed. A 30-day guaranteed rate is of little value to a buyer who must wait 90 days until closing.

b) Term

Where interest rates are going is virtually unpredictable, making it the biggest legalized crap game in Canada. That means there is no easy or right answer when deciding whether to go short-term or long-term on the rate.

When considering the term of a mortgage, keep in mind your own unique needs and circumstances. How long do you expect to stay in the house? How much equity do you have in your home? Could you handle a hefty hike in interest rates (and therefore the mortgage payment)? What is your personality and character (risk taker or risk hater?) Is it a starter home, to be sold in three or four years? What is happening with interest rates? Going up, stable or falling? Often these are difficult questions to answer, considering the house has not even been bought yet! But they will affect the mortgage term selected.

c) Frequency of Interest Calculations

No matter how frequently a mortgage is paid, the standard way of calculating interest in Canada is semi-annually. The more often interest is calculated, the more expensive it is for a borrower. So stay away from mortgages calculated monthly; they will cost you money. Ensure the mortgage is *calculated* semi-annually, even though it may be *payable* monthly, weekly or bi-weekly.

Mortgages in Canada are paid "not in advance." This means the payment is made at the end of the month, not at the beginning like rent. January's rent may be paid January 1st in advance, but the mortgage payment for the month of January is made February 1st, not in advance. This arrangement benefits borrowers, not lenders.

d) Realty Tax Accounts

Many lenders collect 1/12th of the estimated taxes with each monthly mortgage payment, and pay the taxes as the bills are issued. (For weekly or bi-weekly payments, the fraction is 1/52 or 1/26). Convenience is the argument usually advanced by lenders, as it makes budgeting easier. However, a fair rate of interest is rarely paid on the money on deposit in a tax amount —if any interest is paid at all. Yet if the tax account was ever short funds, the borrower is charged interest on the shortfall at the mortgage rate!

To ensure that funds are available when the next tax bill is issued, lenders require that borrowers prepay their realty taxes up to six months ahead of time. Talk about a cash-flow killer. If at all possible, try to pay your own realty taxes.

e) Assumability

Mortgages in Canada are automatically assumable by a subsequent purchaser of the property, without requiring the lender's consent, unless the mortgage contains a restriction to the contrary. Most mortgages today are "limited assumable," making them due and payable at the lender's option if the property is sold. This allows the lender to decide if an existing mortgage can be assumed at that time.

Mortgages are assumed quite easily. By simply closing a resale transaction after any required approval has been given, and paying the vendor the difference between the purchase price and the outstanding mortgage (cash to the mortgage), the purchaser has assumed the mortgage. Rarely are buyers asked to sign a formal mortgage assumption agreement, creating a direct, contractual link between buyer and lender.

f) Portability

Years ago, the following scenario was far too common. Ross and Rachel would "trade up," or sell their current home and buy a larger one with a larger mortgage. However, the buyer of their home did not wish to assume their existing mortgage. That meant Ross and Rachel would incur a hefty prepayment penalty to retire the old loan, and then borrow back that same money (or even more) the same day, possibly from the same lender, to finance the new home purchase.

Enter "portability." It allows borrowers like Ross and Rachel who sell their house and buy another before the mortgage matures to pack up their existing mortgage (and its interest rate and features) just like their furniture, and move it to their new house *without any prepayment penalty*. If a larger mortgage is needed, the rate is blended, like paint, to reflect the proportions of old money (the mortgage from the old home) and new money (the additional money needed to finance the purchase). Of course, this assumes that both the borrower and the property continue to qualify for the new mortgage.

Not all lenders offer portability. Of those that do, many simply refer to it in their literature, without including the clause in the actual mortgage. If that's the case, portability is little more than lender "policy," which can be changed overnight with a directive from head office. So make sure the portability clause appears right in the mortgage.

Portability makes the long-term mortgage viable. With portability, Ross and Rachel don't have to be committed to owning one particular property during the mortgage term, as long as they are committed home owners.

g) Convertibility

Convertibility makes the short-term mortgage viable. Generally available at the short-term closed rate, it lets borrowers "lock in" to a long-term fixed-rate mortgage any time before maturity, usually at no cost, if rates rise mid-term. That makes convertible mortgages the ultimate in flexibility, helping resolve the short-term/long-term dilemma.

Unfortunately, no standard or common definition for a convertible mortgage exists. Different lenders have different convertible terms and requirements: when the mortgage can be converted; if there is any administrative fee; and what happens if the option isn't exercised. And just like with portability, while many lenders claim that their mortgages are convertible, the actual mortgage document is silent on the point.

h) Reducing the Amortization

Interest paid on mortgages is generally not deductible from other income. Therefore, Canadians must strive to retire their mortgages as quickly as possible. When a mortgage is prepaid, the borrower saves both interest and income tax on the money that had to be earned to finance the prepayment. Simply put, say Joe's $500 prepayment saved him $6,000 in interest over the term of his mortgage. Being in the 40% marginal tax bracket, Joe would have to earn $10,000 in income, and pay tax of $4,000, to be left with the $6,000 he saved in interest. That $500 prepayment, in effect, was the equivalent of Joe's earning $10,000 at work.

When a mortgage is amortized over 25 years, it is assumed that the same payment is made every month for that full period of time, with no late payments and no prepayments. Any extra money paid toward a mortgage before it comes due (a prepayment) cuts both its amortization and interest cost. Amortizations can be reduced, and huge savings of interest realized, in four different ways: by choosing a lower amortization (20 years instead of 25); by making a lump-sum prepayment; by boosting the regular mortgage payment over time; and by accelerated fast-pay mortgages (weekly and bi-weekly mortgages).

Regarding this last method, be very careful. Just because a mortgage is paid more often than monthly will not necessarily save borrowers much money. What really matters is how the amount to be paid —be it weekly or every two weeks —is determined. The simplest way to save is to initially ignore the idea of a fast-pay mortgage and book it with a 25-year amortization. Then, just before closing, divide the monthly payment by four for a weekly mortgage or two for a bi-weekly mortgage. That will produce an "accelerated" weekly or bi-weekly payment mortgage, the only type that will make a dent in what borrowers owe.

i) Prepayment Privileges

Many people are surprised to learn that most mortgages are "closed" according to the Interest Act of Canada. They cannot be prepaid or renegotiated before maturity, even on payment of a three months' bonus penalty, unless such a right specifically appears in the mortgage document.

Significant differences exist between "open" mortgages, which allow some money to be prepaid towards the mortgage each year, and "fully open" mortgages, where the borrower can pay off or renegotiate the mortgage at any time.

Another little-known fact is that all mortgages insured by Canada Mortgage and Housing Corporation (CMHC) with a term of three years or more are open after that time by paying a penalty of three months' bonus interest. (The same is not true, though, for mortgages insured by CMHC's competitor, GE Mortgage Insurance Company. It simply honors the prepayment privilege of the mortgage lender.)

Prepayment privileges are literally all over the map. No two lenders offer the same package of provisions. Some distinguishing questions are: how "open" is the mortgage (i.e., the maximum amount that can be prepaid)?; when can a prepayment be made?; can more than one prepayment be made in a year?; what is the penalty charged?; is there a time lag before the mortgage can be prepaid?; and do the prepayment privileges change over time?

For more information about open vs. closed mortgages and prepayment privileges in general, see the chapters devoted to those topics in *Hidden Profits in Your Mortgage* or *The Perfect Mortgage*.

Hidden Costs in Mortgage Transactions

Home buyers are absolutely astounded when confronted with the cost of arranging a mortgage loan to finance a purchase. Al and Lorna booked a $100,000 mortgage with Vaughan Trust, which was registered when their purchase closed on September 11th. Following their HOBS, they got pre-approved for their mortgage before signing the Offer to Purchase. At the same time, they asked about the cost of arranging that mortgage. Imagine their surprise to discover the hidden costs were over $800! Al and Lorna agreed it was better to learn about these deductions now. To do so at the 11th hour would wreak havoc with their budget for closing.

Keep in mind that buyers pay *all* the costs incurred arranging a mortgage when purchasing a resale home. These expenses are "cash" costs, payable up front on closing. Many are even deducted by the lender at source from the mortgage advance, forcing the buyer to make up the difference on closing from their own resources. In Al and Lorna's situation, the net advance was only $99,166.44, meaning they had to give their lawyer the $833.56 shortfall from their own pockets on closing.

Whether any of the following are applicable will obviously depend on the circumstances of the particular mortgage loan.

a) Mortgage Appraisal/Application Fee

Most lenders charge a "mortgage initiation fee" to cover the administrative costs of booking the mortgage (although this fee can be waived on request). Fees of $150 to $200 are not uncommon. However, there's no GST, since the financial service industry is GST-exempt. Another charge is the cost of the appraisal, again between $150 and $200 (plus GST). Ask whether the mortgage application fee covers the appraisal fee or whether they are separate charges. The combined fee to Al and Lorna was $175.

b) Interest to the Interest Adjustment Date (IAD)

Mortgages in Canada are paid in arrears, "not in advance," at the end of the payment period. This leads to a timing issue, and this deduction made by lenders. In its simplest form, it means a buyer/borrower pays the interest for the balance of the month of closing somewhat earlier than normal. Although it is a legitimate charge, the mechanics are usually not well understood. If not properly planned for, interest to the interest adjustment date can devastate a borrower's well-planned cash flow for closing.

Most institutional mortgages are paid on the first of the month, for the month just completed. In Al and Lorna's case, their first mortgage payment will be November 1st for the month of October, the first full month they own the property. But what about the broken month of September? Obviously, Al and Lorna are responsible for paying interest from September 11th to the end of the month. But when is it paid?

October 1st is considered by Vaughan Trust to be the "interest adjustment date" or IAD, the day the mortgage effectively begins to run. The first payment is due one month after the interest adjustment date, or November 1st. To collect interest for the broken period of September, from the date of closing to the interest adjustment date, most lenders deduct it at source from the mortgage advance, calculating the interest daily. Because Al and Lorna's $100,000 mortgage carries a 7% interest rate, this 20-day deduction totals $383.56.

Instead of scooping the interest to the IAD off the top, other lenders make a full mortgage advance on closing, and bill the borrower on the IAD for this interest.

A third approach, one adopted by most private lenders and the odd institutional lender, is to have the interest adjustment date coincide with the date of closing. That eliminates the problem of interest to the IAD. With the first payment due exactly one month after closing, a deduction of interest on closing is unnecessary. Three different solutions to one simple problem. No wonder mortgage financing is so confusing.

With interest to the IAD deducted from the mortgage advance, Al and Lorna in effect are paying on September 11th the interest due on October 1st. One consolation to the cash-flow crisis they face on closing is the fact that no mortgage payment will be due for almost two months, until November 1st. A minor saving grace, which will help Al and Lorna replenish their resources.

Closing earlier in the month (e.g., September 4th) would compound the problem further, as a larger amount would be deducted on closing as interest to the IAD. But closing should not be delayed until later in the month just to minimize this expense. Serious problems plague late-in-the-month closings, as illustrated in chapter 25.

More importantly, interest to the interest adjustment date is an expense that can easily be planned for. Simply multiply the amount of money being borrowed by the mortgage rate, and divide that total by 365. Then multiply the result by the number of days remaining in the broken month. In Al and Lorna's case, the figures looked like this: $100,000 x 7% = $7,000; divided by 365 = $19.1780; multiplying that figure by 20 days = $383.56.

c) Establishing a Realty Tax Account

The taxes on Al and Lorna's home are estimated to be $1,800 yearly. All current-year taxes are paid. Starting November 1st, Vaughan Trust will be collecting $150 with each monthly mortgage payment for taxes. When the interim tax bill for half the year's taxes is issued in late January next year, Vaughan Trust wants to have approximately $900 in the tax account. With only three regular payments to be made before the bill is issued (November, December and January), the lender will be short $450. To cover this shortfall, Vaughan Trust collected $450 from Al and Lorna on closing by deducting $450 from the mortgage advance.

Borrowers who can pay their own taxes save in several ways. First, they can avoid this lump-sum deduction on closing, which ravages a buyer's pre-closing budget. Second, they avoid prepaying their property taxes. By the time each tax bill is issued, Al and Lorna will have paid six months' taxes to their lender before those taxes actually come due. As part of your home-buying strategy, learn if the lender insists on having property taxes paid into a tax account with each payment. If so, you can budget properly for this expense in advance.

d) Mortgage Broker's Fee

Buyers who retain the services of a mortgage broker to handle the paperwork on the mortgage application may have to pay a fee to the broker. (Often, the lender pays the broker's fee, enabling the borrower to use the broker's services free of charge.) If you are using a mortgage broker, know what the fee (if any) will be and plan for it before making any final commitment.

e) CMHC/GE Mortgage Payment Insurance Fees
High-ratio mortgages must be insured with either of these two companies to protect the lender and ensure that the mortgage is paid promptly. Current rates on resale homes range from 1.25% to 2.5% of the amount borrowed. Normally the insurance premium is added to the outstanding principal, thus eliminating any further cash outlays on closing. But borrowers do have the right to pay it on closing. In Ontario, this insurance premium is also subject to an 8% insurance tax, which is payable up-front, on closing. It can't be tacked on to the amount borrowed.

f) Other Insurance
Besides getting payment insurance, borrowers may want to arrange life and/or disability insurance. More details appear in chapter 30.

Every borrower needs an amortization schedule for his or her mortgage. Inexpensive to obtain ($5 to $10), it shows how each mortgage payment is allocated between the principal and interest components, plus the outstanding balance following each payment. Amortization schedules are an invaluable tool in cutting the high cost of mortgage financing. For a thorough explanation of how to order an amortization schedule for a mortgage, and how to take advantage of the information it contains to save thousands of dollars in interest, see *Hidden Profits in Your Mortgage*.

Buyers who want to close their purchase first, followed by their sale several days later, will be interested in the next chapter on bridge financing. After that, as part of the development of a home-buying strategy, it will be time to explore and understand some of the additional charges buyers will face on closing — the so-called "hidden" closing costs.

22
Bridge Financing

Anyone selling one home and buying another should consider arranging bridge financing. It involves completing the transactions in reverse order — the purchase closing days or weeks *before* the sale. Instead of taking the net proceeds from the sale and applying them directly to the purchase the same day (as normally is done), the seller/buyer borrows an amount equivalent to those net proceeds from the bank as a short-term loan to close the purchase. When the sale closes, those funds are returned to the bank, plus interest. Despite the cost, bridge financing considerably lessens the aggravation that accompanies most back-to-back transactions, where the sale and purchase both close the same day.

Sometimes people specifically opt to close their deals on different days, and arrange bridge financing. Sometimes circumstances force them into doing that (the sale closing after the purchase), if closing both deals can't be co-ordinated for the same day. (If the reverse happens, the purchase closing after the sale, it will be necessary to find an alternative place to live during that hiatus!)

Josh and Pam sold their old home on Dinky Drive and bought a new home on Cyclops Crescent. Both deals were scheduled to close May 30th. Obviously, their Dinky Drive sale had to close first, as Josh and Pam needed those funds to close the Cyclops Crescent purchase. Luckily, Rob and Christina, the purchasers of their old home, were moving from an apartment.

Their purchase of the Dinky Drive property was not dependent on any other deal closing first (as often is the case). Still, the lender financing Rob and Christina's purchase would not release the mortgage funds until 10:00 a.m. on May 30th. Those funds had to be delivered to Rob and Christina's lawyer, who in turn would use them to close the Dinky Drive purchase from Josh and Pam. Only then would Josh and Pam's lawyer have the money to close their purchase on Cyclops Crescent.

The time spent waiting for the Dinky Drive deal to close, coupled with the volume of business at the registry office, delayed Josh and Pam's Cyclops Crescent deal from closing until 4:00 p.m. Being on tenterhooks the whole day was only part of their problem. More importantly the movers, who had started loading their truck at 8:00 a.m., were finished by noon. For over four hours, they had nothing to do but sit around as time frittered away at Josh and Pam's expense. Even after the Cyclops Crescent deal closed at 4:00 p.m., Josh and Pam still had to get the keys from their lawyer to gain access to the property. Only at 6:00 p.m. did Josh and Pam finally open the door to their new home. Imagine, having to pay a moving crew for six extra hours. This delay in closing both deals cost Josh and Pam over $450 (plus GST) in extra moving costs.

Lewis and Lily did things differently. Knowing that closing two transactions the same day often means costly delays, they scheduled the closing of their Disco Road sale for that same May 30th; but closing of their Jazz Avenue purchase would take place on May 27th. Since they would own two houses over that three-day period (a weekend), Lewis and Lily had to arrange bridge financing for their purchase.

To their pleasant surprise, Lewis and Lily learned that it was not necessary to bridge finance the whole $150,000 purchase price for their new home. All they had to borrow via bridge financing was their equity in their Disco Road home. The rest of the funds for the purchase on Jazz Avenue, whatever the source — be it the new mortgage or their own resources — would be available regardless of when the purchase closed. Of the $150,000 purchase price, a new $90,000 first mortgage was being arranged, with the vendor taking back a $15,000 second mortgage. The equity in their old home amounted to $35,000, the remaining $10,000 for the purchase coming from Lewis and Lily's own savings. Hence, of the $150,000 purchase price, everything except the $35,000 equity in their old home would be available for closing, whenever that occurred: May 27th, May 30th, any day before, after or in between. So all they would have to bridge finance was that equity in their property, $35,000.

On May 27th, $35,000 of the bank's money was applied to Lewis and Lily's purchase on Jazz Avenue. When the sale of Disco Road closed on May 30th, $35,000 of the sale proceeds, plus interest, was returned to the bank to retire the bridge financing.

What did Lewis and Lily gain by bridge financing? First, May 27th was not a wasted day. Both of them put in a full day at work, picking up the keys to their new home from their lawyer after hours. That evening, they moved several delicate and fragile items into the house, and gave it a once-over cleaning. One bedroom, badly needing a paint job, was done that night. When the movers came to the old house at 8:00 a.m. the next morning, they loaded up the truck, travelled to the new property and immediately began unloading. By 3:00 p.m., the job was done. Saturday night and all day Sunday were dedicated to unpacking, unpacking and unpacking, making the new home "habitable." A quick trip to clean up, reminisce and say goodbye to Disco Road was made early Sunday evening. Monday, while they continued unpacking, the Disco Road sale was closed and the bridge financing paid off. The total cost for the bridge financing: a few hundred dollars. Life was back to normal as of Tuesday. By arranging bridge financing, Lewis and Lily were able to change homes relatively stress-free. And in doing so, they even saved money, compared to Josh and Pam.

As a very short-term unsecured loan, bridge financing is not cheap, but it is not prohibitively expensive either. Most financial institutions levy a set-up or administrative fee (perhaps in the $250 range) plus interest (a common charge being a variable rate of prime plus 2%). Of course, these charges may vary among financial institutions. Before approving the bridge financing, your bank manager will want to see copies of the firm, not conditional, offers on both properties. Additional information may have to be provided, of the amount outstanding on any existing mortgages, plus any amount being borrowed on any new mortgages. All this is needed to verify the net equity in your old home, the maximum amount that will be "bridge financed." As the transactions are processed, a written assurance may be needed from your lawyer that no problems have been encountered to date or were foreseeable in either transaction. You will also have to consent to having the bridge financing secured immediately against either or both properties, if the purchase transaction closes but the sale does not for any reason.

As Lewis and Lily proved, the cost of bridge financing is often money well spent, compared to the additional charges incurred when a sale and purchase both close the same day. Staggering the two closings this way allows a more leisurely move, with less turmoil and grief. Even if bridge financing doesn't save any money, the non-monetary benefits it provides — extra time to clean up the house, paint a room, lay carpeting and unpack, coupled with the aggravation bridge financing eliminates — should not be minimized.

Because the bridge financing loan is unsecured, the lender needs a firm assurance that the funds will be repaid as scheduled. It doesn't want to chase the borrower for the money once both deals are closed. To give the lender first claim on the sale proceeds, buyers like Jack and Elaine sign a bank form called a Letter of Direction, which is addressed to their lawyer. In it, Jack and Elaine authorize their lawyer to pay to the bank from the sale proceeds the amount borrowed plus all accrued interest and administrative charges *before* any money is paid to them. In addition, Jack and Elaine's lawyer must acknowledge in writing that he or she will honor the terms of the Letter of Direction, forthwith, after the sale closes. Only with this pledge, that the funds will be rerouted to the bank immediately after the sale closes, will it release the bridge financing funds needed for Jack and Elaine's purchase.

Bridge financing poses a "chicken-and-egg" dilemma. Banks will not grant bridge financing loans until two firm offers exist. On the other hand, a buyer like Vince cannot make both transactions firm, with two different closing dates, unless he knows bridge financing will be available. To get around this impasse, Vince should make preliminary inquiries and seek informal assurance that a bridge financing loan is possible, before signing the offers and setting the closing dates. Any snags encountered even at this early stage would probably force him to close both transactions the same day. In addition, Vince should learn what the interest rate and administrative costs will be, before making any final contractual commitments. If the expenses are acceptable, Vince can proceed to firm up both offers with staggered closing dates, knowing that the bridge financing can be put in place for closing.

Most financial institutions are reluctant to grant unsecured bridge financing loans unless the purchaser is an established and well-known customer. This is one situation where shopping for a loan will not be helpful. Because lenders are under no obligation to help buyers bridge finance their deals, the best source of funds may well be the bank or trust company you deal with regularly. Often what tips the scale is the actual customer, his or her past dealings with the branch, and his or her reputation.

Another excellent source to contact is the lending institution providing the mortgage financing for the purchase. If the lender gets the mortgage business, the more likely it will provide the bridge financing, too. When Herb and Maryanne met with their bank manager, they discussed bridge financing as well as the terms of the mortgage needed to close their purchase. Both loans ultimately were approved.

Once the two contracts are signed and the two deals are scheduled to close the same day, it is very difficult for existing home owners to reschedule one and consider bridge financing. So if staggering the closing dates appeals to you, or if arranging two different closing dates becomes a necessity (with the purchase closing before the sale), check out bridge financing the transaction as part of your HOBS. This could be one of those rare situations where borrowing money actually ends up being the cheaper alternative!

23

How Much Money Is Needed to Close?

One of the most frequently asked questions is: "How much money is needed to close?" Most buyers are genuinely shocked to hear the answer. Even more important than that reply, though, is when they will learn that figure.

Surprises are for birthdays, not real estate transactions. Being caught short of money for closing produces one of the worst feelings imaginable, totally destroying the enthusiasm for the move. Most so-called "hidden" closing costs (besides the basic purchase price) are known with reasonable accuracy well before closing — often even before the offer is signed! Traditionally, though, the overall amount needed to close — including legal fees, disbursements, transfer taxes and closing adjustments — is only discussed for the first time right before closing. The longer buyers wait to learn about these charges, the more likely they will face a cash-flow crunch on closing.

Frankly, there should be *no* hidden closing costs in any real estate transaction. By asking the right questions of the right people as early as possible, buyers developing their own home-buying strategy (HOBS) can learn how much money is needed to close the deal *before* signing and submitting any Offer to Purchase. This allows buyers to properly budget and plan their finances for closing, knowing how much they can afford to spend and how large a mortgage to arrange. Having the over-all closing charges disclosed early, at the pre-contract stage, is the smart way to buy a house.

Who should provide this information? Unfortunately, real estate agents rarely volunteer it. The news not being overly pleasant, agents are fearful of losing buyer prospects. The best source of information is a real estate lawyer (or notary in those provinces where notaries can process real estate transactions). This can be done either during your preliminary inquiries (when obtaining a price quote) or when reviewing the contents of a draft, unsigned offer with your lawyer. Armed with this information, buyers can prepare for the unexpected — the expenses most buyers know nothing about until the last minute — and properly plan their cash flow for closing.

Hidden closing costs fall into six categories: a) legal fees (plus GST); b) disbursements (plus GST), the out-of-pocket expenses a lawyer or notary incurs; c) provincial transfer taxes; d) adjustments with the seller; e) the cost of arranging deductions made on a mortgage; and f) miscellaneous. When determining how much money is needed to close, all these items are added to the purchase price to determine the gross amount. Deducted from this figure are the deposit and the amount of money coming from other sources such as a new first mortgage (net of any deductions made by the lender), a vendor-take-back or assumed mortgage, or the sale of an existing home (after expenses). The difference is the net amount of money buyers must bring to their lawyer by certified cheque to close the purchase. All these closing costs are payable up front, in cash, on or before closing.

Ed and Joyce are planning to buy a $175,000 home, with a $10,000 deposit. The new mortgage they are arranging will be $130,000, with a further $35,000 being paid on closing. Meeting with their lawyer before the offer was signed, they learned that the legal fees for the purchase and the mortgage will be about $900 (plus $63 GST), disbursements $600 (plus $42 GST), transfer tax $1,475 and adjustments approximately $150. The gross amount needed to close, then, is $178,230. Deducted from this amount are the gross funds for closing. In Ed and Joyce's transaction it is $139,750, consisting of a) the net mortgage advance of $129,750 — the sum of $250 being deducted from the $130,000 gross mortgage advance for i) the application fee ($150) and ii) interest to the interest adjustment date ($100) — and b) the $10,000 deposit paid when the offer was signed. Deducting the gross funds available for closing ($139,750) from the gross amount needed to close ($178,230) gives the net amount required by Ed and Joyce on closing, $38,480. Because Ed and Joyce expected to pay $35,000 "in raw numbers" on closing, the hidden closing costs totalled $3,480.

To avoid being too close to the line, and to avoid any last-minute contingencies, Ed and Joyce set aside another $250, for a total of $3,730. In their own minds, these funds were already committed and spent on closing. If the actual amount needed to close was $3,450, Ed and Joyce would be left with $30 of "budgeted money" and the $250 contingency amount to spend on paint and wallpaper fixing up the house.

For resale homes, a very helpful budgeting rule of thumb is to set aside 1.5% to 2% on top of the basic purchase price for "everything" — all these hidden closing costs. The exact amount needed will depend on a number of factors, such as: in which province you are buying (since transfer taxes differ across the country); your lawyer's fees; whether one or two mortgages are being arranged; and whether your lender deducts interest to the interest adjustment date. Budgeting an extra 1.5% to 2% of the basic purchase price for these closing expenses, "all-inclusive," should be enough in most resale transactions. So brace yourself for it. If Ed and Joyce had used this budgeting number, they would have taken 2% of their $175,000 purchase price and projected $3,500 for closing expenses at the outset, very close to the $3,480 calculated with their lawyer.

Anyone arranging a CMHC-insured mortgage must now demonstrate they have the resources for these closing expenses. Borrowers must be able to cover 1.5% of the purchase price as closing costs, either in cash or by including it in their total debt service calculation, repayable within a year.

(In new-home transactions these closing costs can easily top 2.5% of the purchase price. The reason: additional adjustments with the builder for items such as enrolling the house in the provincial warranty program, and expenses such as water meters/hook-ups, hydro meters/hook-ups, tree-planting fees, and deposits for damage to grading and subdivision services.)

If the figure for these hidden closing costs seems high,

remember that it includes more than just a lawyer's fee. It's the total amount of money needed to close in addition to the purchase price, comprising charges which are payable to many other people — from vendor to lender. It's the number that agents and even some real estate lawyers are reluctant to provide, worried about scaring buyers off. But it's the number that buyers need to know, to avoid the anxiety and stress of being short of money for closing.

What are these hidden costs which buyers must know about and properly budget for?

Legal Fees

What the lawyer takes home at the end of the day for his or her services varies greatly from province to province, region to region within a province, within geographical areas like a city, and from lawyer to lawyer. For more information on the setting of lawyer's fees, see chapter 15.

Disbursements

Disbursements are out-of-pocket expenses lawyers incur on behalf of clients to obtain government clearances, searches and reports, in addition to the cost of the title search. The actual disbursements and amount charged for each item will differ from province to province, from municipality to municipality, and from file to file. Unfortunately disbursements in real estate transactions have been escalating in recent years, as governments have been treating them as a "non-tax" source of revenue. Typical disbursements include:

By-law/zoning and work order report — That the property complies with municipal zoning by-laws, and that no work orders are outstanding. Usual cost: $50 to $100.
Tax certificate — That no realty taxes are outstanding. Usual cost: $25 to $50.
Utility certificates — That no public utility charges — hydro and

water — are outstanding. Usual cost: $10 to $20.

Search of title — Obtaining a copy of the parcel for the property being bought, "pulling" deeds, mortgages and other agreements on title, reviewing and summarizing them. This cost is usually at least $50 or more, depending on the complexity of the state of title.

Registration costs — The cost of registering each instrument on title. In Ontario, the minimum charge to register a document is $50. So registering a deed and a mortgage would cost $100.

Execution certificate — Issued by the local sheriff or land registrar, indicating whether there are any outstanding judgments on file against the purchaser, the vendor or previous owners of the land (plus the condominium corporation, if a unit there is being bought). The searches are conducted twice: once when the title is reviewed, and again on closing. (This gives the parties an opportunity to "clean up" any outstanding executions early, and not delay closing for that reason.) Depending on the number of prior owners of the property, this charge could easily be upwards of $100.

Estoppel certificate — Issued by a condominium corporation, it provides relevant information about the status of the unit as well as any outstanding arrears affecting it. Usual cost: $50.

Subdivision agreement report — That all the terms of any subdivision agreement have been complied with, and that occupancy is permitted. Usual cost: around $50.

Personal Property Security Act search — Shows the existence of liens against any personal property being acquired. Usual cost: around $10.

Other searches — These depend on the nature of the property being bought. For example, a search of provincial rent records may be necessary if all or part of the property is being rented. A report from a conservation authority may also be needed, if lands are subject to its jurisdiction. For rural properties, inquiries must be made about permits and work orders affecting the septic system, and whether any well records exist.

Amortization schedule — Shows the allocation of the mortgage payment between principal and interest, and the balance outstanding after each payment is made. Usual cost: $10 per mortgage.

Transportation and courier charges — Timing is crucial in any real estate transaction. Couriers are absolutely necessary to deliver time-sensitive items (e.g., the net mortgage advance from a lender) to and from a lawyer's office. Typically budget at least $25 for this, plus the cost of two trips to an out-of-town registry office, if applicable (once to search the title, once to close the transaction).

Long-distance telephone charges — If applicable. Usual cost: $10 and up.

Miscellaneous charges — Photostatic, postage and faxing expenses, for example. These can run $25 and up depending on the exact work done in the transaction.

Many of these charges are not subject to GST when incurred. However, since April 1, 1997, clients must pay GST on virtually every real estate disbursement — even those that are GST-exempt by law! The two major exceptions: provincial transfer taxes and the cost of registering deeds, mortgages and discharges.

Two unfortunate practices have developed in recent years. First, some lawyers "lowball" the amount payable for disbursements when giving a price quote (obviously, to get the business), and then hit the buyer with a higher figure on closing. This is an unacceptable practice bordering on professional misconduct, since lawyers are supposed to give a fair estimate of anticipated disbursements when quoting a fee. Second, some lawyers don't make all required searches and inquiries, instead cutting corners to hold down expenses and entice buyers to deal with them. This is professional negligence, plain and simple. All the more reason to get the names of several lawyer references from friends, neighbors, co-workers and family members, and then contact them for fee/closing cost quotes. If one quote seems inordinately low, there's probably a good reason why!

Provincial Taxes

i) Land Transfer Tax

Depending on the province involved, an additional charge is levied whenever title changes hands, in addition to the cost of registration. This special one-time tax must be paid or else the deed will not be registered. In Ontario, for example, land transfer tax is assessed against all properties, virtually without exception, whether they be residential, commercial, industrial, agricultural or recreational. Interspousal transfers of title are exempt, as are estate inheritances.

And these transfer taxes aren't cheap. In Ontario, for example, land transfer tax is applied on an escalating scale: $5 per $1,000 of purchase price for the first $55,000; $10 per $1,000 for that portion between $55,000 and $250,000; $15 per $1,000 for the amount exceeding $250,000; and $20 per $1,000 of purchase price, on single-family homes and duplexes only, on that segment above $400,000.

On Moe's $150,000 purchase, the land transfer tax payable in Ontario was $1,225. It was calculated as follows: ($5 x $55,000) + ($10 x $95,000) = $275 + $950 = $1,225.

ii) Retail Sales Tax

Often, the purchase price includes items of personal property called chattels, most often appliances. If Eli and Karen bought them new (or even used) in a store, provincial retail sales tax would be payable through the merchant. When they are included in the purchase price of a home, retail sales tax technically should be paid as well. (The same is true with GST, too.) But no sales tax is payable on any fixtures acquired as part of the purchase price, since they are already part of the house.

If the chattels have significant value, the buyer should agree with the seller what portion of the purchase price will be allocated to chattels, to avoid problems arising in the future. Because provincial retail sales tax rates are high — in Ontario, it's $80 per $1,000 — the buyer will want to purchase these chattels as cheaply as possible.

Although the offer may contain a list of personal property included in the purchase price, practically speaking the issue of retail sales tax is often overlooked. When used appliances are being bought, what is their value, anyway? Usually nominal, at best. Ignoring the payment of retail sales tax does not mean it should not be paid. Rather, it is simply a statement of reality.

Adjustments

One of the documents to be reviewed with your lawyer before closing is the Statement of Adjustments. It "fine-tunes" the transaction, allocating various charges between the buyer and the seller right up to the day of closing.

But the Statement of Adjustments only reflects the transaction between those parties. Mortgages arranged with anyone other than the seller do not appear on the Statement of Adjustments. When Diane bought Peter's house in an all-cash transaction for $150,000, it meant Diane would be paying Peter $150,000 on closing. The fact that Diane arranged a $100,000 mortgage to finance the purchase was irrelevant to Peter. He did not care how Diane came up with the money. All Peter wanted to see was $1500,000 cash or certified cheque from Diane on closing.

Examine the Statement of Adjustments on the following page. Joseph bought this house from Daniel for $150,000, with a $7,500 deposit. According to the offer, Joseph was to assume a first mortgage of approximately $95,000. Part of the difference was to be paid by Joseph granting a vendor-take-back second mortgage to Daniel for $25,000. The remaining $22,500 was to be paid in cash on closing. This last figure was the "unadjusted" balance due on closing. It is always "subject to the usual adjustments," described later in this chapter.

When told that a further $657.54 was payable for adjustments on closing, Joseph rightfully wanted to know why. The explanation can be found within the Statement of Adjustments. Prepared by the seller's lawyer, the Statement of Adjustments shows how the final balance owing to the seller — the "adjusted" balance due on closing — was calculated.

When examining the Statement of Adjustments, remember that everything in the right-hand column is a credit to the seller, while everything in the left-hand column is a credit to the buyer. All figures are calculated on a daily (or *per diem*) basis. Changing the closing date means all figures must be recalculated. And who is responsible for the payment of all items on the date of closing itself? Joseph, the buyer, even though he does not own it for the entire 24-hour period.

STATEMENT OF ADJUSTMENTS

VENDOR:	DANIEL
PURCHASER:	JOSEPH
ADDRESS OF PROPERTY:	18 Shimshone Road, Thornhill
CLOSING DATE:	April 11 (100 days)

	Credit Purchaser	*Credit Vendor*
SALE PRICE		$150,000.00
DEPOSIT	$7,500.00	
FIRST MORTGAGE: Assumed with Vaughan Trust		
i) Principal as of April 1		
Credit Purchaser	95,165.26	
ii) Interest to April 10		
(9 days) at 7%		
Credit Purchaser	158.84	
iii) Credit in tax account		
Credit Vendor		130.77
SECOND MORTGAGE: Taken back by Vendor		
Credit Purchaser	25,000.00	
TAXES: based on previous year's taxes of $2,018.64		
i) Paid by Vendor — $1,009.00		
ii) Vendor's share — $553.05		
Credit Vendor		455.95
OIL: 909-litre (200-gallon) tank at 35.9 cents/litre (plus GST)		
Credit Vendor		349.17
WATER: for the period January 1 to June 30 — $102.24		
i) Vendor has paid — $102.24		
iii) Vendor's share — $56.49		
Credit Vendor		45.75

ADJUSTED BALANCE DUE ON CLOSING payable to O'Really & O'Reilly or as they may further direct	$ 23,157.54	
TOTAL	$150,981.64	$150,981.64

As any accountant would say, both columns must add up to the identical figure. That means the adjusted balance due on closing is a "plugged" figure, a figure inserted to make both columns match. The difference between the adjusted balance due on closing and the unadjusted balance due on closing — $657.54 here — represents the net amount of the adjustments.

Changing one component on the statement affects the balance due on closing. So if a seller's credit (e.g., taxes) is increased by $50, the adjusted balance due on closing must be increased by $50, too, for everything to balance. If a purchaser's credit (e.g., the assumed mortgage) is increased by $100, the adjusted balance due on closing must fall by $100, for both columns to balance. Alan, as Joseph's lawyer, must independently verify the accuracy of each item on the Statement of Adjustments by obtaining written statements to confirm the information.

What are the "usual adjustments" in a real estate purchase?

i) Sale Price

Always credited to the seller, the sale price is the starting point for the transaction. It comes from the accepted Agreement of Purchase and Sale.

ii) Deposit

The deposit is the money Joseph paid when the offer was signed. Again, it appears in the Agreement of Purchase and Sale. Even though the listing agent may be holding the deposit, the buyer is always credited with the amount. Interest on the deposit, if agreed to, is not usually credited to the buyer on the Statement of Adjustments. Instead, it will be forwarded directly to Joseph by the listing agent shortly after closing.

iii) First Mortgage Assumed

a) Principal

According to the mortgage assumption statement that Joseph's lawyer received from the first mortgagee, Vaughan Trust, $95,165.26 is outstanding after the April 1st payment was made. Assuming the existing mortgage is part of the consideration that Joseph, the buyer, is giving to Daniel, the seller, on closing. The outstanding principal on the mortgage is credited to Joseph, reducing the balance due on closing, as he is taking over Daniel's obligation to pay that mortgage after closing.

The actual amount owing on the first mortgage exceeds by more than $165 the figure for the first mortgage appearing in the offer. Because most offers require that the buyer assume a mortgage for "approximately" a certain sum of money, this minor discrepancy won't threaten the transaction. If the size of the outstanding mortgage is larger than the figure in the Agreement of Purchase and Sale, it reduces the adjusted balance due on closing. If, however, the true mortgage balance is lower than anticipated, the buyer will have to pay that differential to the vendor as part of the adjusted balance due on closing. That's why Daniel's agent must do a mortgage verification before listing the property for sale.

b) Interest

Since mortgages in Canada are paid in arrears and not in advance, Daniel's mortgage payment on April 1st represented the payment due for the month of March. Following that payment, the slate was clean. No interest was owing to the lender, and no interest had been paid in advance to the lender.

When Joseph makes the May 1st mortgage payment, he will be paying interest for the entire month of April, together with the principal component. Why, he asks? He bought the property on April 10th, meaning he didn't own the property for the full month of April. Shouldn't Daniel be responsible for nine days' interest on the mortgage? Vaughan Trust, the lender, really does not care whether Daniel, or Joseph, or both make the May 1st mortgage payment, provided that it is made on time. The question of who makes that payment rests solely with Daniel and Joseph.

Joseph's concern is well founded. One way to ensure that Daniel pays his fair share of the May 1st mortgage payment is for Joseph to collect a cheque from Daniel on closing for $158.84. But what if it bounces? To simplify matters, Daniel gives Joseph a credit on the Statement of Adjustments instead of a cheque for the amount of interest that was Daniel's responsibility — $158.84. If no other adjustments were made, Joseph would pay Daniel $158.84 less than anticipated on closing. Then, when the May 1st mortgage instalment is made, Joseph will pay the total amount normally due that day. It consists of interest from April 10th to May 1st (his responsibility), plus interest to April 10th (Daniel's responsibility, for which Joseph has been reimbursed by Daniel), plus, of course, the principal component. Now Joseph is happy.

c) Credit in the Tax Account

Like many institutional lenders, Vaughan Trust collects 1/12th of the estimated annual taxes from the borrower with each monthly mortgage payment. These funds are kept in a tax account from which the tax bills are paid as issued. After the April 1st payment was made, Vaughan Trust held $130.77 of Daniel's money in this account. Vaughan Trust does not want to get involved in refunding this money to Daniel now that the property is sold and collecting a similar amount from Joseph. To circumvent this, Joseph buys the credit from Daniel by crediting him with $130.77 on the Statement of Adjustments.

iv) Second Mortgage Back

Besides assuming the existing first mortgage, Joseph is giving Daniel a $25,000 VTB second mortgage. Representing an unpaid portion of the sale price, payment of which is postponed by agreement, that $25,000 is credited to Joseph on the Statement of Adjustments on closing. After all, if the transaction between the parties had been structured without any second mortgage, the adjusted balance due on closing would have been $25,000 higher.

v) Realty Taxes

How property taxes are adjusted on closing depends on a number of factors, such as when in the year the deal closes and how much the vendor has paid before closing. Here, the taxes payable for the year of closing have not yet been determined. This is quite common when the transaction closes in the first half of a calendar year. The most up-to-date figure on which to base taxes is last year's bill. If his share is calculated on a daily basis, Daniel is responsible for 100/365ths of the $2,018.64 for property taxes, or $553.05. Yet Daniel has already paid, through the lender, the full interim tax bill of $1,009. Having overpaid the taxes by $455.95, Daniel is reimbursed with this amount on closing, by being credited with it on the Statement of Adjustments.

If the final bill has not yet been issued, some lawyers representing sellers will estimate the current year's taxes by hiking the prior year's taxes by 1% to 5%, depending on the current inflation rate in Canada. What appears on the adjustments then more accurately reflects what likely will be the tax situation for the current year.

On closing, sellers agree in writing to recalculate the realty taxes once the final bill is issued, and to reimburse any money owing to the purchaser. (Buyers are often asked to do the same thing.) Assume that the taxes rose by 1.9%, to $2,056.99. Daniel's share would increase to $563.56, meaning he should have been credited with only $445.44 (the $1,009 paid less his actual share of $563.56) on the Statement of Adjustments. Having been credited with $455.95 on the Statement of Adjustments for taxes, Daniel technically owes Joseph $10.51.

When taxes are adjusted based on last year's taxes, a readjustment of taxes after the final bill is issued often benefits the purchaser, as is the case here. Once the final tax bill is received, Joseph should contact Alan, his lawyer, to determine the amount to be refunded. So should you. Mark down on your calendar to contact your lawyer during the summer about the possible readjustment of taxes in your favor. If the amount owing is sizeable, make sure you receive it! But don't pursue trifles. Most people won't worry about collecting tax adjustments if the amount at stake is $25 or less.

If the transaction had closed in the second half of the year, the adjustment for taxes would have been based on the final tax bill. In such a case, the amount to be adjusted for taxes depends on a) whether the vendor has already paid the full amount of the tax bill and b) whether the buyer will be paying realty taxes directly or through the mortgage lender. Most home owners who pay their own taxes do so as the instalments come due. If the taxes are paid through the mortgage lender, it will pay the *entire* final bill when it is issued (if not yet paid), ignoring the instalment payment plan.

Taxes on Ramon's home totalled $1,800 for the year, and were paid in full by the lender from the tax account it maintained. Anyone closing a purchase from Ramon at the end of July will have to come up with an additional $750 on closing. Why? Since Ramon, through his lender, has paid the entire $1,800 tax bill, Ramon will be credited with 5/12ths of those taxes, or $750, on the Statement of Adjustments on closing.

Elliott recently bought a house where the taxes are also $1,800 annually. Closing is scheduled for the end of July. But only $1,050 in taxes have been paid prior to closing. Because Elliott's lender will be maintaining a tax account after closing, it will deduct at source $750 from the mortgage advance to pay the balance of the year's taxes on closing. With the net advance on the mortgage cut by $750, Elliott will have to come up with an extra $750 on closing — money that's legitimately owing, but which is being paid months before it technically comes due. In this case the $750 is not an adjustment to the vendor on closing, as in Ramon's situation. Instead, it's a deduction on the mortgage. Either way, though, it's money out of the purchaser's pocket on closing, affecting an already tight cash flow.

vi) Home Heating Oil

The only type of home heating energy source that is included on the Statement of Adjustments is fuel oil. Gas and electricity charges are metered, not requiring any adjustment on closing. But only by topping up the oil tank can the amount accurately be determined. Daniel will do this and pay the oil company for the amount of the final oil delivery. Joseph in turn will reimburse Daniel for the value of the full tank of home heating oil (plus GST) on the Statement of Adjustments.

A standard-sized oil tank is 909 litres, or 200 gallons. If home heating oil costs approximately 35.9 cents per litre, or $1.63 a gallon, buyers of homes heated by oil can expect to pay close to $350 as an adjustment on closing, taking into account the GST payable on the oil adjustment, too.

What if Joseph will be converting his heating system off oil right after closing? Why pay for a full tank of oil he will never use? If that's the case, Joseph should insert a clause into the draft offer that no fuel oil adjustment will be made on closing. Frequently, the decision to convert is made after the offer is signed. Where a good rapport exists between seller and buyer, sellers will often co-operate by agreeing to "split the difference," taking a credit for half a tank only, regardless of its actual contents on closing. But there's no obligation to do so.

vii) Water

Most utility accounts are not adjusted; they are metered. A new account is established on the day of closing in the buyer's name, with the final bill sent to the seller. Where a utility is billed on a flat-rate basis, such as the water account in some large metropolitan centres, an adjustment becomes necessary. Here, the total water bill for the 181-day period from January 1st to June 30th is divided into the buyer's share (81 days) and the seller's share (100 days). As Daniel has overpaid his share by $45.75, he is credited with that amount on the Statement of Adjustments.

No adjustment of utility charges is necessary in condominium transactions. Either the charges are calculated on consumption as measured by meter or they are bulk-metered to the condominium corporation and paid as part of the monthly maintenance fee.

viii) Other Adjustments

Other adjustable items include the following: insurance premiums for insurance policies transferred to the purchaser; rent and other rent-related charges for tenant-occupied properties; condominium maintenance (common expense) payments; service contracts for furnaces; and monthly monitoring charges for home security systems. No adjustment is made, though, for telephone charges or cable television fees.

Because insurance policies are typically not transferred from seller to buyer in resale transactions, they are rarely adjusted. Where tenants occupy all or part of the property, the buyer should get a credit for the balance of the rent collected by the landlord in advance for the month of closing, plus any last month's rent or security deposits held by the seller or landlord. If interest is to be paid on the last month's rent, either by contract or provincial law, it should be credited to the buyer as well, calculated from the last day it was paid. Condominium maintenance charges are usually payable monthly, in advance. That means sellers will get a credit on the Statement of Adjustments for any amount overpaid for the month of closing. Condominium reserve funds, though, are only adjusted if the offer specifically provides for it. Adjustments for a service contract for a furnace and monthly monitoring charges for a home security system can only be made if the Agreement of Purchase and Sale specifically provides for it. These are not the "usual" adjustments contemplated by an offer.

Deductions on the Mortgage

Enough is enough! What more can there be? Costs associated with that new mortgage a buyer is arranging, that's what. Most of these must be paid by purchasers on closing, wreaking havoc with their meticulous cash flow.

Whether any particular item applies depends on the circumstances of the specific loan. These are discussed in more detail in chapter 21.

Miscellaneous Expenses

Five charges fall into this category: survey; insurance; home inspection; moving; and bridge financing.

Survey
The buyer may have to order a new survey if none exists or if the present survey is not acceptable to the mortgage lender. See chapter 24 for more information.

Fire Insurance
What will be the cost of the new fire insurance policy the buyer must arrange on closing? See chapter 30.

Home Inspection
How much will the home inspection cost? See chapter 14.

Moving
Whether you move yourself in a rented truck or hire a mover, some expense will be incurred. How large will it be? And remember, a premium is often charged for movers and vans at the end of the month, the "rush hour" for those businesses. All the more reason to schedule a closing date a few days before month-end.

Bridge Financing
For buyers who close the purchase now and the sale later, what will the bridge financing cost be? See chapter 22.

Two points should now be self-evident. First, when asking a lawyer for a fee quote, ask what the estimated overall closing costs will be, too. Second, *learn this information before putting pen to paper.* The time to know what your total financial commitment will be is now, at the pre-contract stage. Waiting until after the offer is signed can cause unnecessary grief and anxiety.

In the space below, prepare both a preliminary Statement of Adjustments as well as a preliminary Statement of Closing Costs. This will help immensely in budgeting properly for a purchase. Ask as many questions as necessary of as many people — real estate agent, lawyer, insurance agent, mortgage broker or lender, and home inspector — as required to get the answers.

STATEMENT OF ADJUSTMENTS

		PURCHASER	SELLER
Sale price			$
Deposit		$	
First mortgage	— principal	$	
	— interest	$	
	— taxes		$

		Purchaser	Seller
Second mortgage	— principal	$	
	— interest	$	
Taxes			$
Oil			$
Water			$
Other adjustments		$	
— rent and related sums			
— condominium maintenance			
Adjusted balance due on closing		____	____
Total		$____	$____

STATEMENT OF CLOSING COSTS

I Fees	— purchase	$
	— mortgage	$____
		$____
II Disbursements	— by-laws/zoning and work order report	$
	— tax certificate	$
	— utilities certificate	$
	— search of title	$
	— registration costs	$
	— transportation and courier charge	$
	— execution certificate	$
	— amortization schedule	$
	— estoppel certificate (condominiums only)	$
	— Personal Property Security Act searches	$
	— subdivision agreement report	$
	— long-distance telephone charges	$
	— photocopy/miscellaneous charges	$____
		$____

	PURCHASER	SELLER
III Provincial taxes — land transfer tax		$
— retail sales tax		$
IV Adjusted balance due on closing (from Statement of Adjustments)		$
TOTAL GROSS AMOUNT NEEDED TO CLOSE		$____

V Mortgage considerations	Amount of new first mortgage applied for	$	
	Less: deductions on the mortgage		
	— mortgage appraisal/ application fee	$	
	— interest to the interest adjustment date	$	
	— establishing realty tax account	$	
	— mortgage broker's fee	$	
	— CMHC/GE mortgage insurance fee	$	
	— life insurance fee	$____	$____
NET ADVANCE ON NEW MORTGAGE			$____

SUMMARY:

TOTAL GROSS AMOUNT NEEDED TO CLOSE	$
LESS: net advance on new mortgage	($____)
DIFFERENCE: approximate net amount needed by purchaser to close transaction	$____

The miscellaneous charges should also be added to this net amount, to give the overall amount of money needed to close:

— survey	$

— fire insurance $

— home inspection $

— moving $

— bridge financing $____

OVERALL AMOUNT OF MONEY NEEDED TO CLOSE $____

24

Surveys

A survey does more than just show the location of a building and other structures (fences, garages and decks) on a property. A survey is a graphic description of the extent of the seller's property. It indicates the size of the lot, its dimensions, the exact location of its boundaries, plus items affecting the property such as fences, hedges, easements, rights-of-way, mutual drives and road widenings. Only with a survey can a buyer know whether the structures on the property are located wholly within the lot lines, and whether there are any encroachments onto the property or onto an adjoining property. Municipalities require a survey to confirm that the location of a building on a property complies with the applicable zoning by-laws, including side-yard, front-yard and rear-yard "setbacks" (the distance between the building and that lot line). Only with a survey can purchasers know exactly how much of the "face of the earth" they are buying.

Occasionally a legal description is at odds with the physical boundaries of a property established by a surveyor. When that happens, the survey prevails. Yes, over the years the courts have consistently said that only surveys, not legal descriptions, are conclusive of property dimensions.

According to the fine print in most standard form resale offers, a seller is simply obligated to deliver to the buyer, before the title search period expires, any survey in his or her possession or control (e.g., with the seller's lawyer). No survey means tough luck for the buyer; get one at your own expense. Yet the purchaser likely will need a survey, especially since a survey is a condition of most mortgage loan approvals. *Therefore, learning whether a survey exists, before the offer is signed, is an essential element of any home-buying strategy.* To ensure that they will get a survey, buyers must specifically require it in the offer.

No survey is needed in a condominium transaction, as a copy of the survey for the complex is filed in the registry office.

One of the first questions Maria's lawyer will ask when reviewing the purchase offer centres on the survey. Anticipating this, Maria should ask her real estate agent about the survey well before any offer is prepared. To be frank, any agent who knows that a buyer like Maria will require mortgage financing should already have inquired about the survey. If no survey is available, or if it's not up-to-date, Maria must be alerted to this possible expense before making any commitment to buy.

Surveys are available from other sources than just the vendor. Occasionally a survey is registered in the registry office. If that's the case, it's available at nominal cost. Sometimes a survey is prepared for a number of adjacent houses. Even though the vendor lacks a survey, one of the neighbors might have a survey that includes the subject property. What a great way to introduce yourself to your future neighbors and save money in the process. When necessary, your lawyer can contact a lawyer who acted for a former owner of the property, to see if he or she has a survey in the file.

Learning whether a survey exists is only the first hurdle. Of greater importance is knowing whether an existing survey is acceptable to the buyer and, more importantly, the mortgage lender. If a survey, however old, is located, it should accompany the offer, so that the buyer's lawyer can review both together. If a mortgage is being arranged, the lender should be given the same opportunity to determine, at the outset, if the survey is acceptable. If it isn't, the buyer still has ample time to deal with the issue before the contract is finalized.

For many years, any survey, no matter how old, was considered suitable. The key was to locate a survey, not to worry about its age or accuracy. But a survey is like an X-ray of a property, taken as of a certain date. No doctor would dare treat a patient using X-rays that are 20 years old. Yet in many transactions, surveys that old or even older were regularly relied on.

To be of any real value to a buyer, a survey should be "up-to-date." Surveyors argue that only a survey prepared for that particular transaction can be considered to be up-to-date. Most people, however, define an "up-to-date" survey to mean a survey "reflecting current conditions" by showing the location of all buildings and structures on the property. Age has nothing to do with the issue. A 40-year-old survey could be up-to-date, if nothing has changed since the survey was prepared. On the other hand, a two-year-old survey is out of date if changes have been made to the property in the interim, such as an addition to the house, the removal of a carport, the erection of a fence or the construction of a deck.

Close scrutiny of the property can quickly determine if a survey is out of date. Consider the survey in chapter 16. Prepared for a brand-new home, this survey technically was out of date by the time the purchase transaction for which it had been prepared closed! Why? The initials C.B.W. (sometimes C.B.F.) on the survey mean the survey was prepared at the concrete block wall or concrete foundation stage. Other surveys boldly state "dwelling incomplete" or "D.U.C." (dwelling under construction). This document is prepared once construction of the house proceeds above grade level, so that the builder can get its first mortgage advance. Of course, much has happened to the property since then: the house has been built! Once even the first course of bricks are laid, the survey becomes out of date. Obviously, the survey does not show what has been added to the property after the C.B.W. stage — the dwelling itself, eavestroughs, downspouts, a driveway, sidewalk, deck or carport.

Practically speaking, the key is to locate an "accurate" existing survey. Having a new survey drawn is expensive — upwards of $750, plus GST. So most mortgage lenders, and therefore most buyers and their lawyers, take a flexible position on the survey issue. They will accept and rely on an existing survey, with one very big if: *if* it accurately depicts the current state of the property, showing the location of the building and all other structures. If there have been no changes, alterations or additions to the external structure of the building from those shown on an existing survey, most mortgage lenders will accept it. To verify this, the lender will want a sworn affidavit from either the buyer or the seller, or both, before advancing mortgage funds. If any buildings, decks, swimming pools, outbuildings or other structures exist on the property which are not shown on the survey, a new survey will have to be drawn. Even if a fence was erected after the survey was prepared, most institutional lenders will still accept it.

Of course, to be acceptable, that "old" survey must be legible, showing the lot and plan for the property, the name of the surveyor, and the date it was prepared. Over time, continuously photocopying a survey makes it unreadable and unsatisfactory. The same with a fax copy of a survey, since the numbers bleed together.

Sometimes it is not clear whether a mortgage lender will approve an old survey. The seller says yes, the buyer says no, and the agent says I hope so. A compromise is to insert a clause into the offer, provided it is still unsigned, allowing the lender to determine whether the existing survey is acceptable. Yes means the buyer is satisfied as well. No means a new survey will have to be drawn. The rest of the clause will spell out who bears the cost and in what proportion.

Even just updating an existing survey does not come cheap. Both field work and research are necessary, resulting in very little savings. Agents who claim that an existing survey can be updated for a nominal sum are fooling both the purchaser and themselves.

Money isn't the only cost to consider when talking about a new survey. Valuable time between acceptance and closing will be lost while the survey is prepared. That research and field work, plus the work drafting the document, will take at least 10 to 14 days. Anyone who buys a house with a "quick closing" may not have enough time to get a clearance letter, based on the information in that new survey, from the building department.

If no survey can be located, or if the existing survey isn't suitable, the big question becomes, who will pay for a new one? Roy faced this problem when he bought a resale home from Raquel. Obviously, Raquel had little to gain by having a new survey prepared, and even less to gain by paying for it. In fact,

Raquel was fearful that a new survey would open a Pandora's Box by disclosing problems that could jeopardize the transaction: items such as encroachments, a boundary inconsistent with the registered title, or structures not wholly within the lot. If an addition had been built too close to a lot line, Raquel would have to get a minor variance to allow it to remain — an additional expense that would also take months to obtain. But Roy was also reluctant to bear the cost of a new survey. It was an additional expense he could avoid if he bought another property.

Surveys are one of those areas where trade-offs are possible, to help strike a deal. An anxious seller may agree in the offer to pay half the cost, a fixed dollar amount or even the entire cost of ordering a new survey, simply to have the offer accepted. Occasionally one or both real estate agents will contribute towards the cost of a new survey to avoid losing a sale. Buyers who fear losing a particular property may decide not to push the issue too hard, knowing what the additional cost will be if they concede the point. In many cases, who will pay for the survey becomes a matter to be negotiated by the parties. Whatever is agreed upon should then appear in a clause in the Agreement of Purchase and Sale, together with a statement of who will be responsible to actually order the survey.

Knowing before signing the offer that no acceptable survey was available, Roy could do one of several things: a) insert a clause into the offer requiring the parties to split the cost of having a new survey drawn; b) insert a "cap" on the amount of the vendor's contribution; c) get a letter from either or both agents, stating how much they will pay towards the cost of the new survey; or d) adjust the purchase price downwards to reflect the fact that he will be bearing the cost of a new survey. After heavy negotiating, and some coaxing by their agents, Roy and Raquel agreed to go 50-50 on the cost of the new survey.

Buyers creating and applying their own HOBS are prudent buyers. They will know whether a survey exists, and whether it is acceptable to both them and their mortgage lender, before the offer itself is accepted.

25
The Offer

In this chapter the contents of an Offer to Purchase (also known as an Agreement of Purchase and Sale) on a resale home will be discussed. Issues relating to the purchase of a resale condominium unit are explored in chapter 20 "Condominiums."

Many offers are drawn as conditional offers, the contract not being firm and binding until one or more items are satisfied. Conditional offers are discussed in chapter 26.

This chapter does not provide a series of precedent clauses to be inserted into an offer that buyers prepare themselves. Rather, it provides food for thought, examining topics buyers will want either included or excluded from an offer prepared by their agent or lawyer, to best protect their interests. Many suggestions in this chapter will not appear in the offer originally prepared by the agent. As part of your home-buying strategy, you must discuss them with your lawyer, and insert them into the offer before submitting it for seller acceptance.

Plain and simple, the document submitted to buy a house is a contract, meaning that basic contract principles apply. For a binding contract to exist, a written offer is needed, followed by acceptance and communication of that acceptance. Few offers are accepted unscathed the first time out. Most are amended by sellers, followed by a series of counter-amendments before mutually agreeable terms are reached. Often, an offer resembles colorful chicken scrawl by the time it becomes firm and binding.

No document is more important to a real estate transaction than the offer. What it contains governs the relationship between the parties up to closing. For that reason, buyers and sellers must be precise and specific. Leave no room for misunderstandings or differences of opinion. If an item is important to you as purchaser, it must appear in the offer in order to be binding on the seller. Otherwise, he or she is under no obligation to comply with the request. If Eli and Karen want the purchase price to include Rochelle's fridge and stove, a clause to that effect must appear in the offer. If there's a paramount rule for real estate deals, it is this: "If it's not in the offer, it's not in the deal."

Negotiating an offer is not for the faint of heart. The time between submitting an offer and receiving the seller's response is extremely nerve-wracking for most buyers, especially first-timers. Was the offer accepted? If not, what changes were made in the counter-offer? The tension, anxiety and uncertainty over what is happening, and whether that time period will be hours or days, are arduous on all but the most seasoned purchaser. During this interval, the best thing buyers can do is put the deal completely out of their minds and keep busy with other activities. Little can be done anyway, since the negotiations rest strictly with the agents and the seller. Worrying won't make a seller accept an otherwise unacceptable offer. So buyers should relax by forgetting about the transaction. The excitement of a house purchase should never be overshadowed by needless concern about events over which the buyer has no control.

What is the scenario when an offer is submitted on a resale home? The buyer's agent, regardless of the agency relationship, prepares the offer without charge. Most real estate boards and associations have a standard form offer which most agents use. Despite what agents may say, the fine print has a distinct "pro-seller" bias. A number of clauses obligate and commit buyers in ways they would never imagine. In addition, many real estate offices use standard "John Doe" precedent clauses, often computerized, which are added to the blank offer, depending on the circumstances.

Once the offer is drawn, and before it is signed and submitted, it should be sent to your lawyer for review, comment and revision. Buyers applying their home-buying strategy will not sign any documents until reading chapter 27, "Do Not Sign on the Dotted Line Until . . ." The reason is simple. Your lawyer should see the offer when he or she can still do something with it, before it is etched in stone. With fax machines so prevalent today, your lawyer can receive a copy of the draft, unsigned offer from the agent in minutes, eliminating the traditional argument that "if you don't move immediately, you'll lose the deal."

Where there is no agent involved in the transaction, the buyer's lawyer must draft the offer, often on the real estate board's standard form, at the buyer's expense.

Negotiating a contract is an art, and experience is the greatest teacher on how to negotiate effectively. All the more reason, then, for buyers to retain an experienced real estate agent. Buyers want to pay the lowest possible price for a property, while sellers want to receive the highest possible price. Skillful negotiations by an agent will encourage each side to re-evaluate their positions, if necessary, so that common ground can be reached. When a meeting of the minds takes place, the parties have a deal.

Try to avoid late-night negotiating sessions. Many home owners have personal recollections of dickering into the wee hours of the morning. When was the last time you did your best work at that hour, let alone purchase a six-figure property? By that time, the parties are tired, especially after a full day at work, making it increasingly hard to think with a clear head. In addition, try to be cool, calm and collected at all times when negotiating an offer, and maintain your objectivity. Never let your emotions carry the day. Negotiate with your head, not your heart. Otherwise, something important could easily be missed.

What happens when the offer is submitted?
Once the offer is signed by the purchaser, the listing agent presents it to the seller. Where an agent is involved, the purchaser often will not meet directly with the seller. In fact, negotiations are often more successful if they are not conducted face to face. Instead, the agents play the role of go-betweens. When the offer is presented to the seller, he or she has three options: accept it, reject it, or make a counter-offer.

Phil wants to buy Adrienne's property. If Adrienne accepts Phil's offer as submitted, the contract becomes binding once Phil is notified, subject to any conditions which must still be satisfied. Notification is usually done by a telephone call followed by delivery of the accepted offer to the purchaser. If Adrienne rejects the offer, that's it. No deal. In most cases, though, a vendor who is not completely satisfied with the terms of an offer will make a counter-offer, also called a "sign-back." That is what happened here. In her counter-offer, Adrienne changes the two unacceptable terms (by increasing the purchase price by $10,000 and deleting the clause that Phil acquire the washer/dryer combination) and initials the changes. All other terms are left the same. For a binding contract to result, the changes must now be initialled by Phil, the purchaser. Considering that Adrienne, the seller, had a limited amount of time in which to make up her mind when the offer was originally submitted, she now returns the "favor" by giving Phil an even shorter period of time to decide what to do!

If Phil agrees to pay the additional $10,000 and not acquire the washer/dryer set, he initials the changes to the offer that Adrienne previously initialled. Once that's done, the offer becomes a binding contract, subject to any outstanding conditions. If, however, Phil will pay only $5,000 more and agrees to Adrienne's washer/dryer clause, he will a) change the $10,000 to $5,000 and initial the change, and b) initial Adrienne's washer/dryer provision, following which he re-submits the offer. Now Phil's offer is technically known as a counter-counter-offer. The initialling done by Phil at this stage is often in a different color of ink, to distinguish the initials of Adrienne's counter-offer from those of Phil's counter-counter-offer. (If the offer becomes very messy, a new "clean" offer should be prepared.)

This volley of papers between Phil and Adrienne continues until either all the proposed changes are acceptable and initialled by both sides or no agreement can be reached and the negotiations end. Tenterhooks time for Phil and Adrienne!

If and when the offer is accepted, a copy is sent to each party's lawyer, even if one or more conditions remain outstanding. Any amendments or waivers of conditions are also delivered, when they become are available.

Once the offer is accepted, the transaction takes on a sacred quality. "There shall be a binding Agreement of Purchase and Sale between the purchaser and the vendor." Ominous words. For this reason, buyers must be acquainted with some of the key elements of an offer. While the typed-in clauses distinguish one offer from another, the wording of the printed form should not be ignored. Printed-form clauses are not unalterable. They can, should and must be changed if they do not adequately protect a buyer's interests or reflect his or her concerns.

The Purchaser (Buyer)

The purchaser is the person who signs the offer, and who is obligated to close the transaction. Determining who should be the buyer is not always a simple matter.

Gary and Judy, a married couple, are buying a house. For business reasons, title will be registered in Judy's name alone. Because Gary does not own the house, his creditors cannot seize it if his business fails. (This arrangement — people in high-risk jobs putting title to the matrimonial home in the name of the other spouse — is commonly used by professionals such as doctors, dentists, lawyers and accountants.) Therefore, only Judy should sign the offer as purchaser. If Gary signs the offer (either alone or with Judy) and the seller is taking back a mortgage, Gary must sign that mortgage either as owner or as guarantor. The reason: the seller dealt with Gary as one of the purchasers, and is looking to his "covenant" on the mortgage. Obviously, this defeats Gary's intentions. But if only Judy signs the offer as purchaser, Gary can't be forced to sign the vendor-take-back mortgage in any capacity, as he was not a party to the original contract.

Occasionally, one spouse is not available to sign the offer when it is prepared. Charley was out of town when the offer was signed by Lucy, his wife. But they want title to be registered in both names. No problem. Before closing, Lucy can direct, in writing, that title be taken in her name alone (in accordance with the offer), in Charley's name alone, or in both her name and Charley's name. Written directions of this sort are very common.

The Vendor (Seller)

The vendor is the person selling the property. Occasionally, an agent does not know whether a husband or wife or both are the registered owners of the property. Where a matrimonial home is involved, most provincial family law legislation prevents one spouse from selling it without the written consent of the other spouse, even if the other spouse is not a registered owner of the property. To avoid any problems from arising in the future, both the husband and the wife should sign an offer to sell a matrimonial home, whether or not both technically own it. If a non-titled spouse doesn't sign the offer, thus not signifying consent to the transaction, there is a greater chance he or she will refuse to sign the deed and other closing documents.

The Property

The property should be described in as much detail as possible. The municipal address should appear, as well as its legal description. This will help the buyer's lawyer begin the title search as soon as possible after acceptance. Any easements, rights-of-way or mutual drives affecting the property must be stated, as well as the dimensions of the property as verified by the survey or deed. Use caution when relying on an old tax bill for property dimensions, since the numbers are nothing more than an estimate. Even the practice of describing a property "as per vendor's deed" can be dangerous. What if those dimensions have changed over time, due to a road widening or an expropriation?

The expression "more or less" often appears in an offer, to describe the frontage and depth of the property. To the surprise of many buyers, that expression actually helps sellers if the dimensions are not exactly as stated in the offer. When the boundaries of a property are clearly marked, and the offer states the lot dimensions "more or less," courts usually say that "what you see is what you get," even if the discrepancy is far from minor.

Paul and Carol bought a house where the offer said the

property had a depth of 110 feet "more or less." Its true depth was 98.5 feet, resulting in a 10% shortfall in lot area. However, the boundaries were clearly visible (the property being a corner lot with a lane in the rear), and the offer did contain the words "more or less." Therefore, Paul and Carol were not entitled to any compensation or reduction in the purchase price. Use of the words "more or less" qualified the lot dimensions appearing in the offer, minimizing their relevance.

The Purchase Price

This is the "compensation package" a buyer will pay to acquire a property. If Moe buys Larry's house for $100,000, Moe must give Larry $100,000 of "consideration" on closing. Cash is only one of three different types of consideration a buyer can give a seller on closing. Consideration can consist of the following: cash (payment now); a vendor-take-back or VTB mortgage, a deferred payment of the purchase price (payment later); or the assumption of an existing obligation on an outstanding mortgage ("cash to the mortgage"). Of course, it could also be a combination of all three. If a buyer arranges his or her own mortgage, the transaction between the buyer and seller becomes an all-cash transaction. Several examples will explain how a $100,000 purchase price can be paid with different types of consideration.

Alan and Hannah bought a house for $100,000. On closing they will assume the existing mortgage for $65,000. Since the deposit is $5,000, Alan and Hannah must pay a further $30,000 on closing. Their total equity in the property is $35,000 and the total received by the seller is $35,000 (the seller's equity in the property).

Aron and Frieda are also buying a house for $100,000. They will be assuming the existing mortgage for $55,000 and are arranging a $10,000 second mortgage with a bank. Having already paid a $5,000 deposit, Aron and Frieda will be paying $40,000 to the seller on closing — the $100,000 purchase price less the $55,000 mortgage assumed, less the $5,000 deposit. Of this $40,000, $10,000 is coming from the new second mortgage and $30,000 from their own funds. Aron and Frieda's total equity in the property is therefore $35,000 — the $30,000 of their own money paid on closing plus the $5,000 deposit paid when the offer was signed. The total received by the seller for her equity in the property: $45,000 — the $100,000 purchase price less the $55,000 on the assumed mortgage.

Elliott and Michelle also paid $100,000 for a home. They arranged a new first mortgage for $65,000. With a $5,000 deposit already paid to the Sue, the seller, Elliott and Michelle will be paying a further $95,000 to her on closing — $65,000 from the mortgage and $30,000 from their own funds. Their total equity in the property: $35,000. The total received by Sue for her equity in the property: $100,000. For Sue it was an all-cash deal, although Elliott and Michelle had to borrow money to pay that.

The amount of cash paid is adjusted right down to the date of closing on the Statement of Adjustments. More information on this topic appears in chapter 23.

What is the proper price to put in an offer?
After consultation with the real estate agent, and depending on market conditions, the price inserted is often anywhere from 5% to 10% below the expected ultimate purchase price. Most reasonably priced houses are sold for slightly less than their asking price. It's a given that buyers want to pay the lowest possible price for a home, while sellers want to receive the highest possible price. If the price in the offer is too high, the vendor might accept the offer immediately, leaving the buyer to wonder how much lower a price would also have been acceptable. Going in too low could insult the seller, to the point that he or she will not entertain any further offers from that purchaser. Generally speaking, if the offer is reasonable and "within the ballpark," the offers and counter-offers begin to fly until either a deal is struck or negotiations break off.

The purchase price in your first offer should never be the maximum price you are prepared to pay. Because it will probably be necessary to adjust your price upwards, leave yourself ample negotiating room within your maximum price range.

When no agent is involved (i.e., in a private sale), determining

how much to offer for a house is very difficult. Unless buyers
have done extensive homework comparing real estate listings
and sales, it is not likely they will know the true market value of
a property. As it is human nature to set a high price for property,
vendors will probably value their property at the high end of
the price range. Without the benefit of an agent to advise on
property values, a buyer could easily wind up paying more than
market value for the home.

To deal with this situation, some buyers in private-sale transactions will have a real estate appraiser value the property. The
cost of an appraisal report is relatively small, generally in the
$200 range (plus GST). Armed with this information, a buyer
has a much better idea of what a property is worth, and what
price to offer for the property. But there's a sizeable downside
risk in doing this. If the buyer isn't successful buying that
house, the cost of the appraisal is money totally wasted.

Deposit

Most people incorrectly equate the deposit with the downpayment. A deposit is only the money paid by the purchaser at the
time the offer is submitted. The downpayment, on the other
hand, is the total amount of money, including the deposit,
being paid to the vendor on or before closing. So if Joseph and
Carla are buying a house with a $10,000 deposit and a further
$20,000 on closing, their total downpayment is $30,000.

Deposits serve two purposes. If the deal closes, the deposit is
credited as a part payment of the purchase price. But the
deposit is also a guarantee that the buyer is serious about proceeding with the transaction, since it can be lost if the deal does
not close as scheduled.

*Buyers who want to receive interest on their deposit must specifically
ask for it in the offer. Otherwise, no interest is payable.* Three criteria
must usually be met for interest to be paid on a deposit. First,
the deposit must be at least $5,000, the minimum amount for
the listing agent to buy an interest-bearing term deposit
to mature on closing. Second, the interval from acceptance to
closing must be at least 30 days. That's the minimum period of

time for which a term deposit will be issued. Finally, the buyer must provide his or her social insurance number to the agent. Interest on a deposit is taxable to the purchaser; hence the need for the SIN.

Technically, the listing agent is not a party to the offer, as he or she does not sign it. This means the purchaser has no legal recourse against the agent if the request to place the deposit in an interest-bearing account is not honored. Still, most agents do honor the interest clause in an offer if the above criteria are satisfied.

What happens to the deposit?

In most cases, the purchaser's uncertified cheque, payable to the listing broker in trust, accompanies the offer. Once the offer is accepted, the agent will have the cheque certified and will hold the deposit in trust pending completion of the transaction.

In a private-sale situation, the vendor's lawyer should hold the deposit in place of the listing agent. So make the uncertified cheque payable to that lawyer, in trust. *Never pay the deposit directly to the vendor.* To do that is to play with fire. Try recovering money from a seller if the deal falls through, once it has already been spent! It's a lot easier to chase a lawyer than an unco-operative vendor.

Buyers who earn interest on a deposit will receive a T5 Supplementary from the agent or lawyer holding the deposit, either with the interest cheque or before February 28th the following year. This interest is taxable, to be declared when filing your next income tax return.

As purchasers, Kevin and Sheri paid a $10,000 deposit when they signed their offer. After closing, the deposit (which is now the seller's money) was ready to be distributed. The $78.57 in accrued interest was paid to Kevin and Sheri. Then the $9,630 commission (including $630 GST) was deducted from the deposit and put into the agent's bank account. The remaining $370 was forwarded to the seller. What if the deposit had been only $5,000? Since the $9,630 commission (including GST) would exceed the $5,000 deposit, the agent would keep the entire deposit after closing, after paying the accrued interest to Kevin and Sheri, and bill the seller for the balance.

If the transaction does not close, the deposit can be tied up for years in litigation, to be released in one of two circumstances: a) the seller and buyer mutually agree how the deposit should be distributed; or b) a court determines the issue.

How large a deposit should be submitted with an offer?

Whether or not the deposit earns interest, buyers like to pay the smallest deposit possible. Once the deposit leaves their hands, buyers feel they've lost control of their funds. By contrast, sellers like the largest possible deposit. Too small a deposit is unsatisfactory, as the buyer has put little of his or her own money at risk, meaning there is little to prevent the buyer from simply walking away from the deal. Larger deposits not only indicate a greater willingness of the purchaser to proceed with the transaction, but also give the seller a bigger fund to claim, if the transaction is aborted.

Not surprisingly, agents also have a stake in getting a large deposit. Getting paid on closing is much easier if the commission, or the lion's share, is held in trust by the listing broker. Larger deposits are possible when they are placed in an interest-bearing term deposit, agents argue, because buyers do not suffer any loss of interest. With total commissions in the 5% to 6% range (plus GST), agents routinely recommend that the deposit be at least 5% of the purchase price, rounding the figure upwards where appropriate. So on a purchase of $145,000, the deposit is $7,500.

If you are in a back-to-back transaction, where one property is being sold and another purchased the same day, be sure the amount of the deposit paid on your sale does not exceed the amount of commission payable (plus GST). Otherwise, you could inadvertently find yourself of short funds for the purchase.

Glen sold his house for $150,000 cash, as did Donna. Neither had a mortgage against their house, and both were buying another house the same day. The commission owing on each sale was 6% of the purchase price (plus GST), for a total of $9,630. Therefore, each would net $140,370 from their sale. Accompanying Glen's offer was a deposit cheque for $12,000. Of course, Glen's agent was proud of how large a deposit he got from the purchaser. However, on closing the sale, Glen would only receive $138,000 from the purchaser. The other $2,370 wouldn't be available for Glen from his agent until several days after closing, leaving Glen $2,370 short to close his purchase. That sent him scrambling for funds just days before closing.

By comparison, the deposit paid on Donna's sale was only $8,000. Since she would receive $142,000 on closing, immediately after closing she would pay the remaining $1,630 to her real estate agent, leaving her with the necessary $140,370. Because the deposit paid did not exceed the commission owing (plus GST), the full $140,370 Donna expected to receive on closing her sale was available at that time, ready to be used on her purchase. Despite agents' protestations, it *is* possible for too large a deposit to be paid when an offer is signed.

While there is no "right" amount for a deposit, generally it should not be less than 2% or greater than 5% of the purchase price.

Balance Due on Closing

The balance due on closing is the amount of money paid by the buyer to the seller on closing. Where the buyer assumes the mortgage or the seller takes back a mortgage, the balance due on closing is the purchase price less the deposit, less the amount of the mortgage. If the buyer is arranging his or her own mortgage financing, the balance due on closing between the buyer and seller is the purchase price less the deposit *only*. After all, between buyer and seller it's an all-cash deal, requiring the balance of the purchase price to be paid to the seller in cash on closing.

Different ways the balance due on closing can be paid are discussed earlier in this chapter, under the heading "Purchase Price."

Dates

Four key dates appear in an offer: the irrevocable date; the completion date/closing date; the title search date; and the "conditional" date, the date when outstanding conditions must be satisfied. Each has its own importance in a real estate transaction. The first three dates are examined below, while the conditional date is discussed in detail in chapter 26.

Irrevocable Date

Richard and Angela signed an Offer to Purchase on December 2nd. This offer has an irrevocable date of 11:59 p.m. on December 5th. This means Lou, the seller, has until one minute before midnight on December 5th to decide whether or not to accept their offer. During the period from December 2nd to the irrevocable date, Richard and Angela are not allowed to revoke or cancel their offer. It remains outstanding, and ready for acceptance. (Despite this, courts have said that a buyer can still revoke the offer during this irrevocable period prior to acceptance, unless the offer is signed and a seal is affixed next to the buyer's signature. That's just one of several reasons why offers are "sealed.") If the irrevocable date passes and Richard and Angela are not advised that the offer has been accepted, there is no deal and there is no obligation by either party to continue negotiations. If Lou wishes to make a counter-offer before the irrevocable date passes, the irrevocable date should be changed, to give the purchasers enough time to consider the counter-offer properly. (In addition, the body of the offer should be amended to state that the counter-offer is now coming from Lou, the seller.)

How much time should buyers give sellers to make up their mind?
Again, there's no right or wrong answer. Usually, no more than two or three days are given, which should be more than ample for a seller to review the offer, consult a lawyer, and decide what to do. The time given by sellers to buyers on sign-backs and counter-offers is much less, sometimes as short as a few hours, as little remains to be decided to strike a deal.

Completion Date/Closing Date

This is the date the deal closes, the seller gets his or her money, and the buyer becomes the owner of the property.

A closing date should only be set after careful thought. Sufficient time must be given to the buyer's lawyer to search the title and obtain the clearances and reports essential for a complete title opinion. With too short a time to closing, oral replies rather than written clearances will have to be relied on. To process a transaction properly, allow at least 30 days between acceptance and closing.

Be sure the scheduled closing date is not a weekend or a holiday. Occasionally, an agent relies on a previous year's calendar, or forgets about a statutory holiday, and schedules closing for a date when the registry office is closed. Unless the closing date is changed by mutual consent, closing is moved to the last business day *before* the scheduled date, not afterwards.

Don't let the agents automatically schedule closing for a Friday, the last day of the month, the last Friday of the month, or just before a long weekend — rush hour in the registry offices. While the agents may feel they are doing both parties a favor, they are really doing more harm than good! After all, there is no magic in closing a deal on any of these days. A transaction can be closed just as easily, and probably faster, on a Tuesday than on a Friday, or on the 9th or 19th of the month than the 29th.

Fridays and month-ends are high-volume days at the registry office, making delays and lineups to register instruments inevitable. Jim and Tammy found this out the hard way. Their purchase closed on the last Friday of the month, the busiest day that month. Although the movers were fully loaded and ready to move everything into the new house at 12:00 noon, the sheer volume of business in the registry office meant Jim and Tammy could not get the keys to their new home until 4:30 p.m. There was little their movers could do for over four hours except sit and wait at Jim and Tammy's expense — several hundred dollars (plus GST). Ironically, they could have closed the deal and moved two days earlier but decided against it, as it would have cost them another $75 in carrying costs for the house. Talk about being penny-wise and pound-foolish!

Many agents recommend a month-end closing because they think it is most convenient. Nothing could be further from the truth. Closing at the end of the month does not save buyers any money, since adjustments are calculated on a daily basis anyway. Obtaining mortgage proceeds any other day is not a problem either, because mortgage lenders advance funds every day of the month, even though the mortgage may be payable on the first of the month. In fact, the reverse is true: obtaining mortgage funds is often harder at the end of the month, when everybody else needs mortgage money to close their purchase, too. Given the opportunity to review an offer before it is signed, most lawyers will suggest a change in closing dates away from Friday, the last day of the month, or the last Friday of the month.

There are other good reasons why buyers should steer clear of closing their transactions at these peak periods. Many movers charge a premium, upwards of 10%, at the beginning and end of each month. It's the law of supply and demand at work. Nor do "do-it-yourselfers" get a break either. Rental trucks are always in heavy demand on weekends and at month-end. Sometimes a premium rate is charged during those times. Regardless of when you close, remember to book a mover or van early.

Even sellers should shy away from a Friday closing. They face three extra days' interest (four when it's a long weekend) when paying off a mortgage following a late-in-the-day Friday closing. That can be quite a financial drain. Remember this when trying to convince the seller not to close on a Friday!

Whenever possible, all buyers — both those who presently own a home and those who rent premises as a tenant — should try to close their purchase several days before vacating their old premises. This provides a valuable "overlap" period, a chance to clean up, fix up, repair or paint the new home before moving in, at nominal cost. Buyers moving from an existing home who wish to benefit from this overlap will have to arrange bridge financing. For further information on this topic, see chapter 22. The additional cost to apartment dwellers of maintaining two residences for a short period of time is not all that great. If the apartment rents for $900 a month, the cost of carrying both places is only $30 per day. That's a small price to pay to avoid the "rush act" on closing. Whether moving from an apartment or from a house, having two residences for a very short period of time allows buyers to move into their new home leisurely and with dignity. That's the way it should be.

More and more offers also specify a time by which the deal must be completed on the day of closing, e.g., 6:00 p.m. Without any time limit in the offer, closings are legal as late as 11:59 p.m. the day of closing, even though the land registry offices have long since closed. More importantly, buyers like Billy are entitled to vacant possession of the house "upon completion." So if the deal closes at 4:00 p.m. and Vince, the vendor, hasn't moved out by that time, Billy can sue Vince for extra moving costs incurred after 4:00 p.m. This eliminates a legal quirk that allowed Vic to give vacant possession to Billy anytime up to 11:59 p.m. the day of closing — a terrible inconvenience for Billy.

Title Search Period

This is the period of time given the buyer's lawyer to search the seller's title and raise any defects such as outstanding liens. Usually it is a blank on the offer that must be filled in, either with a number or a fixed date. The standard amount of time given to search title is 30 days. If the offer is silent on the point, by law the buyer's lawyer has 30 days from acceptance to search title. Why, then, do buyer's agents continuously limit the amount of time for the title search to between 15 and 20 days? Don't they realize how a short time period prejudices the purchaser? *To protect your own interests, be sure the title search period is a minimum of 30 days.*

Conditional offers must be dealt with somewhat differently. By taking the draft, unsigned offer to your lawyer for consideration before signature, you can ensure that the title search clock won't inadvertently start to run while the offer is conditional. Fred and Shirley signed an offer September 1st with a title search period of 21 days. The financing condition was satisfied and waived on September 15th. This left Harry, their lawyer, only six days to complete his title search and raise any title defects. Fred and Shirley's agent should have inserted a clause into the offer that the title search period would only begin to run *after all conditions were removed,* not simply after the offer was accepted. Another alternative is to fix a specific date when the title search period will end, a date well beyond the last day of the conditional period.

Unless buyers give firm instructions to the contrary, few lawyers do anything with an offer while it is conditional. This prevents the lawyer from running up a huge legal bill if the condition is not satisfied. When a conditional offer is signed, clearly advise your lawyer if any work should be done before the condition is satisfied and waived.

Warranty and Condition

Two words often wrongly interchanged in offers are "warranty" and "condition." Don't confuse a condition in an offer with a conditional offer, examined in the next chapter. Buyers must remember that an important legal distinction exists between a warranty and a condition. Depending on the particular issue, buyers must instruct whether it is to be phrased as a warranty or a condition in the offer.

A *warranty* is a minor promise that does not go to the heart of the contract. If a warranty is breached, the buyer cannot simply cancel the contract and get out of the deal. All he or she can do is close the transaction and then sue the seller for damages. When Sid bought his house, Gordon, the seller, warranted that the appliances would be in good working order on closing. Although the stove did not operate properly on closing, Sid was still obligated to close the transaction. After closing, Sid had the stove fixed, with Gordon paying the bill.

By comparison, a *condition* is a promise which is fundamental to the very existence of the offer. A breach of a condition allows the buyer to back out of the deal before closing and recover his or her deposit. It was the condition in Perry's offer that the property be zoned for duplexes which allowed him to terminate the transaction when he learned the zoning only permitted single-family residences.

Anything so important that you might want to cancel the

contract if the statement is not correct should appear in the offer as a condition rather than a warranty, Too often, though, matters of great concern, such as urea formaldehyde foam insulation, appear in offers as warranties. This severely limits a buyer's remedies if a breach is discovered before closing. Remember, *to back out of a deal, the issue in question must be a condition, not a warranty.*

Chattels and Fixtures

Chattels are items of personal property in a home by their own weight alone, although they may be connected by pipes and wires. Examples of chattels are fridges, stoves, washers and dryers. Fixtures are items of personal property that are affixed or attached to the home. Becoming part of the property itself transforms a chattel into a fixture. Examples of fixtures are doors, windows, and electric light fixtures. An area rug is a chattel, while wall-to-wall carpeting securely attached to the floor is a fixture. To simply say that "floor coverings" are included in the purchase price is ambiguous, since it does not specify whether they are a chattel or a fixture. While the distinction between chattels and fixtures is often black and white, there is also a huge grey area between them. What about an electronic garage door opener system? Are the hand-held units chattels but the motor/receiver attached to the garage a fixture? And isn't one useless without the other? What about a central vacuum system? Are the pipes and canister fixtures but the accessories chattels?

What is the rule on chattels and fixtures? All fixtures stay with a house while no chattels are included in the purchase price, unless the parties agree otherwise in the offer. Therefore, any chattels a buyer wishes to acquire when purchasing a home must be specifically included and listed in the offer. Otherwise, the buyer does not get them, and the seller has the legal right to remove them from the house. The reverse is true for fixtures. Because they are already part of the house, all fixtures — including electric light fixtures — automatically stay with the house and are included in the purchase price, whether or not they are listed in the offer, unless the seller specifies in the offer which fixtures he or she will be removing before closing. Space is left in most blank standard form offers to list those chattels which are included and those fixtures which are *not* included in the purchase price. (In many newer offers, a space appears for rental equipment, too, such as a hot water heater or home security system.) Obviously, everyone wants to avoid any misunderstanding on what the buyer is acquiring as part of the purchase price and what the seller can take. And properly categorizing what is a chattel and what is a fixture is no easy task. To minimize mistakes and sidestep these legal niceties, prudent buyers will leave nothing to chance. Everything that is included in the purchase price — both chattels and fixtures — is listed in the offer. When in doubt, spell it out, in the offer. State clearly whether a particular item stays with the house or goes with the seller. That's the only way a buyer can ensure that "what you see is what you get."

Too often, insufficient attention is given to the chattel clause. To simply state that the fridge, stove, washer, dryer, and dishwasher are included in the purchase price is not enough. Be specific. For equipment, list the color, make and model number, plus serial number, if available. That's the best way to protect yourself in case an item is switched before closing. (It does happen.) Other items like window coverings should be described by color, style, design and location to avoid future confusion.

In the offer, the seller should warrant that the personal property being acquired will be free of liens and encumbrances on closing. No one wants to buy appliances, a furnace or an air-conditioning system if a finance company has a lien on them for unpaid money.

The seller should also warrant that the chattels and fixtures, as well as the plumbing, heating, electrical, air-conditioning and mechanical equipment, will be in good working order on closing. A warranty to this effect should be delivered on closing. Most people automatically assume the chattels and fixtures will be in good working order on closing. Not so. Silence in the offer means they only have to be in the same state of repair on closing as when the offer was signed. If the washer wasn't working when the deal was struck, the vendor doesn't have to fix it.

Adding this warranty to the offer reminds sellers of the need to repair anything that breaks down between acceptance and closing.

Some equipment may still be governed by guarantees or warranty plans. If so, insert a clause into the offer requiring the seller to assign or transfer them on closing.

Sometimes fixtures are to be removed, with replacements being substituted. A common example is the chandelier in the dining room that the vendor wishes to take to his or her new house. The vendor may agree to install a new light fixture in its place. If this is the case, state clearly and completely what is to be done. Describe what the replacement fixture should look like. Leave nothing to the seller's discretion. Otherwise, if nothing is said in the offer about a replacement fixture, the purchaser will find a hole in the ceiling where the old light fixture once hung.

Retail sales tax and GST may be payable on the used appliances being acquired from the seller of the house. See chapter 23.

Appendix A is a list of the items of personal property most often appearing in a resale offer. Use this checklist to help decide which chattels and fixtures to include when submitting your offer.

Surveys

The topic of surveys is examined in detail in chapter 24.

Utility Charges

Final utility accounts can be a problem when left unpaid by sellers. The buyer's lawyer will ensure that all "regular" bills issued before closing are paid by the seller on or before closing. When a property is sold, though, a special request is made by the buyer's lawyer for a final meter reading on the date of closing. It is this final bill, based on consumption from the last regular reading date to the date of closing, that causes all the headaches. The biggest problem is the fact that it's not issued until after closing, and can't be paid until then.

Matt and Ruth faced this dilemma when they bought a house from Tom on March 28th. The last regular hydro meter reading was February 15th; the next one was scheduled for April 15th. The final hydro bill, for $96.31, was issued April 12th and covered the period from February 15th to March 28th, the date of the final meter reading/closing. It remained unpaid for months. Although Tom had agreed in writing to pay all utility charges to the date of closing, it was a toothless commitment. Tom had left the country with no forwarding address.

Why should Matt and Ruth even be concerned about Tom's unpaid account? Because public utilities have the legal right to place a lien against a property for any unpaid utility bills. (Included here are hydro and water charges, but not those of telephone, cable TV or privately owned gas companies.) Then they can be collected as taxes — a "super lien" which ranks even higher in priority than a previously registered first mortgage — no matter who incurred the expense and no matter who now owns the property. With the bill remaining unpaid for many months, the municipality added the $96.31 to Matt and Ruth's tax bill. Ultimately, they ended up paying an expense which rightfully belonged to Tom.

If all previous bills have been paid to date, the amount owing on this final bill should not be too large. To best deal with this potential problem, insert a clause into the offer requiring the seller's lawyer to hold back sufficient funds after closing to pay the final utility accounts when issued. The buyer would also be notified when they were paid. With such a clause in their offer, buyers like Matt and Ruth can rest assured that the final bill based on the final meter reading will be paid, either by the seller or the seller's lawyer. Despite what many people think, any clause requiring a holdback of funds must be added to the offer. It's not part of the standard form contract.

Urea Formaldehyde Foam Insulation (UFFI)

While the thinking on UFFI has changed in recent years, purchasers who want the maximum protection possible should make it a condition of their offer that the property is not, and never has been, insulated with urea formaldehyde foam insulation. This is different from a conditional offer as described in the next chapter. If it is a condition or essential term of the offer, buyers who learn before closing that the property is or was insulated with UFFI can back out of the deal. More information on UFFI appears in chapter 34.

Work Orders and Zoning

Municipalities prescribe standards for the maintenance and occupation of properties. When these standards are not met, a deficiency notice is sent to the owner, followed by a formal work order. Sellers are supposed to disclose whether any deficiency notices or work orders have been issued, but that is not always done. Too often, a purchaser learns of these violations for the first time when a work order report is requested by the municipality. Understandably, buyers do not want to bear the cost of bringing the property up to municipal standards, unless this was a term of the offer (the property being bought "as is").

To protect buyers like Sandra, the offer should contain a warranty from the seller (Hal) that there are no deficiency notices or work orders affecting the property, both when the offer is signed and on closing. Furthermore, any violations that exist or arise before closing must be complied with at Hal's expense. Too often, standard form printed offers don't include this clause. Instead, Sandra is simply given a set period of time to "satisfy herself" that there are no outstanding deficiency notices or work orders. If any exist which Hal is "unable or unwilling" to remove and which Sandra will not waive, the deal is over. That's not too much protection for buyers like Sandra, considering how Hal's reluctance to comply with a work order could cost her the deal.

Of course, Sandra's lawyer can add such a warranty to the offer, provided he or she is given a chance to review the draft, unsigned offer. Only by clearly spelling out the seller's obligation to comply with any municipal violations, can a buyer like Sandra ensure that the deal will close without her being saddled with any unexpected expenses after closing.

Besides work orders, a buyer's lawyer checks out how the property is zoned, whether the location of the building and other structures on the property comply with the zoning requirements, and whether its current use may lawfully be continued. Municipalities are notoriously slow in providing these reports to lawyers. Buyers can do themselves a favor by giving their lawyers as long as possible, preferably until closing, to raise outstanding work order and zoning violations with the seller.

An offer should also state how the property is presently being used, and whether this is a permitted or a legal nonconforming use. Too often, the generic term "residential" appears. So be specific. If you are concerned about whether a building is a legal triplex, say so in the offer. By comparing this with the municipal zoning report, a buyer's lawyer can establish whether the present use can be legally continued.

Future use of a property is another matter. Most offers say there is no representation that any future intended use of the property is lawful, except as specifically stated in the offer. So if a minor change of use is planned (e.g., construction of an addition at the rear, or renting out a basement apartment), that future intended use should appear in the offer. This will enable the buyer's lawyer to confirm whether the existing zoning will accommodate the proposed use. Where the property is to be used in a substantially different way, the offer might have to be made conditional on rezoning the property before closing. Otherwise, the purchaser would have to close the transaction even though the property cannot be legally used as anticipated.

Rights of Access and Inspection

As strange as it sounds, once the offer is accepted, the buyer has no further right to inspect or even enter the home unless specifically permitted in the offer. (Making the offer conditional on having it inspected by a professional home inspector is discussed in chapter 14.) Understandably, most buyers want to enter the house at some point between acceptance and closing, to measure windows for drapes and window coverings, the kitchen when purchasing appliances, and room sizes for carpeting, paint and wallpaper. Equally important is the right of access to view the house a day or two before closing, to ensure that everything is "okay." Most sellers are reluctant to give buyers unlimited access, fearing they will find fault with the home that could jeopardize the transaction. While many sellers will voluntarily permit reasonable access to buyers, this is no assurance the seller won't be obstinate. To solve this problem, the offer should contain a clause giving the buyer the right to enter the premises a set number of times, in the presence of the vendor, at mutually agreeable times, *for specified purposes only*, such as taking measurements. Even with this clause, sincerity and friendliness may result in further rights of access.

Another clause says that the purchaser acknowledges having inspected the property before submitting the offer. That means buyers must thoroughly examine it before putting pen to paper. All the more reason, then, to make the offer conditional on getting a satisfactory home inspection report within a few days of acceptance, an issue tackled in chapter 14.

Clear Title

Buyers should receive "good and marketable" title on closing, subject to "permitted encumbrances" listed in the fine print. Many aren't contentious: development agreements, provided they have been complied with; minor easements for utility services to this or adjacent properties (if the "adjacent proper-ties" component bothers you, cross it out); and easements for drainage, sewers, public utility lines, telephone and cable TV lines, provided they "do not materially affect the present use of the property." The important issue of registered restrictions is discussed below.

Virtually all offers say that the seller must discharge all mort-gages, charges, liens and other encumbrances (except those specifically being assumed) from title on or before closing, at his or her own expense. This is an obvious statement, since no buyer wants to inherit the vendor's obligations. Sellers, though, face a real dilemma with this clause. How can they get a mortgage off title for closing? Few lenders will provide a discharge before the mortgage is paid in full. "Cash on the barrelhead" is their motto. In almost all cases, the mortgage will not be discharged "on or before closing." Even if it is paid off on closing, the formal discharge won't be registered until *after* closing.

Normal conveyancing practice is for the seller's lawyer to receive the funds to discharge the mortgage on closing, and pay them to an institutional lender immediately after closing. In addition, the seller's lawyer delivers a "personal undertaking" to the buyer's lawyer on closing, to obtain and register a discharge of that mortgage as soon as possible afterwards. Practically speaking, this is the only way a deal can close when a mortgage must be discharged and the discharge is unavailable for closing. That explains why agents often insert a clause into an offer forcing the buyer to accept the seller's lawyer's personal undertaking to discharge an institutional mortgage, if it's not in hand on closing. (If the lender is a private individual, the discharge should be available for registration on closing.)

Registered Restrictions

While municipalities regulate the use of land through zoning by-laws, many subdividers when developing an area impose their own, tighter restrictions on land use. They register a "building scheme" against the title to the lots in the subdivision, containing a series of building and use restrictions. Most restrictions are imposed to improve the esthetic appearance of the subdivision: no external TV antennae; no clotheslines; no permanent parking of campers, vans, and trucks on the driveway; and no repairs of automobiles on the driveway. The local municipality may not have a by-law prohibiting TV satellite dishes, but the developer's building scheme may disallow them. Most building schemes have a "sunset" clause, meaning they only run for a fixed period of time — 10 or 20 years — after which they automatically expire.

Standard form offers state that a buyer will accept title to a property subject to any registered restrictions, provided they have been complied with. This clause could prove to be a mine-field for many buyers, who do not know at the pre-contract stage if any restrictions exist. Steve and Anita found this out the hard way. They signed their offer without first taking it to their lawyer. All along they wanted to install a satellite dish, but said nothing about it to anyone. Just days before closing, Steve and Anita learned that satellite dishes were prohibited by a registered restriction on title. Herb, the present owner of the house, did not have a dish, so he was complying with the restrictions. Therefore, Steve and Anita were obligated to close the deal and accept title subject to the registered restrictions, since Herb had not violated them before closing! Because they did not properly spell out this future intended use in their offer, Steve and Anita had no grounds to back out of the deal. Literally, they were caught by the fine print.

If a future intended use of a property is important, buyers like Steve and Anita should do one or more of three things:

a) Insert a condition into the offer that no restrictions are registered on title, or delete the printed-form wording by which you agree to take title subject to registered restrictions, provided they were complied with.
b) Ask if the future intended use (like a satellite dish) is prohibited by either by-law or registered restriction. Then, to protect yourself further, add a condition — not a warranty — to the offer, that the specific use is not prohibited in either manner. This way, if you suddenly learn before closing that the future intended use is not allowed, you can refuse to close the purchase, without jeopardy. The time to raise these concerns is before the offer is signed, not afterwards. Let the agent do some legwork, if necessary, to see whether that proposed use is permitted.
c) Obtain and review a copy of the restrictions ahead of time, to learn whether the proposed use is excluded. Who should provide it? The vendor. Practically speaking, of course, very few buyers do this.

It's too bad sellers do not disclose the existence of these registered restrictions in an offer. The way most standard form offers are worded, sellers do not have to provide information about registered restrictions unless they are not being complied with. Keep in mind that not all homes are subject to registered restrictions. They usually affect homes less than 20 years old.

Although developers establish the registered restrictions, rarely do they police them after all the lots in the subdivision are sold. Furthermore, if the subdivider is given the power to "waive, alter and modify" these restrictions for specific lots, the building scheme may not even be enforceable. In other words, if the restrictions themselves give the developer the right to pick and choose which properties will be exempted from the restrictions, the restrictions are likely toothless in law. While that may be a saving grace for some buyers dissatisfied with the terms of the registered restrictions, it's far from an adequate answer. Granted, most buyers will honor the terms of a building scheme, simply because it exists. But that does not change the fact that registered restrictions are a trap for the unwary. The best way to deal with them is to consult a lawyer before signing any offer.

Representations and Warranties

One of the last clauses in the offer, bulging with legalese, says it all: "This Agreement shall constitute the entire agreement between the purchaser and the vendor. There is no representation, warranty, collateral agreement or condition which induced either party to enter into this Agreement of Purchase and Sale, other than as expressed herein in writing." Translation: if it's not in the offer, it's not in the deal. And since the second sentence is a disclaimer, anything said that influences your decision to buy must appear in the offer. So if Jack, the seller, tells Jill, the buyer, that the air conditioner is in good working order, such a clause must appear in the offer. Otherwise, it's as though Jack never spoke those words. This is all the more reason why a lawyer should independently and objectively review the offer before it becomes a binding contract. A lawyer's job at this stage is not to "rewrite" the offer or be a deal-breaker (unless specifically hired for that reason). It's to make sure the purchaser understands what's in the contract and to verify that the offer says what it's supposed to say, with no glaring omissions and no hidden zingers.

Goods and Services Tax (GST)

Most people assume that resale homes are automatically exempt from the GST. They aren't, automatically. Yes, most resale homes are exempt from GST — provided they meet specified criteria. But when it comes to taxation matters, never assume anything.

A "used residential complex" (bureaucratic lingo for a resale home) is exempt from GST if the vendor has not claimed any input tax credits against the house. That could arise if the owner used the house for commercial purposes, such as operating a business there. If the vendor claimed input tax credits, that could taint the house and subject it to GST. Of course, buyers are responsible for paying the GST, while sellers are responsible for collecting it.

An important (but little known) section of the Excise Tax Act, the legislation that created the GST, encourages buyers like Ellen to make "reasonable inquiries" whether the sale of a resale home is an exempt supply. If so, Ellen is not responsible for paying GST even if the seller, Rob, provided incorrect information, unless Ellen knew the information was wrong.

The simple solution is for Ellen to add a clause to the offer in which Rob "certifies" that the transaction is an "exempt supply" for GST purposes, with a "certificate" to be delivered on closing. (That "certificate" isn't a government-prescribed form, nor is it issued by Revenue Canada. Instead, the word simply describes how Rob's statement should be delivered to Ellen: as a certificate). Then, unless Rob and Ellen are in cahoots, Ellen is off the hook for the payment of GST.

Unfortunately, many standard form offers either are silent regarding GST or butcher the clause, making it useless. So a "GST clause" will likely have to be added to the printed form.

Cottages and rural property are another issue. Here, it's not just the type of property that determines if GST is payable, but the type of seller, too. If buyers aren't careful, they could inadvertently find themselves subject to GST.

Sales of recreational and other personal-use real estate such as country and vacation properties or hobby farms are exempt from GST if the vendor is an individual who doesn't use it in a business, and if the vendor is not in the business of selling such properties. But if the seller is a corporation or a partnership then GST is payable! In other words, the question of whether GST must be paid depends on who owns the property. That's a real trap for the unwary. To avoid making a 7% mistake, prudent cottage buyers will have to learn more about the vendor at the pre-contract stage. Not asking the right questions about the vendor could be costly.

Even though resale homes are generally GST exempt, it's still levied on many of the services involved in a real estate transaction: lawyer's fees; most disbursements; real estate commission (an important issue if the purchaser will be paying commission to a buyer broker); home-inspection charges; appraisal costs; and surveyor's fees.

An Expression to Avoid

An expression cavalierly used in real estate is "to the best of my knowledge and belief." Buyers should avoid it whenever possible, because of its profound legal impact.

Hannah was interested in buying Rodney's house. Several years ago, Rodney built a garage next to the dwelling. But no new survey was ever prepared to confirm that the garage was sited far enough from the side lot-line to satisfy the municipal zoning "setback" standards.

Understandably, Hannah was concerned that the garage might not comply with those zoning requirements. So she asked Rodney to warrant in the offer that the property, and in particular the garage, complied with all municipal zoning by-laws. Rodney insisted on qualifying it with the expression "to the best of my knowledge and belief." Hannah's refusal to accept it created a stand-off.

Hannah's concerns were well founded. If Rodney's warranty

about the zoning was limited by the phrase "to the best of my knowledge and belief," Hannah could only sue Rodney successfully if the opposite of the statement in the offer was true. Hannah would have to prove not only that the garage violated the zoning by-law, *but also that Rodney knew* the garage didn't comply. An uphill battle, since Rodney, with no survey, honestly didn't know if the garage breached the zoning.

Smart buyers will ensure that the expression "to the best of my knowledge and belief" is absent from their offers.

Special Clauses

Particular circumstances may require the drafting of special clauses to meet the situation. The precise wording of the clause is absolutely crucial, as it is intended to deal with a specific concern. For this reason, it is usually better that the clause be prepared by a lawyer, properly trained in drafting contracts, rather than by a real estate agent.

Mark and Lee noticed water stains on the walls and ceilings of the resale home they were thinking of buying. Bob, the seller, assured them the problem had been repaired years earlier. In addition to the conventional home inspection clause, their lawyer added a clause allowing a roofer to investigate and test the soundness of the roof. Knowing they had left nothing to chance, Mark and Lee felt quite relieved when no problem was found.

Whenever special clauses are needed, tell your lawyer about them as early as possible, giving him or her ample time to consider and prepare the appropriate wording.

Can Houses Be Bought and Sold on a Sunday?

Sunday is the most popular day of the week to view and attend open houses. Over the years, many real estate agents would have loved to submit an offer on a Sunday after buyers saw an appealing house. Rarely was that done, though, as the Lord's Day Act of Canada invalidated any contract made on a Sunday.

In April 1985, the Supreme Court of Canada unanimously

held that the Lord's Day Act infringed on the freedoms guaranteed in the Canadian Charter of Rights and Freedoms. Based on this case, any real estate offer made, submitted or accepted on a Sunday is valid. No longer is it necessary for a seller and buyer to anxiously await the stroke of midnight, with pens and paper at the ready, before signing an offer. Real estate liberation preceded the changes in Sunday shopping legislation across Canada!

With this legal obstacle out of the way, agents may now try to persuade buyers to submit an offer the same day they view a house. Of course, buyers applying their HOBS won't do this. Instead, they will wait until their lawyer has had a chance to see the draft offer the following morning. Remember, there is no "cooling-off" period for resale homes, allowing buyers to change their minds within a limited period of time after the offer is accepted and cancel the deal. Therefore, buyers must avoid getting caught up in the hoopla and emotion of buying a house, and not be pressured into signing that same day. A home should be bought with the head, not the heart. Time is needed to think things through carefully and rationally. If necessary, play dumb and say "never on Sunday." No one wants to go too far on a Sunday and wake up with regrets on Monday. Be absolutely sure before making that commitment. Once the die is cast, there is no turning back.

26
Conditional Offers

When an unconditional offer is signed by the buyer and accepted by the seller, it becomes "firm and binding." Often there's a meeting of the minds on the basic terms of the contract — price, deposit, chattels/fixtures, payment terms and closing date — but several loose ends must still be tidied up before the buyer is ready to proceed. If these points cannot be resolved, the buyer wants the right to cancel the deal. Other people, not parties to the contract, are usually involved with satisfying these outstanding items.

When this happens, to protect themselves buyers will insist that a "conditional" offer be prepared, as part of their home-buying strategy. Although a deal has been struck, the contract is in suspense, "subject to" the conditions being satisfied and waived, usually quickly. If and only if this is completed within a set period of time does the piece of paper become a legally binding and enforceable contract. Otherwise the deal is off, as though it never existed.

Two or more conditions may appear in an offer, depending on the particular transaction. Whenever a conditional offer is drawn, and whatever the condition may be, buyers must be certain they fully understand what the condition says and how it works, as not all conditions are alike. Noncompliance with the exact terms of a condition can have disastrous consequences.

Stan's situation shows how a conditional offer typically works and when it can be used effectively. Without too much difficulty, he was able to negotiate the terms to buy Rochelle's house on an "all-cash" basis on closing. While he had been pre-approved for a mortgage, Stan (always the cautious fellow) still wanted to be 100% sure he would have the financing in place for closing. So his offer was made conditional on obtaining satisfactory mortgage financing within seven days after the offer was accepted. If the mortgage offer fell through, the deal with Rochelle that never really had been a deal would be off. Once Stan got confirmation that the mortgage had been approved, he waived the condition, making the contract firm and binding. Conditional offers, then, give buyers time after an offer is accepted to straighten out and satisfy these specified loose ends.

A typical conditional clause (this one dealing with arranging mortgage financing) might read as follows:

> This offer is conditional on the purchaser arranging satis-
> factory financing on or before _____, and notifying
> the vendor or his agent in writing before that date.
> Otherwise, this offer shall become null and void, with the
> deposit to be returned to the purchaser without interest
> or deduction. This condition has been inserted for the
> sole benefit of the purchaser, who reserves the sole right
> to waive it at any time at his option.

Here, the offer is not "firm and binding" until the buyer arranges satisfactory financing within a specified time and the vendor or the vendor's agent is given written notice of this fact. Usually, this is done by the purchaser waiving the condition in writing, within the specified time.

A properly drafted conditional clause should state the following:

1. The condition to be satisfied.
2. How long the buyer has to satisfy the condition. Avoid saying that the buyer has 7, 10 or 15 banking or business days after acceptance to waive the condition. This old-fashioned approach leads to confusion when there are intervening weekends and holidays. And what is a banking or business day today anyway, considering that shopping is

legal seven days a week and some bank branches are open on weekends? Choose a set number of calendar days, or better yet, fix a specific date by which the condition must be satisfied.

3. What happens if the condition is not met, and what steps (if any) must be taken to kill the offer. Two different kinds of conditions can be inserted into an offer: self-destructing and self-fulfilling. In the above clause, if the buyer cannot arrange financing within the specified time, the offer will self-destruct. Nothing has to be done for the contract to end and for the purchaser to get his or her deposit back. The offer will automatically die a natural death.

Self-fulfilling conditions are the total reverse. The contract does not die, but automatically becomes firm and binding, unless the buyer does something to cancel the deal within the specified time. If the buyer is unable to arrange financing, he or she must notify the vendor or the vendor's agent of that fact to kill the contract. Silence doesn't kill the contract; it keeps the contract alive! With a self-fulfilling condition, doing nothing automatically renders the contract firm and binding, not null and void. For this reason, *always insist that a condition be self-defeating. Self-fulfilling conditions are dangerous.* Make sure a positive step is needed to keep the deal alive, rather than to destroy it.

4. What steps are necessary to fulfil (or destroy) the condition. What type of notice is required, written or oral? Even if oral notice is allowed, prudent buyers will put it in writing. To whom can it be given? The seller alone? The listing agent? The seller's lawyer? Any of these people? How can it be given? During what period of time?

5. That the buyer's deposit will be returned to him or her without interest (unless otherwise agreed upon) and without deduction. Clarify this at the outset, to avoid any misunderstandings.

6. For whose benefit the condition has been inserted, and who can waive it. The condition appearing above stated that it existed for the buyer's benefit, making it abundantly clear that only the buyer, and not the seller, could waive it.

Sometimes, a buyer may want, or need, to waive a condition and firm up the offer even when it has not been satisfied. Mitch and Paula faced this dilemma when they bought their house. The formal written mortgage commitment had not been delivered by 4 p.m. the day the condition on financing expired, although they had received oral approval. With a competing offer more attractive to the seller waiting in the wings, Mitch and Paula decided to waive the condition, even though it technically was not satisfied.

Obviously, waiving a condition based on oral representations is risky. To minimize the risk, try to seek additional information before making any final decisions. Why has the condition not yet been fulfilled? Is only paperwork involved? When will it be available? Is it better to lose the property altogether, or waive an unsatisfied condition?

Many real estate boards, associations and offices have their own "John Doe" standard form conditions, dealing with numerous situations. The applicable clauses are either noted on a sheet of paper and added to the offer when it is prepared, or lifted off a series of precedent clauses on a computer screen. Either way, very little thought is given to the specifics of the situation and the precise wording of the condition. It is always dangerous to be a slave to a precedent clause. Conditional clauses should be carefully reviewed and revised where necessary, tailored to suit the needs of the particular transaction. The best approach is to forward the offer with the conditional clause to your real estate lawyer before signing it, for his or her review, input and opinion.

When a transaction is made conditional, it is usually for one of five reasons — for the buyer: a) to have the property examined by a home inspector; b) to arrange satisfactory mortgage financing; c) to be approved to assume an existing mortgage; d) to sell his or her existing property; or e) to review and approve the condominium documents.

a) Home Inspection
Without this clause, buyers have no right to inspect the property themselves, or have it inspected by a home inspector, in the period between acceptance of the offer and closing. Today, it is

quite common to make the offer conditional on having a home inspector examine the property within a set period of time. A properly worded inspection clause requires that the purchaser be satisfied with the contents of the home inspection report, and that the buyer notify the seller in writing of this fact, thus waiving the condition. If the inspection reveals problems which cannot be resolved between the parties, the deal ultimately self-destructs before it becomes a binding contract. To know how much time to insert in the offer for the home inspection to be conducted, check with your home inspector *before* the offer is signed.

b) Financing

Another common conditional clause involves financing. Although they may have been pre-approved for a mortgage, most buyers still lack formal approval for their financing when they submit an offer. (Usually, a formal commitment is only available once a property is actually bought.) Therefore, they are very reluctant to sign an unconditional offer. If the seller and buyer can agree on the basic terms of the deal, "financing" is the classic situation where a conditional offer makes sense — where the firming-up of the contract depends on the actions of a third party.

Many offers are very specific on the terms of the mortgage a purchaser like Tina must arrange: the principal, the maximum interest rate, the term, the payments, the additional clauses and so on. Once a mortgage is available on the stated terms, Tina is obligated to waive the condition and close the deal. More flexibility is available, though, by making the offer conditional on Tina arranging "satisfactory financing" within a specified time. While that means Tina must use her best efforts to try to obtain satisfactory financing, she doesn't have to proceed with the deal if the terms ultimately offered (e.g., the amount, rate, prepayment features) are not satisfactory to her, acting reasonably. So Tina can't just sit back and let the conditional period lapse if she develops cold feet about the deal after signing the offer. But if Tina isn't happy with the mortgage terms available, acting reasonably, she can still walk away from the deal. Obviously, sellers do not like "satisfactory financing" clauses in offers, but such clauses are a fact of life.

As with home inspections, leave ample time to get the final written approval for the mortgage. Learning this is easy. In Tina's case she should ask her lender at the time she is pre-approved just how long it will take. Where a pre-approved mortgage has been issued, two or three days' days "turn-around" time should be enough. And Tina shouldn't let anyone convince her that an abbreviated period of time is better. If Tina had wanted to waive the condition before the approval was granted, her offer would not have been made conditional on financing in the first place!

c) Being Approved to Assume an Existing Mortgage

Traditionally, mortgages were automatically assumable by a buyer without having to be approved by the lender to assume it. In the early 1980s, lenders began inserting clauses into mortgages giving them the option of deciding whether a buyer could assume an existing mortgage. If the buyer is not allowed to assume that mortgage then the seller must pay it off in full when the sale closes. Most mortgages today contain these "limited assumability" or "due-on-sale at the lender's option" clauses. Permission to assume is not automatic, especially if the mortgage rate is considerably lower than the prevailing rate in the marketplace.

Darryl and Michelle were going to buy a house, and wanted to assume a limited assumable mortgage with Beaver Bank at 7% with a remaining term of three years. (The current rate for a three-year mortgage was 9%.) Their lawyer inserted several clauses into the unsigned offer. First, the offer was made conditional on Beaver Bank approving Darryl and Michelle to assume the mortgage within a set number of days of acceptance. They agreed to apply immediately after acceptance to assume the mortgage, and to provide full financial information to the lender. As a self-fulfilling condition, it would be waived automatically once they were approved to assume the mortgage. However, what if Beaver Bank rejected their application to assume the mortgage? Then Darryl and Michelle, *at their sole option*, would be given a set number of additional days to arrange satisfactory financing from an alternative source and waive this condition. (If they decided not to exercise this option, the deal would be null and void at that time.) Giving Darryl and Michelle this option was very reasonable, as Beaver Bank could reject their application to assume the existing mortgage.

Here is what happened. Beaver Bank would not allow Darryl and Michelle to assume the existing below-market-rate mortgage. Exercising the option, Darryl and Michelle applied elsewhere for a mortgage and were approved. However, before waiving the condition, Darryl and Michelle insisted that the purchase price be reduced by $1,000, to compensate them for the extra financing costs they would incur.

d) Sale of Purchaser's Property

One way to resolve the sell-first/buy-first dilemma is to sign a conditional offer. A buyer with an existing home to sell submits an Offer to Purchase another home conditional on the current home being sold. (Be sure the conditional clause makes it clear that "selling" means signing the offer, not actually closing the deal.)

This is exactly what Fred and Wilma did. They owned a house on Bedrock Circle, and were interested in buying Barney's house on Stoney Drive. Fred and Wilma's offer to buy the Stoney Drive property was made conditional on selling their Bedrock Circle home by April 30th. Otherwise, the offer on Barney's house would be null and void. The sole benefit/ right to waive clause mentioned earlier was also inserted in the offer, in case Fred and Wilma wanted to firm up the Offer to Purchase before selling their existing home.

Barney was rightly concerned that the conditional offer with Fred and Wilma would effectively take his property off the market until April 30th. This would prevent Barney from trying to sell his property to anyone else during that period, while the deal with Fred and Wilma was in a state of legal limbo — sold but not really sold.

To resolve the seller's dilemma, an escape clause is commonly inserted into a "conditional on sale" offer. Buyers should expect to see this when the condition might be outstanding for a long period of time. According to this clause, Barney can continue to list his house for sale during the conditional period, even though it has been sold conditionally to Fred and Wilma.

If Barney is presented with another acceptable offer, he must advise Fred and Wilma in writing. Then the ball is in Fred and Wilma's court, to decide within a very short period of time (48 hours, generally) whether to waive the condition in their offer. If they waive it, their offer to buy Barney's house on Stoney Drive becomes firm and binding, without Fred and Wilma first having sold their Bedrock Circle property (a potentially dangerous move, if they still can't sell their house before the purchase from Barney is scheduled to close). If Fred and Wilma decide not to waive the condition, Barney is free to sign the other contract, making Fred and Wilma's offer null and void.

How long should Fred and Wilma be given in the conditional clause to sell their existing home? Obviously, from their point of view, the longer the better. For Barney, the seller, the reverse is true: the shorter the better. Barney does not want to tie his hands for too long, even though he does have an escape clause in the offer. The reason? Many agents are reluctant to submit an offer on a home that has already been sold conditionally, fearful that all their work may be in vain if the buyers (Fred and Wilma, here) opt to waive the condition. The norm for "conditional on sale" clauses is 30 to 60 days.

Where a property is sold conditional on the buyer selling an existing home, the involvement of the real estate agent intensifies. Elliott, the selling agent on Barney's house (or the listing agent if only one agent is involved), will insist on getting the listing to sell Fred and Wilma's house. Real estate agents adore this situation, called a double-ender transaction. Elliott not only is the selling agent on Barney's house, but also becomes the listing agent on Fred and Wilma's house. If he can sell their home within the allotted time, Elliott stands to win big; he earns two commissions! To sell Fred and Wilma's house, Elliott will ask for a long listing period, at least as long as the conditional period in the contract with Barney, say 60 to 90 days. Then he tries like mad to sell their house.

Sellers in this situation like Fred and Wilma face additional pressure to sign a sale contract. After all, if Elliott can help Fred and Wilma sell their Bedrock Circle home, the picture is complete and he has earned two commissions. If not, Fred and Wilma are left with their old house and Elliott earns nothing.

See why selling first has its advantages! See, too, why choosing a real estate agent when buying a house is so important. The agent Fred and Wilma used to buy their new house turned out to be the agent they had to use to sell their old house! For this reason, buyers applying their HOBS are advised to consider all the consequences of submitting an offer conditional on selling an existing house, before proceeding any further.

Having to retain Elliott as the listing agent for the Bedrock Circle property could have its pitfalls for Fred and Wilma. While he may be well acquainted with the real estate market in Barney's community, that may not be the case for Fred and Wilma's area. Lack of familiarity with comparable market values there could result in his recommending a sale for less than the house is actually worth.

Some agents working for large real estate firms avoid this problem by transferring the listing to a local office near Fred and Wilma's home. This way, an agent more familiar with the area can service the listing, eliminating most of these concerns.

e) Review of Condominium Documents

Unless purchasers of a resale condominium unit learn more about the project, its financial health and its rules and regulations early on, they are literally buying a pig-in-a-poke. They could be stuck with a series of unacceptable restrictions, or even wind up inheriting the vendor's financial headaches.

Standard form resale condo offers provide little assistance to buyers. Vendors simply state how much is payable monthly as the common expenses (or maintenance) and what it includes. Because the reserve fund won't be adjusted, the amount on deposit isn't disclosed in the offer. And vendors meekly warrant that no special assessments are contemplated by the condo corporation "to the best of their knowledge and belief." The offer doesn't even clearly say that the vendor on closing will pay any special assessments levied against the unit before closing.

How can buyers like Steve and Evelyn, who have been developing their HOBS, protect themselves? By making the Offer to Purchase conditional on them reviewing and approving the condominium documents for the project — a current Estoppel Certificate, financial statements, budget, Declaration, By-laws,

Rules and Regulations, management agreements and insurance certificates — a developing trend in real estate.

Steve and Evelyn should leave themselves enough time to get these documents. Since it will take the condominium corporation a few days to issue them, and several more for Steve and Evelyn (and likely their lawyer) to digest what they say, the offer should be made conditional for 10 days after acceptance for this purpose. Otherwise, the deal is null and void. While vendors and their agents may not like such a long conditional period, anything shorter could be insufficient.

What should be examined in these documents? While the Estoppel Certificate will state if the owner is behind in paying the maintenance, any arrears shouldn't jeopardize the deal, as the account will be brought into good standing by the vendor on closing. But it's also crucial to learn about any lawsuits involving the condo corporation — either suing or being sued. The same is true for any special assessments or possible increases in common expenses, and any substantial alterations/improvements to the common elements. Planned hikes or changes here could easily convince Steve and Evelyn to change their minds.

One of the key facts disclosed in an Estoppel Certificate is the size of the reserve fund. Does it have a healthy credit balance? To calculate a unit's share, multiply that unit's proportion of common interest (appearing in the Declaration) by the total in the reserve fund. Too small a fund could mean higher common expenses or even a special assessment in the future, if significant repairs are needed.

The budget indicates where money will be spent over the coming years. Large sums allocated to replacing common elements and other assets could indicate that the project is starting to show its age, meaning higher maintenance fees down the road.

Both the Declaration and the Rules and Regulations should be reviewed in order to learn about house rules. What is the greatest concern to most purchasers? What the rules say about pets. As noted earlier, not all rules and regulations appear in the Rules and Regulations. Some are buried in the Declaration, the condominium's constitution, making them virtually unalterable.

Details on parking and locker units appear in the

Declaration, too. Whether they are owned, leased, exclusive-use or allocated should be disclosed here. The right to use an exclusive-use common element — balcony or patio — should also appear.

Making the Offer to Purchase conditional, in order to obtain and be satisfied with the contents of the condo documents, makes good sense. Steve and Evelyn will be bound by those items if they proceed with the deal. To learn what they say for the first time after the transaction becomes firm and binding is absurd.

Other Conditions

Obviously, these will depend on the circumstances of the particular transaction. And the rule-of-thumb to follow, simply stated, is: "If it's not in the offer, it's not in the deal."

If the buyer's lawyer is unavailable and an offer must be submitted (despite what the buyer's HOBS says), the offer may be made conditional on the buyer's lawyer reviewing and approving the contents of the offer. (See the next chapter for a typical clause.) For rural properties, the offer could be conditional on the buyer having the quality of the drinking water tested and approved as potable. Sometimes, the seller must do something to the property before closing, such as clean the furnace, paint the exterior or repair the shower. If so, the work to be done must be clearly spelled out in the offer. Also, the right to re-attend on the premises between acceptance and closing, to ensure that the required work has been done properly before closing, must appear in the offer. Otherwise, as the offer boldly states, "This Agreement shall constitute the entire agreement between the purchaser and the vendor. There is no representation, warranty, collateral agreement or condition which induced either party to enter into this Agreement of Purchase and Sale, other than is expressed herein in writing."

While conditional offers provide buyers with the maximum in flexibility, there is a trade-off that must be recognized. Unconditional offers always receive a better reception with sellers, because they are not concerned about external events determining whether the deal is on or off. An unconditional offer becomes firm and binding by signature alone. Agents often recommend that an unconditional offer be presented, as it looks better, cleaner, and more inviting to a seller. Buyers who are confident they can sell their present house or arrange financing may decide to go in firm, unconditionally, using this to their advantage in negotiating other concessions from the seller — price, appliances, survey and so on. However, buyers must be absolutely certain they can sell their house or arrange mortgage financing. Otherwise, submitting an unconditional offer can be like playing with fire. If the house can't be sold or the financing falls through, the purchase contract is still legally binding and enforceable, and the buyer can get burned — badly.

The same is true with a larger number of conditions in an offer. Stacking the offer with conditions is a definite turn-off for the seller. So if any of the potential conditions can be satisfied ahead of time, do so. The fewer the conditions, the more appealing the offer to the vendor.

When market conditions heat up (e.g., during a seller's market), buyers are often told by their agent that the only way they can acquire a particular house is to submit an offer that isn't conditional. With multiple offers to be presented, agents often argue that "the cleaner the offer, the more likely it will be accepted." While that may be a very practical answer, it's very simplistic — and downright dangerous. No house is that good a deal, if the buyer can't afford to close (because mortgage financing hasn't been arranged), or if the buyer will inherit the seller's headaches (because a home inspection won't be conducted). No house justifies throwing caution to the wind. Signing an offer is serious business. Signing an unconditional offer is making a firm commitment to buy on the stated terms. Think twice before spurning a conditional offer.

If seller and buyer can agree on all the key points between them, the seller should not be reluctant to sign a conditional offer, giving the buyer a reasonable amount of time to satisfy a condition. In fact, conditional offers can sometimes benefit a seller. No one wants to find themselves in Morris and Benny's situation. Benny signed an unconditional offer to buy Morris's house. The offer should have been, but was not, made conditional on Benny arranging satisfactory financing, the agent talking Benny out of the condition. Because Benny could not get the necessary financing, the deal did not close, and the matter ended up in court. Both parties (plus the agent) then faced years of expensive litigation.

Better to be safe than sorry. Unless you, as a buyer, are absolutely and positively certain that a would-be condition can be satisfied, go for the conditional offer. It is better to lose a particular property than to sign a contract which cannot be completed.

27

Do Not Sign on the Dotted Line, Until . . .

As has been repeatedly emphasized in this book, signing an offer is serious business. Like any contract, it becomes a firm and binding legal document once it is accepted (unless there are outstanding conditions), with rights, duties and obligations to be performed by both parties on a specific date. Therefore, buyers must be certain they can and will live up to these obligations, well before signing it.

When buying a resale property, there is no "cooling-off" period during which buyers can cancel a deal after the offer is accepted. Therefore, one of the key features of your home-buying strategy is the step of taking the draft offer to your lawyer for review and comment, *before* it is signed.

Many real estate agents claim that it is unnecessary for buyers to see a lawyer before signing the offer. After all, agents argue, the offer is a standard printed-form agreement with "boilerplate" clauses. Even the typed-in clauses that supposedly distinguish one offer from another are standard "John Doe" precedent clauses used extensively by real estate offices. What more could a lawyer possibly add?

Realistically, nothing could be further from the truth. Standard form offers are slanted in favor of sellers and therefore have their own shortcomings for buyers. While the John Doe clauses added by a real estate agent help to deal with specific issues raised by a buyer, too often the wording is imprecise and unclear, failing to adequately protect a purchaser. Of greater concern from a legal point of view is not what the offer includes, but rather what it omits. Few real estate agents have had the same intensive training and experience in drafting contracts as lawyers. Granted, if the deal closes as scheduled, any inadequacies become academic. However, if problems do arise, everyone will regret that a lawyer did not have the opportunity to comment on the offer ahead of time. When the potential consequences of an improperly drawn offer are coupled with the dollar amounts involved, purchasers should be encouraged to have the draft, unsigned offer reviewed by a lawyer.

Fewer than 10% of all buyers of residential real estate take offers to lawyers before they are signed, a fact that is both surprising and distressing. Only that small minority can benefit from the unique three-pronged opportunity seeing a lawyer at this stage presents:

1. To ensure that the contract adequately protects the buyer, properly incorporating both his or her wishes and intentions. Often, a lawyer will raise an issue that was previously overlooked. Or the lawyer may make suggestions, based on experience, that will save buyers money. A prime example is the need for a survey (required in virtually all mortgage transactions) and the proper drafting of the survey clause, so an acceptable survey will be available.
2. To ensure that the buyer fully understands what the offer says and the obligations flowing from it. Frank and Joyce were glad their lawyer explained in detail the "conditional on financing" clause in the offer that the agent prepared, drafted as a self-fulfilling and not a self-defeating condition. Frank and Joyce finally understood what had to be done if the mortgage could not be arranged.
3. To review and have explained the basics of mortgage financing, plus the hidden costs in a real estate transaction. Buyers can budget properly for these items now, rather than face a cash-flow crisis right before closing.

Sometimes it is said that lawyers want to review draft, unsigned offers because it allows them to pump up their fees. This comment is both unfair and untrue, since this initial contact with a lawyer costs buyers far less than they might think — if anything.

Many lawyers do not charge for time spent reviewing and commenting on the offer or making minor changes or suggestions. After all, a lawyer acting for the buyer of a resale property must read the offer in its entirety before processing it. Timewise, it makes no difference whether the offer reviewed is in draft or executed form. No additional fee should be charged simply for reviewing a draft offer (assuming it is later signed and the deal closed). So why not give the lawyer this opportunity before the offer is signed, before the terms of the contract are set, while the lawyer can review it, revise it, suggest additions or deletions, and generally comment on it? Once the ink is dry, this opportunity for input is gone forever.

If the offer is poorly drawn, requiring a major rewrite or significant modifications, the lawyer obviously will charge for his or her time. But that's money well spent, considering how the offer as originally drawn was so deficient. Imagine what might have happened if you hadn't taken the unsigned offer to the lawyer for review! When the amount of money at stake is compared to this *possible* cost, it is incredible that not all buyers do contact lawyers before signing offers. It could be the best investment a buyer makes in the property.

The only additional time for which a buyer should be billed is consultation time — time spent with a lawyer before the offer is signed, examining its terms in greater detail, revising the document, if necessary, and discussing other issues such as mortgage financing at length. In large part this is determined by the client anyway, depending on how much time is needed in consultation.

If you are going to arrange a consultation, save time by having the draft offer sent to your lawyer in advance. (Often, the real estate agent does this by fax.) This gives him or her the opportunity of reviewing it without your being there. Then, when the appointment begins, it's right down to business! The alternative is to sit and watch your lawyer read the offer — not a terribly exciting time.

Some real estate agents are apprehensive about lawyers seeing buyers and discussing the terms of an offer before it is signed. Often, the agent exerts pressure on the buyer to sign the offer now, fearing the lawyer will be a "deal breaker." Again, this is an inappropriate comment about the legal profession. The role of a real estate lawyer at this stage is to amend clauses that are not in the buyer's best interests and raise issues that either have been overlooked or are still unclear in the buyer's mind. A real estate lawyer must ensure that prospective purchasers know their legal rights and obligations, that they fully understand them, and that they appreciate the financial commitment they will be making on signing the contract. Genuinely sincere real estate agents who have their client's best interests at heart will offer no resistance when a buyer wants to have the offer reviewed by a lawyer before it is signed.

Real estate lawyers rarely "blow the deal." Granted, buyers occasionally do withdraw from negotiations at this stage. Sometimes the offer is deficient as a contract. More often, though, buyers realize the financial difficulties they would face, either in closing the transaction or in carrying the property afterwards. Inevitably, the lawyer is fingered as the culprit for the deal falling through, for having talked the buyer out of the deal. In actual fact, the deal never should have been struck in the first place.

With no financial stake in the transaction at this stage, a lawyer can provide a buyer with unbiased objectivity. Seeing a lawyer at this stage helps plant a buyer's feet back on the ground before any final decisions are made, rather than letting emotion carry the day.

Do not expect your lawyer to pass judgment on two questions: a) the purchase price and b) the ultimate decision whether to proceed with the transaction. Real estate agents know the market in an area much more intimately. It is their role, based on the resources available to them, to advise buyers on market values and purchase price. Lawyers are hired to concentrate on the "legalities" of the transaction. However, an experienced real estate lawyer often can tell if an offer is "in the ball park" for other properties in the area. Similarly, an experienced real estate lawyer can provide invaluable assistance on mortgage financing, qualifying for a mortgage, and government assistance programs. Still, the final decision to sign the offer and continue with the transaction must rest with you as purchaser, and only you.

If a private sale is involved, the offer normally drawn by the real estate agent must be prepared instead by the buyer's lawyer, at the buyer's expense. The cost incurred, usually upwards of $200, could end up being a blessing in disguise. This need to have an offer drawn forces buyer and lawyer to come together early, to discuss all aspects of the transaction.

Without question, timing is crucial in submitting an offer. Despite the convenience of fax machines and any prior arrangements that may have been made with your lawyer, he or she may simply not be available to review the offer when you want to submit it. If that happens, insert the following condition into the offer, to give your lawyer ample time to protect your interests:

> This offer is conditional on the purchaser's lawyer, Alan G. Silverstein, having an opportunity to review this offer, determine that it is satisfactory to the purchaser, and approve it in full without requiring any changes whatsoever. To satisfy this condition, a letter to this effect shall be delivered to the listing agent on or before 11:59 p.m. on _____. Otherwise, this offer shall become null and void, with the deposit being returned to the purchaser without interest or deduction. This condition has been inserted for the sole benefit of the purchaser, who reserves the sole right to waive it at his option.

Few sellers will deny a buyer this opportunity, especially on a weekend, if the time given is reasonable — 48 hours or less.

By including this clause in their offer, Bobby and Jenna accomplished two things. First, it gave their lawyer ample time to pass judgment on the contents of the offer, exactly what Bobby and Jenna wanted. Second, it effectively gave them a short cooling-off period they otherwise would not have had, to reconsider what they had done and possibly even cancel the contract after it had been signed. If Bobby and Jenna changed their minds and decided not to proceed with the transaction, it might be possible for them to back out of the deal. Only one change — any one clause their lawyer found to be unsatisfactory, acting reasonably — and the entire contract would be nullified.

Cardinal Rule — Despite any pressures that may be brought to bear, do not sign on the dotted line until the offer has been thoroughly reviewed by your lawyer. If absolutely necessary, make the offer conditional on your lawyer reviewing and approving the contents of the offer.

28

The Buyer's Role from Contract to Closing

Congratulations! The offer has been accepted. While you may think that much of the work now shifts to the lawyer, in reality there remains much for a buyer to do besides just packing. To make the transition as smooth as possible, here are 10 tasks for buyers in the interval between the contract being accepted and closing:

1. Contact your lawyer and arrange for him or her to get a copy of the accepted offer as soon as possible. A photocopy will suffice if you only have one original and want to keep it. While the real estate agent will also be delivering the offer to your lawyer, your extra effort can get the lawyer working for you that much sooner.

    If for some reason the lawyer is seeing the offer for the first time, arrange for an appointment as soon as possible after the offer is accepted, even if any conditions are still outstanding. (Most lawyers won't proceed further with the offer while any conditions remain unsatisfied, to hold down expenses in case the conditions can't be waived.) Be sure to review with your lawyer the anticipated closing costs, including fees and disbursements (and GST on both), provincial transfer taxes, estimated closing adjustments and mortgage deductions, as well as the approximate amount of money needed to close, all explored in chapter 23.

    Also review with your lawyer how you want to "take

title" — be registered on the title to the property. Several different possibilities exist, especially in spousal situations. (See chapter 33 for more information.) Full names, birth dates and spousal status of all persons to appear on the deed are generally required.

Numerous clearances, reports and certificates must be obtained from various government departments before closing. Many real estate lawyers now ask that a disbursements retainer of several hundred dollars be sent to them shortly after closing, in partial payment of the total disbursements to be incurred.

As part of your home-buying strategy, you should learn early on whether a survey is available and if it will be acceptable to the lender. Otherwise, the survey can be an unexpected financial burden. If you haven't discussed the issue of a survey with your lawyer yet, do so immediately. Buyers of resale condominiums don't have to worry about a survey, however; the condominium plan is the survey for the project.

2. Satisfy any outstanding conditions (e.g., arranging a mortgage, being approved to assume an existing mortgage, conducting a home inspection, selling an existing house or reviewing condominium documents) *immediately*, within the time frame and in the manner set out in the offer. Very short time periods usually apply to these conditions, and the clock is already ticking. Be certain you fully understand whether the conditions are self-defeating or self-fulfilling, and what time is allotted for compliance. Also be sure you know what must be done either to keep the deal alive or to kill it if the conditions can't be satisfied. Contractual conditions must be strictly complied with.

An individual condition can be deleted from the offer by waiving that specific condition. This becomes necessary if the conditions have different "compliance" dates. Once all conditions have been satisfied, and assuming the conditions are self-defeating, the agent must prepare a waiver of the conditions, to be signed and delivered to the seller before the prescribed time expires. Be sure this is done promptly and without any slip-ups. Once it is done, the

offer is "firmed up," the contract becoming "firm and binding." (If the conditions are self-fulfilling, the deal is
automatically kept alive on the compliance date, unless the
purchaser sends a notice to the vendor to kill the deal.)

At this stage, most people like Joe and Tillie say, "We
have bought a house." Legally speaking, that's not true.
With an unconditional offer, all Joe and Tillie have
acquired is a legal interest in that property. They will not
have really "bought" the house, in terms of owning it,
until the deal formally closes.

3. Once you receive the formal mortgage commitment, send
    it to your lawyer as quickly as possible, together with your
    contact person's name and his or her telephone number.
    If you are assuming an existing mortgage, provide this
    information to your lawyer once you have been approved
    to assume it. Confirm the amount being borrowed, the
    interest rate, the term, the amortization, the payment,
    how often it will be paid, and the prepayment privileges.
    See if it will be necessary to bring a blank cheque to the
    meeting with your lawyer for future pre-authorized pay-
    ments, or a series of postdated cheques for those
    payments. Review what the final mortgage advance will be,
    and any deductions to be made from that advance (for a
    tax account, interest to the interest adjustment date, plus
    the application fee).

4. Only funds on deposit for at least 90 days can be withdrawn
    under the Home Buyers' Plan, the RRSP program that
    allows first-time buyers to use up to $20,000 of their RRSP
    funds tax-free and interest-free when buying a first home.
    To participate fully in the Home Buyers' Plan, make your
    maximum contribution to your RRSP as soon as possible,
    and most definitely at least 90 days before closing. For more
    details on the Home Buyers' Plan, see chapter 9.

5. Buyers who are presently tenants must either cancel their
    lease or transfer their tenancy/sub-lease their current
    apartment, if permitted. To avoid problems, be sure to
    give the landlord the amount of notice required in the
    applicable residential tenancy legislation. If in doubt,
    check it out with your lawyer. Try to arrange an overlap, so

that the lease terminates shortly after the date of closing. This will make moving considerably easier.

6. Since most residential insurance policies are not transferable, arrange fire insurance coverage as soon as possible, to take effect the date of closing. Coverage should be for the full insurable value *of the building only* (not the land), on a replacement cost basis. A certified copy of the insurance coverage, showing the names of any lenders in the loss payable clause, should be forwarded to your lawyer before closing. If this is not possible, as an absolute minimum ensure that an insurance "binder" letter is available for closing from your agent or broker, showing the name of the insuring company, the amount of coverage and its expiration date, as well as the lenders' names in the loss payable clause. Purchasers of condominium units only need to arrange condominium unit owner's package insurance. It does not have to be sent to your lawyer for closing.

7. Normally, your lawyer contacts the local gas, hydro and water departments for final meter readings the day of closing. New accounts are also to be established in your name on closing, with the final bill sent to the vendor or the vendor's lawyer. Occasionally, though, slip-ups do occur, especially on busy closing days or month-ends. That's why many buyers do a "double-check" with the local utilities a few days before closing, just to be sure. Better to be told that the matter will be done, than find yourself without utility service following closing.

Buyers are responsible for contacting the telephone and cable television systems and any home security company themselves. Lawyers do not contact these companies, as their outstanding charges are not a lien against a property.

For homes heated by oil, the seller arranges to fill the oil tank on closing. The seller is then credited with the cost of a full tank of home heating oil on the Statement of Adjustments. Ask whether an extended warranty or service contract is in effect on the furnace, and if it is assignable. With the name of the company previously servicing the furnace and supplying oil to the property, the buyer can arrange for both a continued supply of oil and the maintenance of the furnace after closing. No one, especially in the dead of winter, wants to find their oil tank dry because arrangements for a regular oil "drop" in the days following closing fell through the cracks.

8. Arrange for your move as early as possible, whether you are hiring a mover or renting a van. Packing takes an enormous amount of time — more than you think! Get several quotes from movers or for a rental van. Remember that demand is highest in the middle and at the end of the month, on Fridays (especially the last Friday of the month) and the week before Canada Day and Labour Day.

9. Organize who to notify about your change of address. Send change of address cards to people you know and companies you deal with — from the post office to magazine subscriptions. And don't forget to contact the provincial motor vehicle department about your driver's licence. Failure to notify them could lead to a fine. See chapter 32 for more details.

10. Plan to meet your lawyer to review and sign the closing papers one or two days before closing — *not the actual closing date*, when so many other things must be done. Even if the property will be registered in the name of one spouse only, *both* spouses must attend the pre-closing meeting to sign the closing documents when a matrimonial home is being purchased and mortgaged.

    At the pre-closing meeting, your lawyer will review the total amount of money needed to close. Included will be the amount for fees, disbursements and GST on those items. Arrange to deliver to your lawyer the total amount of money needed to close no later than 2:00 p.m. the business day before closing. A certified cheque, money order or bank draft is needed, payable to your lawyer in trust. These arrangements are necessary for the transaction to close as early as possible the day of closing (what most buyers want). At that time, get information about any payments due shortly after closing — on a mortgage, to the tax department, or to the condominium corporation for maintenance.

Bonus Idea — What's the most commonly asked question in a real estate transaction? "Where and when will the keys be available for pick-up?" Getting keys into your hands as soon as possible after closing is also of great concern to your lawyer.

Everyone knows that buyers want their keys promptly so they can start unloading the moving van. For most resale deals, keys are normally delivered to your lawyer by the vendor's lawyer at the Land Registry Office on closing. Then they are returned to your lawyer's office for pick-up by you. That means those keys make a long trek on closing day from the house to the seller's lawyer's office, to the registry office, to your lawyer's office, and then back to the house!

To save valuable time and avoid that from happening, see if other arrangements can be made for the keys. Contact the vendor several days before closing to see if the keys can be left with a trusting neighbor, to be released after closing. Or arrange to obtain them directly from the vendor after he or she has moved out of the house. Another option is to have the vendor leave the keys with the listing agent (who, generally, is located close to the home), so that you can pick up the keys there after closing. If necessary, they can also be picked up from your lawyer at the registry office. If any alternative plans are made for the keys, be sure to tell your lawyer so he or she won't expect to receive them on closing. Buyers who do their homework can save considerable time and stress, exactly when the family is most anxious to move into its new home.

Meeting with your lawyer a day or two before closing and delivering the closing proceeds at that time are crucial if the keys are to be available as soon as possible on closing. Yet it is impossible for your lawyer to guarantee a precise time when the keys will be available, since it is impossible to give a precise time when the transaction will be completed (the exact time depending on when the seller's lawyer is ready to close the deal). Realistically, buyers should not expect to receive the keys until mid-afternoon the day of closing at the earliest.

29

The Lawyer's Role from Contract to Closing

According to your home-buying strategy, selecting the lawyer to handle your purchase is one of the first decisions made, never the last. With full knowledge of its contents, once the offer is accepted your lawyer can immediately start processing it.

Exactly what a lawyer does every step of the way is not of great concern to most purchasers. What they really want to know are the end results: where do I sign; exactly how much money do I bring in; and when will the deed be registered and the keys be available?

Usually, the first step in processing a purchase is searching the title to the property. Most offers give the buyer's lawyer a very short time to examine the title and to raise title deficiencies. Because the title search period is generally 30 days or less, even if closing is months in the future, getting the search underway quickly is extremely important. If the legal description appeared in the draft offer your lawyer reviewed, all it will take is your phone call advising that the deal is firm, for him or her to start the search. Receipt of the accepted offer can come later. Most lawyers wait until all conditions are removed before searching title; this keeps expenses down in case a condition is not satisfied or waived and the deal aborts. The need to contact a lawyer before signing any offer again becomes self-evident. Consider the case of Ray, a buyer, who makes initial contact with a lawyer several days after the offer is accepted. With that delay, precious time on that title search clock has been lost forever, to Ray's disadvantage.

A title search is a historical investigation of previous ownership and prior dealings with the property. Depending on the
province and the land registration system involved, this could
involve examining all registered instruments affecting the title
going back 40 years, to ensure an unbroken "chain of title." A
lawyer's title opinion is based on the information appearing in
the search of title.

Rarely are formal engagement contracts signed between a
lawyer and his or her client in real estate transactions. Despite
this, the standard of care for real estate lawyers is that a purchaser must be provided with a formal legal opinion, stating
that the buyer becomes the registered owner of the property on
closing with a "good and marketable" title. Good means appropriate for the buyer's purposes, while marketable indicates that
it is adequate to be conveyed to someone else, now or in the
future. To meet this standard, a lawyer must investigate the title
in the prescribed manner. Following a careful review of the title
search, a letter will be sent to the seller's lawyer (called a requisition letter) setting out matters that must be dealt with, on
or before closing.

Probably the most common requisition raised is the need
for the seller's existing mortgage to be discharged, if the buyer
is not assuming it on closing. Most other requisitions involve
outstanding monetary expenses: taxes, utility charges, condominium expenses and mortgage payments. These are easily
satisfied on closing, the seller simply paying the amount owing
to the appropriate creditor from the closing proceeds. To
ensure that these sums are paid promptly, the buyer often gets
a credit from the seller on the Statement of Adjustments for the
amount outstanding. Then the buyer's lawyer pays the amount
owing to the seller's creditor, right after closing.

Occasionally, a search of title reveals other outstanding and
unexpected matters, such as a utility easement, a right-of-way or
mutual drive, or registered restrictions. All of these detract
from the "perfect" title buyers expect to receive, legally known
as "fee simple" (the most extensive, unrestricted and unconditional interest in land a person can enjoy).

A properly drawn offer will disclose these title qualifications
at the outset, so that buyers and their lawyers know precisely
what to expect in the search of title. Some of these situations

are dealt with in the fine print in many standard form offers. For example, the buyer may agree to take title subject to minor easements to public utilities for the supply of domestic utility service. Or, the buyer may agree to take title subject to registered restrictions, provided they have been complied with. (For more information, see chapter 25.)

Occasionally, the search reveals a serious title deficiency not disclosed in the offer. A 25-foot underground sewer easement ran diagonally across the property Paul and Kelly were buying, but their offer said nothing about it! However, the search of title revealed its existence. Because a lawyer must follow the terms of the deal reached by his clients, Paul and Kelly's lawyer immediately contacted them about this discrepancy. After advising Paul and Kelly of the legal implications, and discussing the situation with them thoroughly, their lawyer also recommended what course of action to follow. They should seek a reduction in the purchase price, since the affected area would substantially interfere with their use and enjoyment of the property. Paul and Kelly gave their lawyer written instructions to proceed on this basis, since the terms of the contract would have to be altered. Ultimately the deal did close, with this drop in the purchase price.

Prudent lawyers will obtain a written acknowledgment from purchaser clients before closing, listing all items that the title will be subject to, even those originally disclosed in the offer. Having such a document signed is quite helpful, since everything affecting "perfect" title is noted, discussed and approved before title and money change hands, eliminating any future possible disagreements.

Besides the title search itself, many "off-title" searches are conducted, too. Clearances, reports and certificates must be ordered from different government departments, usually a month or so before closing. For example, a certificate is ordered to ensure that all realty taxes have been paid to the date of closing, and to learn whether any additional charges such as local improvements have been levied against the property. The local municipality is contacted, to ensure that the property complies with all zoning by-laws and to learn if any work orders or deficiency notices are outstanding. A check is also made with the local utilities — hydro, water and gas — to see if any of their charges are outstanding. At the same time, they are notified that the property has been sold and who will be the new owner. A request is also made to each for a final meter reading on the day of closing, with the final bill to be sent to the seller's lawyer.

Besides these, compliance letters are sought from any municipality which has registered an agreement on title, such as a development or subdivision agreement. A search is conducted for unpaid judgments (technically known as "executions") against the seller and prior owners. Personal property security records are checked to see if any liens, encumbrances or chattel mortgages affect any personal property being acquired. For "tenanted" properties, a search of rent records is necessary in those provinces where rents are subject to government regulation.

In condominium transactions, an Estoppel Certificate must be ordered from the condominium corporation. This certificate contains information about arrears of common expenses for the unit and whether any legal actions are pending by or against the condominium corporation.

Where rural property is being acquired, a number of additional inquiries are conducted. These include searching for well-water records and learning whether the sewage disposal system (septic tank) has been approved by the provincial environment ministry.

The purpose behind all these searches is to ensure that no liens or other deficiencies affect the property. Buyers are paying their lawyers to ensure that no accounts are in arrears and that no outstanding government infractions exist, so that the buyers can acquire the property with a clean slate on the date of closing. A fee is charged for most of these searches and reports. The cost of obtaining this information represents the out-of-pocket disbursements buyers incur when purchasing property.

Surveys were discussed in detail in chapter 24. If no survey can be located, or if the content of the existing survey is unacceptable, arrangements should be made to have a new one drawn as soon as possible. Preparing the new survey will take several weeks. Even more time will then be needed to obtain a by-law and work order report based on the contents of that survey. On request, your lawyer will arrange to order a new survey.

Once received, the survey should be carefully reviewed to

ensure that the dimensions of the property, the size of the lot and the extent of title correspond with the particulars stated in the offer. Any encroachments onto this property by adjoining properties, or by this property onto adjoining properties, should be noted. Written instructions from buyers to their lawyers to close the transaction despite these encroachments (some of which may have long existed) is customary. Some lawyers also require written instructions from the purchaser to close, if no survey exists or if the survey is old but acceptable. Any qualifications to the lawyer's title opinion resulting from this reliance on an old survey are indicated here as well.

The survey for the house Sam and Roz are buying was prepared in 1973. Nothing has changed on the survey since it was prepared. If they use that old survey to close, their lawyer's title opinion will be subject to any changes to the property that might have occurred between 1973 and the date of closing, that a new survey would have revealed. Not only has full disclosure been made to Sam and Roz about these matters before closing, but they provided their lawyer with written instructions to close the purchase with this survey. The likelihood for any misunderstanding has been considerably reduced.

The draft deed, Statement of Adjustments and other closing documents are reviewed by the buyer's lawyer upon receipt. To ensure its accuracy, a buyer's lawyer must independently verify the contents of the Statement of Adjustments. Any discrepancies should be raised and resolved with the seller's lawyer as soon as possible.

The lawyer's role in the mortgage transaction depends on how the purchase is being financed. Three different ways exist to finance it: by the purchaser assuming an existing mortgage; by the purchaser granting a new mortgage to a lender; and by the vendor taking back a new mortgage from the purchaser.

Where an existing mortgage is assumed, a mortgage assumption statement is sought from the lender. Particulars sought include the following: the outstanding principal as of the last payment; the interest rate; the amount of the payment; the maturity date; the status of any tax account; whether the mortgage is assumable; plus any prepayment privileges. This information is then compared with the clauses in the offer dealing with the mortgage, plus the mortgage as registered on title.

Where a new mortgage is being arranged, the lender's instructions will list the many documents that must be prepared before the funds can be released. Usually, the buyer's lawyer is allowed to act for an institutional lender, too, saving the buyer money. Draft documents prepared by the buyer's lawyer are sent to the lender for approval, and arrangements are made to have the net mortgage advance available for closing.

In a vendor-take-back mortgage situation, the buyer's lawyer prepares the draft mortgage, based on the wording in the offer. It is then sent to the seller's lawyer for approval.

Don't be afraid to discuss matters with your lawyer or ask questions that concern you. Your lawyer has been hired for that very purpose! Also, buyers, especially first-time home buyers, must never worry that their questions are too simple or too basic. Although your lawyer and his or her staff may have been asked the same question innumerable times, you don't know the answer. Otherwise, you would not be asking the question. To assist buyers, some lawyers provide "information booklets" that answer many of the routine questions commonly raised by purchasers. Even if you receive such a booklet, never leave important questions for the final meeting. Ask them as they arise, to the lawyer or his or her staff. An unanswered question can become an unresolvable problem if not dealt with promptly.

As noted in the previous chapter, plan to meet with your lawyer to review in detail the Statement of Adjustments and sign the closing papers *a day or two before closing*. By that time, the exact amount needed to close should be known. Try to avoid signing papers the actual closing date unless absolutely necessary. In most cases, papers can be signed well in advance. Who knows what can happen the day of closing? The car could break down; the children could be sick; inclement weather could make travel impossible; or a hydro blackout, fire or robbery could effectively close off part of the city. Then what? For most buyers, a lawyer's office is the last place they want to be on the day of closing; they really want to be in their new home! So make the date of closing your last choice for the pre-closing meeting, never your first.

Signing the papers on closing day itself actually delays the closing. Remember that no keys are delivered to buyers at that meeting. Before keys to the new home are available, the deal must already be closed! How, then, can buyers like Dick and Liz, who did not meet their lawyer until 11:00 a.m. on closing day, expect to receive their keys early? Following that meeting, their lawyer had to deposit the funds into her trust account and certify the closing proceeds. Only then could the transaction be closed in the registry office. As Dick and Liz learned, closing-day meetings inevitably mean late-in-the-day closings with the seller's lawyer and an even later delivery of keys.

The situation is even worse for people with back-to-back transactions, selling an existing home and buying another the same day. Unless bridge financing has been arranged, the sale must be closed before the purchase, as the funds needed for the purchase will only be available after the sale has closed. Obviously this will further delay the closing of the purchase. Anything that will expedite the deals closing, such as meeting the lawyer one or two days in advance, is encouraged.

Closing proceeds are often obtained from different sources — the buyer and the mortgage lender (and the bank, if bridge financing is being arranged). The funds are assembled in the buyer's lawyer's trust account, to be disbursed on closing. Unless told otherwise, buyers must deliver a certified cheque, money order or bank draft to their lawyer, payable to the order of their lawyer, in trust. Arranging for a lawyer to be "in funds" early is just as important as signing the closing papers early.

Joel and Nancy were asked to bring the closing proceeds to their lawyer when they met at noon the day before closing. Already concerned about the extra cost this involved, they also wondered why the net proceeds for the new mortgage being arranged were also being delivered the day before closing. Then they realized that the overall cost to them was quite small. Assuming that the interest cost on their own money and the mortgage for one day averaged 7%, the cost on the $150,000 Joel and Nancy needed to close was only $28.76.

Joel and Nancy applied their HOBS both in meeting with their lawyer a day before closing and in arranging for him to have the closing funds that same day. Delays in closing are usually attributable to delays with buyers — and in particular, hitches in getting the closing proceeds. By comparison, most sellers are ready to close early the day of closing. Once their paperwork is signed, seller's lawyers are simply awaiting receipt of the sale proceeds from the buyer. (Occasionally, though, the seller's lawyer may be unable to close the transaction until later in the day, too.) Because everything was completed the day before closing, Joel and Nancy's purchase was closed by noon and they had their keys by 1:00 p.m.

When it comes to real estate closings, the early bird catches the worm! By meeting with their lawyer a day or two before closing, and putting him in funds at that time, buyers like Joel and Nancy have a fighting chance of completing their purchase early on the scheduled closing date and getting possession with a minimum of delay. If this saves them even one hour's moving time, they wind up further ahead financially, despite the nominal cost involved. To close as early as possible on the day of closing, meet your lawyer no later than the day before closing. In addition, make sure the closing proceeds are delivered by 2:00 p.m. the day before closing.

Few documents will be given to buyers at this pre-closing meeting, other than copies of the "money" items such as the Statement of Adjustments. With the upcoming move, no one wants to run the risk of losing important legal documents in transit. Copies of all relevant papers will accompany the reporting letter.

The lawyer's role in the real estate transaction does not end with closing the transaction, registering the deed and mortgage, and delivering the key to the purchaser. Immediately after closing, the tax department and the condominium corporation (if applicable) must be given the names of the new owners of the property. Any outstanding charges credited to the buyer on the Statement of Adjustments must be paid. An amortization schedule should be ordered for any new, assumed or vendor-take-back mortgages, too.

A complete summary of the work performed by the buyer's lawyer appears in the reporting letter. Since proper preparation of this letter takes time, expect it to be delivered about a month after closing. Certain detailed information is needed right after closing, though. Included here are the mortgages (the date of the first payment; the amount of the payment; where payment should be sent; the mortgage number), property taxes and condo maintenance payments. Remembering everything explained at the pre-closing meeting is not easy, so get this information from your lawyer at that time. Some lawyers will also send an interim report containing this information to purchasers in the days after closing. Often, this is the first letter buyers receive at their new home address.

Separate reporting letters, including the title opinion, are prepared and sent to the purchaser and mortgage lender. Copies of all relevant documents such as the deed, mortgages, amortization schedules, Statement of Adjustments and survey should accompany the report. A proper reporting letter is not simply a form letter with the blanks filled in. It should be specifically tailored to, and include relevant information about, this particular transaction. Because most buyers are very concerned about the "money aspects" of the transaction, a proper reporting letter should provide a detailed commentary explaining every item in the Statement of Adjustments. The calculation of every credit should be outlined, with a copy of the document verifying the item accompanying the letter. Deductions made by the mortgage lender at source should be clearly explained and documented, too. Special instructions received from the client before closing should also be discussed in the reporting letter.

The lawyer's bill will indicate the fees charged (plus GST), as well as the amount incurred for each disbursement (plus GST where applicable). In addition, a Statement of Receipts and Disbursements will provide a complete accounting of the funds received in a lawyer's trust account from all sources, and to whom the money was disbursed.

Properly prepared, the detailed commentary of the reporting letter, accompanied by copies of all relevant documents, should answer all outstanding questions a buyer may have. Besides providing a permanent record of the transaction for the purchaser, the reporting letter will also form the basis for any further dealings with the property. Be it for a sale or mortgage financing, your lawyer should be able to pick up where he or she left off, at some future date, simply by reviewing the reporting letter.

30
Insurance

Everyone buying a house knows that "fire insurance" is needed. How much to arrange, the different coverages that are available, and the impact of a mortgage on insurance coverage are discussed later in this chapter.

However, buyers will likely also encounter two other types of insurance when discussing "mortgage insurance": term life insurance and mortgage payment insurance. Loosely applied, the term "mortgage insurance" can refer to any of these three categories. So when asking about "mortgage insurance," distinguish between insuring the property, your life, and the payments to the lender.

Home Insurance

Calling this "fire insurance" ignores the many different ways a loss can occur. When arranging this type of insurance, make sure the home and its contents are protected. Personal liability coverage is needed, plus coverage against theft. These are available in the so-called "home owner's package" offered by many insurance companies.

Most insurance policies offer standard protection against loss by fire and specified "named" or "extended perils," including explosions, falling objects, vehicular impact, lightning, riots, vandalism, windstorm and smoke damage. Some insurance policies provide a more comprehensive "all-risk" coverage (for a higher premium), protecting against more possible sources of loss, although certain exclusions and deductibles exist even here.

Like most buyers, Ian and Marie are financing their purchase with a mortgage, arranged through Punch Trust. If the building burned totally to the ground, the insurance money would replace the building as security for the loan. The lender would then want first claim to those funds. As Punch Trust has an insurable interest in the property, Ian and Marie should ask their insurance agent to show it as first mortgagee in the loss-payable clause of the insurance policy. When the mortgage is paid off, the interest of Punch Trust will then be deleted.

Paperwork takes time. Few insurance policies are available for closing, although they take effect that day. To satisfy lenders that the required insurance is in place, insurance agents issue "binder" letters for closing, indicating that it has "bound" or arranged insurance coverage. A binder letter contains full particulars of the insurance coverage in effect: the insurer, the amount of coverage, the policy number, the expiry date, together with the names of the lenders in the loss-payable clause. Except for in the case of condominium units (where condominium unit owner's package insurance is arranged), home buyers should arrange for the binder letter to be delivered to their lawyer as soon as possible before closing. In turn, it will have to be forwarded to the lender for approval. Aware that adequate insurance has been arranged, with the policy to follow, most lenders will then advance the mortgage proceeds on closing.

How much insurance coverage is required? When answering this question, too often buyers only consider the size of the outstanding mortgages. Actually, that should be ignored when determining the amount of insurance coverage to arrange. Instead, what should first be considered is the "full insurable value" of the building (the premises). This coverage guarantees that the building is insured to the maximum. Seriously consider optional coverage on a "replacement cost" basis, too. This ensures that the cost of rebuilding the dwelling *at current prices* will be paid by the insurer, without any reduction for depreciation. Despite any nominal premium for full insurable value coverage on a replacement cost basis (sometimes available at no additional cost), only it guarantees that a home will be replaced with one of similar type and quality in the event of an insurable loss. And that is true even if the loss exceeds the current insurable value of the home. In other words, guaranteed replacement cost eliminates any concern of underinsuring a house. But the replacement cost endorsement isn't available on all properties. Usually, it's limited to owner-occupied homes, not investment real estate.

How does this replacement cost endorsement work? First, the building must be insured for 100% of its insurable value as determined by the insurer (say, $100,000 for Davey's home). If his home was totally destroyed, and the cost of rebuilding it was $110,000, replacement cost coverage means Davey's insurer would pay the full cost of replacing the building ($110,000), even though the policy limit was $10,000 less.

An important point to remember is that the land component of a property does not have to be insured. Land does not burn. Even if a home is totally destroyed in a fire, the lot still exists. Only the house must be rebuilt, not the lot. Where a mortgage lender has the property appraised, find out the separate values given to the land and the replacement cost of the building. This will help greatly in knowing how much insurance coverage to arrange.

Unfortunately, some lenders require that the full amount of the mortgage be insured, even if it exceeds the full insurable value of the property. Clauses like these cause both headaches and extra expense for purchasers.

Rob and Laura bought a property for $150,000. The lot is worth $45,000, the full insurable value of the house being $105,000. If they book an $80,000 mortgage, Rob and Laura will need at least $80,000 insurance coverage to satisfy the lender. Of course, Rob and Laura should arrange $105,000 coverage, the full insurable value of the house. Here the size of the mortgage ($80,000) is less than the value of the house ($105,000).

Ward and June's situation is the reverse. Although they are buying the identical house for $150,000, their mortgage will be $120,000. Unlike in Rob and Laura's situation, here the amount of the mortgage ($120,000) exceeds the value of the house

($105,000). Now the problems begin. Because the full insurable value of the dwelling is only $105,000, any greater coverage is really unnecessary. Nothing is being insured for that extra $15,000 except the land. Nevertheless, their lender, Spring Farm Trust, insisted that the full amount of the mortgage — $120,000 — be insured, forcing Ward and June to overinsure their house and pay the premium for $15,000 of worthless coverage. Unless their lender agrees to accept only $105,000 in insurance coverage, Ward and June have little choice but to comply. Although the difference in premiums is small, it is still an unnecessary expense for unnecessary coverage.

Even today, some lenders adamantly refuse to advance mortgage proceeds unless the full amount borrowed is insured, even though the full insurable value is less. No law says lenders can only demand insurance coverage for the full insurable value of the building. And that irritates borrowers.

Most lenders insist that the Standard Mortgage Clause approved by the Insurance Bureau of Canada be attached to the policy. What is this and why is it so important? Insurance is arranged and paid for by borrowers, to protect lenders. Only rarely do lenders deal directly with the insurance company. In the event of a loss, could the insurer pay the insurance proceeds to the lender, someone it never dealt with? This Standard Mortgage Clause allows insurance proceeds to be paid directly to a mortgage lender, despite the lack of a contractual link between lender and insurer. With this clause, lenders are also assured that coverage will not be cancelled without the lender first receiving notice (so that they can pay the insurance premium, if necessary, and add the premium to the mortgage debt). Most insurance policies today contain the IBC Standard Mortgage Clause as a matter of course.

Insurance policies on resale homes are arranged for a term of one year. Unlike years ago, insurance policies on residential homes are not assignable to a new owner of the property. Therefore, buyers shouldn't expect the seller to transfer his or her insurance to them on closing. As part of their home-buying strategy, prudent buyers will start shopping for insurance early, well before closing, obtaining quotations and comparing coverage, to get the best possible terms. Use the form at the end of this chapter to record the information provided by different insurance agents. And make sure the insurance coverage takes effect from 12:01 a.m. the date of closing, too.

When shopping for insurance, consider dealing with an insurance broker who deals with a number of insurance companies. A better overall package should be available from one of the many insurance companies the broker deals with. True insurance agents work for, market and sell the product of only one insurance company. Your chances of getting the best possible deal are somewhat restricted when dealing with an insurance agent.

Insurance on condominiums, both townhouses and apartment units, is handled totally differently. Both the condominium corporation and the unit owners must arrange separate insurance coverage on the property it owns. For further information, see chapter 20 on condominiums.

One final word about home insurance. If a fire hit your home or a thief ransacked your house, would you know exactly what was lost? The more precise information you can give the insurance company, the fuller the recovery. So compile a complete inventory of personal possessions, prepared on a room-by-room basis. Each item should be described in detail, including serial numbers. Some people even videotape the contents of their house. One copy of the list or tape should be kept in a secure location *outside the house,* such as a safety deposit box. Many police departments will loan engraving guns to residents at a nominal or no charge. A unique identification code, such as a social insurance number, can then be marked on personal property such as TV sets, stereos, VCRs, appliances, cameras, china, tools and the like. This way, if any property is stolen and later recovered, returning it to its rightful owner becomes considerably easier.

In the space below, make a list of the insurance quotations received. Don't forget: any lenders must be shown in the loss-payable clause of the insurance policy.

Insurance Agencies
Name
Address
Phone number
Contact person
Amount of coverage
Insurer
Cost
Replacement cost coverage?

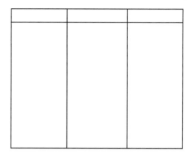

Term Life Insurance

Many institutional mortgage lenders offer term life insurance to borrowers at a nominal premium. If the borrower dies while the mortgage is outstanding, the insurance proceeds are used to pay off the loan. For this reason, often it is called "mortgage insurance." But it's really only declining-balance term insurance, available from almost any life insurance agent.

Because the insurance is arranged on a declining-balance basis, the coverage falls as the principal owing is reduced — by either regular payments or any prepayments. Each time the mortgage is renewed, the cost of insurance should theoretically fall, too, reflecting the lower amount outstanding at that time (subject, of course, to any offsetting increase because the borrower is now a little bit older than before). Once the mortgage is paid off, this term insurance coverage ends, too. While it's available at many lenders, few make it mandatory. Similar coverage can also be arranged for illness and disability.

When considering whether to buy this type of insurance coverage through the lender, stand back and ask yourself, do I have sufficient life insurance in case I die to pay off my obligations and leave sufficient funds from which my family can live comfortably? If not, compare the premiums charged by different insurers for the same product before automatically signing up with the lender. Often, rates for group level-balance term life insurance are cheaper at work, through an organization or club, or even through an alumni association, than those charged by the lender. So, as is often the case in real estate, shop around.

Another reason borrowers like to arrange their own term insurance coverage is to name the beneficiary of the funds on death. Gary arranged $100,000 group level-balance term life insurance through his alumni association, naming wife Roberta as beneficiary. When Gary died, the balance owing on his mortgage was $85,000. Of the $100,000 that Roberta received, $85,000 was paid to retire the mortgage, while she kept the other $15,000. If Gary had booked $100,000 declining-balance term life insurance through his lender, it would have been the beneficiary of the insurance proceeds on his death. While the $85,000 mortgage would have been paid off, no excess funds would have been paid to Roberta.

Mortgage Payment Insurance

High-ratio mortgages, where the owner has less than 25% equity in the property, are riskier investments for lenders than conventional mortgages, which do not exceed 75% of the lower of the purchase price and appraised value. For institutional lenders to grant a high-ratio mortgage, they want some guarantee that the mortgage will be repaid in case the borrower defaults. *To protect the lender,* borrowers must arrange mortgage payment insurance on the full amount of the mortgage. This type of insurance is available from two sources: a private insurer, GE Capital Mortgage Insurance Canada (GEMICO), and a federal agency, Canada Mortgage and Housing Corporation (CMHC).

The one-time premium paid by the borrower does not come cheap. Insurance premiums are 1.25% of the total mortgage when the loan-to-value ratio is between 75% and 80%, 2% when it's between 80.1% and 85%, and 2.5% of the total mortgage for loan-to-value ratios from 85.1% to 90%. (That same 2.5% premium applies to mortgage loans with loan-to-value ratios between 90.1% and 95% for participants in the First Home Loan Insurance Program discussed in chapter 8.) Note that the insurance premium is paid on the whole amount of the mortgage, not just the part exceeding 75% of the appraised value, the "high-ratio" portion at risk.

While borrowers have the option of paying the insurance premium up front on closing, most lack the funds to do so. Instead, thcy opt to add the mortgage insurance premium onto the amount being borrowed. So if Howard and Bonnie are arranging 90% insurance coverage on their $150,000 purchase, the insurance premium will be 2.5% of the $135,000 mortgage, or $3,375. Adding it to the amount borrowed means Howard and Bonnie's mortgage will be registered for $138,375. In addition, the normal processing fee ranges from $75 to $235. And in Ontario, the insurance premium is also subject to provincial sales tax. Both these charges must be paid in cash on closing; they cannot be tacked on to the mortgage principal.

While capitalizing the insurance premium helps Howard and Bonnie's cash flow for closing, it also means the insurance premium itself will bear interest for years to come. Given an interest rate of 8% over the mortgage's 25-year amortized life, Howard and Bonnie will pay an extra $25.76 monthly for that insurance premium, or an additional $4,351.56 in interest over those 25 years (on top of the $3,375), to assure their lender that they (Howard and Bonnie) will make their mortgage payments punctually.

Despite what many people think, mortgage payment insurance does not make the mortgage payment for borrowers in case they default so that they don't have to pay it. Instead, the insurer pays the lender the overdue payments, with the insurer then pursuing the borrower for that money. Although mortgage payment insurance premiums are paid by borrowers, the coverage protects lenders!

Don't forget that all CMHC-insured mortgages with a term of three years or more are open after three years on payment of three months' bonus interest, regardless of the lender's "normal" prepayment privileges. This is one of the major benefits of having CMHC provide the mortgage payment insurance coverage. With GEMICO mortgage insurance coverage, on the other hand, the lender's usual prepayment policies still apply.

Mortgage payment insurance exists to help people with good incomes but less than 25% for a downpayment buy their first home. But it doesn't come cheap. *So avoid mortgage payment insurance unless absolutely necessary.* With a little advance planning as part of your HOBS, or by participating in the Home

Buyers' Plan (described in chapter 9), you may be able to cut the amount being borrowed slightly and drop into a lower mortgage payment insurance category. So crunch those numbers carefully.

31

Closing — The Moment Everyone Has Waited For

Closing takes place at the local registry office. Many law firms use trained paralegals called "conveyancers" to handle the mechanics of actually closing the deal. Meanwhile, the buyer's lawyer is in his or her office where he or she can easily be reached by that client, the conveyancer, and other people whose deals are closing the same day. Knowing where their lawyer will be on closing, and that he or she will be available if the need arises, is very reassuring to most buyers. Last-minute instructions can easily be relayed by a client, through the lawyer's office. Information that the deed has been registered and where keys will be available for pick-up can be easily conveyed to the client, through the lawyer's office. On busy closing days, a lawyer's office becomes a "central command," the hub-of-the-wheel through which all communications are funnelled.

Closing a deal is not nearly as mysterious as it sounds. Everyone with a HOBS (home-buying strategy) should have signed the closing papers a day or two before closing. The funds from the various sources should be ready for delivery to the lawyer by mid-day the day before closing. Draft documents should have been submitted and approved by each lawyer ahead of time. At the prearranged time on the closing date, the buyer's conveyancer hands the closing proceeds, any vendor-take-back mortgage and other required closing documents to the seller's representative. In return, the seller's conveyancer delivers the deed and keys, any undertakings and any other required documents. Everything is carefully checked against the closing instructions provided by each lawyer. Once done, the conveyancers wait their turn to register the closing documents (deed and mortgage). Not until that has been completed can each side release to their respective clients the items received from the other side on closing.

Buyers with back-to-back deals must close the sale of their old home first, before completing the purchase of their new home that same day. This results in unavoidable delays in closing the second deal.

Chris was buying Danny's house. Before that deal could close, Chris's sale to Bob had to be completed. Because Chris was closing both his sale and his purchase the same day, he expected some delay in closing the purchase from Danny. What Chris didn't know was that Bob was selling his house to Alan that same day, too, a deal that had to close before either of Chris's transactions. The flow of money on closing resembled dominoes falling — looking like this:

Alan → Bob → Chris → Danny

Poor Chris. Not one but two deals had to close the same day, before his purchase could be completed. That meant the keys to his new house weren't available until very late in the day. Of course, if Chris had arranged bridge financing, all this could have been avoided (see chapter 22).

The system of land registration in much of Canada is very primitive and highly labor-intensive. A concerted effort is underway to facilitate computerized searches and electronic registrations, but it's far from complete. While the exchange of documents on closing can be completed in just a few minutes, the problems encountered in registering the deed and mortgage usually account for lengthy delays. On rush hour at the registry office — Fridays, the end of the month, Fridays at the end of the month and just before a long weekend — registration clerks are unable to handle the sheer volume of business. Hours can be spent in lineups, waiting to "get registered." That's why it's better to schedule closing for an off-day. Even on quiet days, afternoons are much busier than mornings. That's another good reason to meet in advance with your lawyer and push for an early-morning closing.

As noted in chapter 28, the biggest headache of all, and the most commonly asked question, is, "When and where will the keys be available for pick-up?" So try to make an arrangement with the vendor in the final days before closing, through the agent if necessary, to keep the keys near the property on closing.

Occasionally, buyers get keys to the house before the deal closes. Although making alternative arrangements to get keys on closing is encouraged, moving into the house before closing is risky and never recommended, no matter how inconvenient the wait may be. Taking possession before closing involves serious risks. As the purchaser, you are considered to have waived all outstanding title deficiencies. In effect, that forces you to close the deal. More importantly, you immediately assume liability for the house and anyone entering it. What if a mover injures himself before the deed is registered? Granted, it's annoying to have the keys in hand and not be able to use them. But prudent buyers will never use the keys to the house until the deal has closed.

Often, only one key is given to the buyer on closing. Any other keys can be found in the house, usually on the kitchen counter. Purchasers of condominium units should ensure that either the various keys (to the building, the garage, the mail box and the recreational facilities) are delivered on closing or they are left in the unit on closing. Garage-door openers and access cards are often turned in to the management office by the vendor just before closing. To have them re-issued, the purchaser must pay a refundable deposit to the property manager.

When does a seller like Sam have to vacate the property? When can a buyer like Brian move in? Immediate access to the property is a pressing concern to all buyers, except those who are bridge financing their purchase or are keeping their apartment for several days after closing.

Of course, before Brian is legally entitled to possession, the deal must be closed and the deed registered. Rarely does either Sam or Brian know precisely the moment this happens. While their lawyers or conveyancers are in the registry office, Sam and Brian could be anywhere — in the process of moving, at work, in a car, even at lunch. Despite what people say, few sellers deliberately delay moving out. Most sellers like Sam are just as anxious to get out of their old house and into their new house as Brian is to move into Sam's old house. Typically, sellers vacate a property by early to mid-afternoon, allowing the buyer to start moving in at that time if the deal has closed.

Practically speaking, courtesy and co-operation are the answer. On his lawyer's recommendation, Brian spoke to Sam the night before closing and made arrangements to get the keys directly from Sam. At 1:30 p.m. Sam was notified that the deed to Brian had been registered. On moving out at 2:15 p.m, Sam gave his keys directly to Brian, who began moving in immediately.

Many offers say Vince, the seller, shall give vacant possession of the property to Phil, the buyer, on completion, without specifying either the time when the deal must close or the time when vacant possession must be available. Must Vince be completely moved out by the time set for closing? Can Phil recover from Vince any additional costs incurred, especially the extra amount paid to the mover, if Vince moves out after the deed to Phil is registered? To the surprise of many buyers, the answer is no. Unless the offer contains a specific time when the deal must be completed and/or vacant possession must be available (a clause which is becoming increasingly common), Vince technically can deliver vacant possession to Phil at any time up to 11:59 p.m the day of closing. That being the case, it is impossible for Phil to recover damages from Vince if keys are available at any time the day of closing. All the more reason why buyers should — no, *must* — co-operate with sellers. Of course, if the offer specifies a closing/vacant possession time, even a time by which the deal must be closed (e.g., 6:00 p.m.), Phil can sue Vince for moving costs incurred after that hour.

Communication is a two-way street. As much as clients want information from their lawyer on closing, lawyers will also have information to relay to, and possibly questions to ask of, their clients. Simply put, a buyer's lawyer must be able to reach the buyer at *all times during the day of closing*. Some people stay at work and are easy to reach. Many, though, move on the actual day of closing, making them unavailable for extended periods of time. The change-over in telephones is one reason; running errands is another. Unless you are constantly in reach with a cellular telephone, give your lawyer the phone number of someone who can reach you quickly despite your day's activities: a relative, a neighbor — at the old home, the new home, or both — even a friend at work. And keep a pocket-full of quarters or a pay-phone calling card handy. Then check in periodically with your contact, to see what is happening, or has happened! With developments at the registry office and the move happening independently, buyer and lawyer must be able to keep in touch during the day, either directly or indirectly. Everyone wants to avoid the situation where the deal has closed but the buyer can't be reached! Co-ordination of communications the day of closing is crucial.

32

After Closing — A Buyer's Work Is Not Yet Done

To most buyers, getting into their house seemed like a titanic struggle. So much has happened since they first went house-hunting several months ago. Now that they own their own home, Dave and Denise may feel it's time to sit back, relax and start enjoying it. True, but not yet. Much remains to be done as part of "the move" besides simply unpacking those mountains of boxes.

Several obvious items will require immediate attention. Few resale homes are in "move-in" condition. Walls may have to be painted or wallpapered, while floors and carpets may need cleaning. Minor repairs may be required, too. The benefit of closing now and moving in later — the overlap for tenants or bridge financing for existing home owners — soon becomes apparent. Cleaning, painting and fixing up a vacant home is much easier and saves an enormous amount of time compared to moving furniture and boxes from room to room. To move in first and then spruce it up is like putting the cart before the horse.

One of the first things to do immediately after closing is change the locks (or at least the tumblers) on every door. While several keys may have been delivered on closing or left in the house itself, who knows how many other keys remain in the hands of friends, neighbors, relatives, in-laws, babysitters and children of the former owner? To secure your home properly, start by changing the locks. Seriously consider upgrading the locking system at this time, if necessary, by installing deadbolt locks.

Notify *everyone* of your change of address. Start with the post office. Unfortunately, no longer will it redirect mail to the new address free of charge. If the redirect period (usually six months) is too short, then renew it on its expiry. Change of address cards are available at the post office for friends, neighbors and family members.

Who should be contacted with the change of address? An easy answer is to record all mail received for at least a month before closing, and everyone you deal with during that time. Appearing on the list will be the names and addresses of credit card companies, magazines, the doctor and dentist, and banks. A quick flip through your wallet will add several more names to the list. *Be sure to notify the provincial department of transport about the change of address for both your car ownership and your driver's licence, within the required time, usually less than a week.* Failing to do so could lead to a fine.

Diarize two weeks after closing as the day when a cheque for interest on the deposit should be received, if arranged in the offer. If nothing has been received by then, contact your lawyer.

Expect to receive your lawyer's formal reporting letter about a month after closing. Some lawyers send an interim report shortly after closing, containing details about upcoming payments. List the names, addresses, payment dates, amounts payable and account numbers for items due the first month after closing (see below). If no interim report is sent, get this information from your lawyer either at the pre-closing meeting or right after closing.

	Payment Dates	Name	Address	Amount Payable	Account Number
First mortgage					
Second mortgage					
Realty taxes					

Condominium
maintenance

Other items

When a transaction closes in the early months of a year, the adjustment for realty taxes is based on the amount levied for taxes the prior year. So if closing takes place before the final tax bill is issued, contact your lawyer during the summer about the possible readjustment of realty taxes in your favor.

Many essential items will be needed in the days and weeks following closing, if not already owned. While this list is not exhaustive, items to acquire include garbage cans, snow shovel, lawn mower and other lawn accessories, rake, hose and nozzle, sprinkler, shears, lawn fertilizer and spreader, household tools and supplies such as a hammer, wrench, pliers, screwdrivers, nails and screws, and rock salt or sand to remove ice. Get to know the owner of the local hardware store. You will be seeing much of him the first few months after closing!

As soon as possible after closing, obtain the following emergency numbers, especially if 911 does not exist in your community. Place them near your phone. The time to look them up is now, not when you need them.

Police

Fire

Ambulance

Hospital

Poison information centre

33

Facts to Know About Owning a Home

From the moment an offer is accepted, purchasers must become instant experts on many topics. Consider this chapter a primer on these points.

Title

One of the first questions a buyer will face once the offer is accepted is how he or she proposes "taking title" to the property. In everyday English, what the lawyer really wants to know is how the buyer will be described in the deed and on title. To simply reply "co-owners" is inadequate, as several different types of "co-ownership" situations exist. More must be known about the buyer's intentions, especially in the event of death.

i) Joint Tenancy
The first thing to know about holding title as joint tenants is that it has absolutely nothing to do with being a tenant! Where a husband and wife decide to take title together, it's usually as joint tenants. This provides the survivorship arrangement most married couples want. If one joint tenant dies, the property automatically goes to the other joint tenant by survivorship.

Harvey and Charlene took title to their house as joint tenants. If Harvey dies while Charlene is alive, she will automatically own it outright, by the mere fact that she has survived

Harvey. The house will not even be included as an asset of Harvey's estate, to be disbursed according to his will. Nor is it included in the value of Harvey's estate for probate purposes. Property passes on a joint tenancy to the surviving joint tenant *before* the assets of the deceased's estate are distributed. If Charlene dies while Harvey is still alive, the reverse holds true. By the mere fact of death, title to the property automatically passes to the surviving joint tenant. Joint tenancy is not limited to "husbands and wives." However, it has little practical use elsewhere except, perhaps, for common-law couples.

ii) Tenants in Common
Again, this expression has nothing to do with a tenancy. Taking title as tenants in common means the named parties own equal shares of the property. Tenants in common is often used where two or more unrelated people own a property together, such as common-law couples, business associates or persons living in shared accommodations.

Mickey and Carol are living together, unmarried, and took title to their home as tenants in common. Automatically, each owns a 50% share of the property, which can be sold to someone else if desired. As the survivorship rules do not apply to tenants in common, on Mickey's death his share of the property becomes part of his estate. It passes either to the beneficiary named in his will or to the beneficiary entitled to his estate by law if no will exists. His share does not automatically pass to Carol, as it would in a joint tenancy situation. That means his 50% interest in the house could go to someone other than his co-owner, Carol. Actually, that's what happened. Because Mickey named his brother Vic as his sole beneficiary in his will, Vic and Carol have become co-owners of the property on Mickey's death, as tenants in common.

If the respective shares are not owned 50-50, then the title should specifically state that. So if Carol contributes 60% of the purchase price and Mickey 40%, Carol will hold a 60% interest in the property, while Mickey has a 40% interest.

iii) One Name Only
Where either a husband or wife is self-employed or in a high-risk

job, title to the matrimonial home is often registered in the name of the other spouse. That is exactly what Dave, a self-employed businessman, and wife Denise did when they bought their home. Denise became the sole registered owner of the property, to protect the home from creditors. The theory behind this arrangement is quite simple. If Dave's business encounters financial difficulties, the matrimonial home cannot be seized and sold by his creditors. After all, Denise owns it, not Dave.

iv) Family Law Issues

Many provinces have reformed their family laws over the years. In many parts of Canada today, it is very difficult for the spouse who owns the matrimonial home (the titled spouse) to sell or mortgage it without the written consent of the other, non-titled spouse. In Ontario, for example, Denise cannot sell or mortgage the matrimonial home without Dave's written spousal consent. The need for Dave to consent to any dealings with the matrimonial home does not mean Dave has any property rights to it. Instead, all Dave has is a personal right to remain in the home until he consents to any transaction affecting it. This distinction between property rights and personal rights is crucial.

Practically speaking, when a matrimonial home is involved, both spouses (both Dave and Denise) must sign all documents if it will be sold or mortgaged, regardless who is the registered owner. If Dave and Denise both own it, obviously both must sign the deed to convey the property. If Denise is the sole titled spouse, Denise must sign the deed as owner, while Dave signs the deed to grant his spousal consent, releasing his personal rights to the property. The same holds true in reverse if Dave and not Denise is the sole registered owner of the matrimonial home.

Spousal consent replaced the ancient English concept of dower. While dower protected only women, spousal consent applies equally to both men and women. Not all properties are affected this way, though, only the matrimonial home. Therefore, if Denise owns an investment property in her own name, she can sell it without obtaining Dave's spousal consent.

Squatter's Rights

A legacy inherited from English land law is the concept of "adverse possession," commonly known as squatter's rights.

People constantly wonder if they can gain (or lose) title to a piece of land this way. The problem with squatter's rights arises because fences are not always located where they should, precisely along the boundary line. Sometimes they waiver to one side or the other. Occasionally, part of a building — an eavestrough or roof overhang, for example — encroaches onto the adjoining property. Taking the notion that "possession is ninetenths of the law" to the limit, adverse possession prevents landowners from making any claim to the affected land after a fixed period of time, usually 10 years. For possessory title to be gained or lost this way, the occupation and possession by the "squatter" must be continuous, unambiguous and undisputed, to the exclusion of the registered owner.

The fence between Al and Jeff's property is improperly placed; it is located one foot north of the boundary line between their properties. According to the doctrine of adverse possession, if the owner of the property to the south (Al) can establish the quality of possessory title required by law for the required period of time, he can gain title to the area between the property line and the fence, even though Jeff is the registered owner of that land.

Thankfully, the antiquated concept of adverse possession has been abolished in many parts of the country, where a newer and more precise land registration system has been instituted. If that applied to the misaligned fence between Al and Jeff's property, Jeff (the owner of the northern parcel) would never lose title to the area in dispute, no matter how long the fence has existed in its present location. Only by checking with your lawyer can you learn which land registration system applies to your property, and therefore if the notion of squatter's rights also applies.

Construction Liens (Mechanics' Liens)

Practically every home owner at some time hires a tradesman to do work on his or her property. Stuart and Lily might put an addition onto the house, or Frank and Carol might finish their basement. Both the tradesmen who work on the property as well as the suppliers of material add value to property. If they are unpaid for their efforts, provincial law gives them the right to register a lien against the property. If the nonpayment continues, the property can even be sold to satisfy the outstanding debt, provided that the procedural rules are strictly followed. This lien, previously known as a mechanics' lien but now called a construction lien, prevents owners of land from realizing a windfall — having work done and materials supplied at their request without paying for it.

Construction liens are one of the most confusing and least understood areas of the law affecting home ownership. Anyone contemplating any major construction or renovation work to their home should read and reread the following paragraphs until the complexities sink in. Perhaps a meeting with your lawyer would be in order to review and understand the relevant legislation. A mistake, misunderstanding or miscalculation, however innocent or unintentional, could end up costing you big time.

Wayne and Sandra are having their basement finished. The total contract price: $20,000. Under the construction lien legislation, they must withhold a set percentage of the price of the services and materials actually supplied under the contract (generally called the "value of the work done") until a fixed number of days after work on the contract is substantially completed. (In Ontario, for example, construction contracts for less than $250,000 are considered to be substantially completed when 97% of the work is done.) The money retained this way is known as the "holdback." Years ago, the holdback was 15% of the value of the work done, and the holdback period was 37 days from substantial completion. The newer construction lien acts have reduced the holdback to 10% of the value of the work done, while extending the holdback period to 45 days. Once the holdback period expires, the holdback can be released, provided that no construction liens are registered against the title to the property.

Why the holdback? Who benefits from it? In most construction situations, a general contractor is hired by the property owner to do the work. The general contractor in turn hires subtrades (subs) to perform specific components of the overall contract. For the work to be done on Wayne and Sandra's basement, they signed a contract with General Contractors. In turn, it hired the necessary subtrades: drywall, electrical, plumbing, heating, and so on. While Wayne and Sandra may pay money to General Contractors on schedule, that's no assurance General Contractors will pay the subs in a timely manner, or at all.

Everyone has heard horror stories of contractors absconding with funds or going bankrupt. If all the money that could be released at any point in time was paid to the general contractor, absolutely nothing would be left for the subs. With a construction lien holdback, the subs are guaranteed that some money will still be available from the project if the general contractor defaults in honoring its contracts with them. How? Instead of releasing the holdback funds to the general contractor, the owner by law retains them until the prescribed time has passed — to be paid to the subs, if necessary. Of course, if the subs aren't paid in full for their work, they can sue the general contractor for any shortfall, assuming it still exists and is solvent. The holdback, then, is money retained by the owner of the property for the benefit and protection of the subtrades.

Buyers planning any home renovations or home improvements after closing must be familiar with their obligations under the relevant construction lien legislation, and their potential liability for noncompliance. In Ontario, for example, payment representing only 90% of the value of the work done at any point in time can be released without jeopardy to a general contractor until the 45-day holdback period expires. (Note that the 10% holdback continues to grow over time, the value of the work done increasing as work progresses.) For major projects, an architect issues periodic certificates stating the value of the work done, which facilitates the release of funds. In smaller jobs, where no architect is involved, determining the value of the work done and whether a contract has been substantially completed depends on the circumstances of each specific case.

Complicating the situation is the payment schedule in most small contracts, stating what percentage of the contract price is to be paid at various stages of construction. Often the amounts payable this way exceed the value of the work done at that point in time. Making payments according to this payment schedule, ignoring the actual value of the work done, can have disastrous consequences for home owners.

When Wayne and Sandra signed their $20,000 contract, General Contractors, like most contractors, required a sizeable deposit. Five percent of the contract price was paid on signing the contract, and a further 20% when work started. This was needed, of course, to buy materials. According to the payment schedule, another 35% was to be paid when the wood frame was erected, and 25% more when the drywall went on. The final 15% was to be paid on completion. No mention of any construction lien holdback appeared in the contract. Also, the percentages payable were based on the contract price, not the actual value of the work done. Because the progress payments exceeded the value of the work done at any point in time, Wayne and Sandra unwittingly placed themselves at considerable financial risk.

Once they had paid 25% of the contract price to General Contractors, Wayne and Sandra had already paid too much money by law. Any material suppliers or initial tradesmen working on the house who didn't get paid would have the right to register a lien against the property. Although $5,000 had been paid on the contract, the value of the work done was only $2,000. This meant that Wayne and Sandra should have paid only 90% of the $2,000, or $1,800, to General Contractors (the other 10%, or $200, being the holdback at that stage). If the property was liened at that time by a subtrade for nonpayment by General Contractors, Wayne and Sandra can forget about the $3,000 paid in excess of the value of the work done. They paid it at their jeopardy, and now must absorb the loss. Not only that, but Wayne and Sandra are also responsible for the 10% ($200) holdback to the subtrades based on the value of the work done. This is money that will have to be paid, in effect, a second time. The cost of their mistake: $3,000 overpaid plus $200 for the holdback, for a total of $3,200.

To prevent situations like this from arising, never give the general contractor a large sum of money up front as a deposit. If he states that considerable funds are needed to buy materials, only give him what's needed for the initial materials. Or, offer to pay for that initial delivery of materials yourself, on the contractor's behalf. Since less money is paid to the contractor directly, and since you and not the contractor own those materials, the likelihood of problems is reduced.

Double jeopardy in payment of the holdback is also possible during the course of construction. Suppose the electrician registered the first lien on the project when $17,000 had been paid to General Contractors according to the payment schedule. In actual fact, the value of the work done was only $12,000. General Contractors then abandoned the contract. Assuming that Wayne and Sandra could get another contractor to finish the job for $8,000 (the difference between the $20,000 contract price and the $12,000 work done to date), construction of the basement would cost $26,200 — a lot more than the original contract price. How was that $26,200 calculated? It consists of a) the $17,000 paid on the old contract; b) the $8,000 still to be paid on the new contract; c) the $1,200 that should have been, but was not, held back, for which Wayne and Sandra continue to be responsible. Granted, they have legal recourse against General Contractors for that extra $6,200, if it can be found and still has any money.

Most contractors insist on being paid in full once the work is completed. *Don't do it. Never pay a construction contract in full at that stage.* Contractors rarely voluntarily tell home owners that a holdback of 10% of the total value of the work done is needed for 45 days after the contract is substantially completed. Don't be afraid to tell a contractor what your legal obligations are, and that you will be retaining 10% of the contract price (which is now the total value of the work done) until the holdback period expires. If Wayne and Sandra pay the full contract price on completion, and a lien is registered within the 45-day period, they will have to pay the $2,000 represented by the holdback a second time. That's double jeopardy.

Full discussion of and agreement on how much money will be paid and when, together with the question of holdbacks, is imperative *before* any construction or home renovation contract is signed. If necessary, amend the contractor's standard form agreement to say that all amounts required by law will be held back, for the period of time required by law. If the contractor objects, there's one simple answer: don't deal with him. Also, never accept the argument, often presented, that owners can waive their construction lien obligations, and that a contractor's quote is lower because there will be no holdbacks. Plain and simple, that's wrong. Owners must retain the statutory holdback for the prescribed period of time by law to protect the subtrades, not the contractor. Home owners who turn a blind eye to construction lien holdbacks may learn the hard way that a "cheap" contract ended up costing a lot more than what was bargained for!

To be absolutely sure no construction liens have been registered, and that the holdback can be paid out with impunity, title to the property should be "subsearched" or quickly reviewed once the lien holdback period expires. The cost involved is small, compared to the peace of mind it brings.

Realty Taxes

Realty (or property) taxes are collected by most municipalities in two stages, with an interim bill and a final bill. Jack and Jill paid realty taxes of $2,000 last year. The interim taxes this year will be one-half of this amount, or $1,000. Issued early in the year, the interim tax bill is payable in two, three or four equal instalments, depending on the municipality. Once the final taxes have been determined, usually in late spring or early summer, the final tax bill is issued, again payable over several instalments. Since Jack and Jill's taxes went up 2.5%, or $50, this year, their total taxes this year will be $2,050. With $1,000 having been paid on account, the final tax bill totals $1,050.

For many years, nonpayment of property taxes was a cheap way to borrow money. The interest penalty charged on overdue taxes was well below the current rate for bank loans. Today, overdue instalments bear interest at rates similar to or higher than those charged in the marketplace.

Some (but not all) municipalities give a discount for early payment of tax instalments. So check it out. It could be to your advantage to prepay your property taxes.

Upon receiving their tax bill, whether interim or final, many home owners send postdated cheques to the tax department, payable on the dates the instalments fall due. Interest penalties arising from late payments can be avoided this way.

Unpaid realty taxes place a serious strain on the cash flow for a municipality, as all other taxpayers must shoulder the financial burden of it not receiving anticipated revenue on time. To ensure that municipalities collect the money justly owing to them, unpaid property taxes are a special lien against the property, ranking even higher than a first mortgage! Because they wish to remain at the front of the line at all times, many mortgage lenders collect a portion of the estimated annual realty taxes from borrowers with each mortgage payment, whether that's done monthly, weekly, bi-weekly or semi-monthly. Taxes are then paid to the municipality by the lender as the tax bills are issued, from the realty tax account it maintains.

Utilities

Like realty taxes, unpaid municipal hydro or water charges can be enforced as a lien against a property. This approach is fair, for if the land benefiting from the utility did not bear the burden, all the other users would be subsidizing that property. With unpaid utility bills being a lien against a property, part of your lawyer's job is to ensure that those bills are fully paid, up to and including the date of closing.

Lien rights do not exist in favor of telephone companies, privately owned gas companies or cable television systems.

Land Registry Systems

In old England, real estate titles were established by delivering to buyers a deed box containing all previous deeds to the property.

When the earliest statutes were passed in Canada allowing the registration and recording of deeds and mortgages, this practice was continued, with one important variation. The provincial government maintained a master deed box in each county called a "registry office," where everyone could store their deeds. To establish good title, it was still necessary to search the historical records of title for many years. Over time, a new land registration system was introduced which considerably simplified the searching of titles, where the government actually guaranteed the title of the owner appearing in its records. The older format is known as the "registry system," while the newer scheme is called "land titles."

The development of a new land registration system has also resulted in changes in terminology. Traditionally, the document by which land was transferred was known as a deed. Money was borrowed by the property owner issuing a mortgage to a lender. Both could easily be identified with the words "This Indenture" appearing at the top of the first page. Replacing these terms in the newer system are the expressions "transfer" and "charge." While the legal effect of these documents is slightly different from their predecessors' effect, what they mean to the public is the same.

It is impossible, simply by looking at two adjacent properties or two different streets, to determine which land registration system applies. Whether a particular property is governed by one system or the other is immaterial, although searching titles in the newer land titles system is considerably easier.

Many home owners, like Maurice and Martha, unable to locate their deed, grow panicky, fearing a loss of their property. They can rest assured. Obtaining replacement proof of ownership is easy. Two copies of every deed are signed by the seller and delivered on closing. The buyer receives one copy, while the second is filed at the registry office, where it is permanently recorded and stored or microfilmed. Since the provincial government — the owner of the deed box — is the keeper of everybody's deeds, all Maurice and Martha must do is have their lawyer obtain a copy of their deed from the registry office.

Most people are astonished to learn that a land registry office is a hall of public records. Armed with a legal description (obtained, perhaps, from the tax office), anyone can discover a wealth of information about a property. For a nominal charge, you can learn the name of the registered owner, the price paid for a particular property, and even particulars of mortgage financing. This is essential information for appraisers and real estate agents, who need to know what similar properties have sold for in an area.

34
Urea Formaldehyde Foam Insulation

Urea formaldehyde foam insulation (UFFI) was used to re-insulate the walls of older homes, starting in Canada in the mid-1960s. Its heyday was reached in the late 1970s, fallout from the energy crisis of the mid-1970s. That's when the Canadian government, under the CHIP Program (Canadian Home Insulation Program), offered government grants as an incentive to upgrade home insulation levels. One of the approved forms of insulation was UFFI.

With growing reports that formaldehyde gas seepage was causing health problems (like dizziness, nausea, nosebleeds and eye/nose/throat irritation), UFFI's use was permanently banned by the federal government on December 17, 1980. An estimated 80,000 homes were insulated with UFFI before its ban. (See "UFFI: Acceptance of the Unacceptable Product," by Lloyd Tataryn, *Canadian Consumer Magazine*, Vol. 14, Num. 6, June, 1984, page 35.)

Selling a home with UFFI is not illegal, but "UFFI homes" still carry a definite stigma in the real estate industry. Not every-one wants to buy a UFFI-insulated home. And while the impact of UFFI has been re-evaluated over time, that should not affect the inquiries every home buyer must make on the UFFI issue. Plain and simple, buyers through their agents must discover, and vendors must disclose when asked, whether a particular home is now or ever has been insulated with UFFI.

Obviously, no home built since 1981 can have UFFI in its

walls. But newer, brick-front homes are not the problem, since UFFI was never used as a primary insulator. Instead, the concern is with older homes, where UFFI was injected into the walls as a re-insulator.

In most resale transactions, vendors give a warranty that the property is not and never has been insulated with UFFI. Although this would appear to resolve the question, it actually raises more questions than it answers.

If the person selling the house owned it during the entire period of time when UFFI was an acceptable insulator, he or she knows firsthand that UFFI was never installed. Rarely, however, is that the case. What if the property Archie and Edith bought in 1978 is being resold now? Do they absolutely know that the property was never insulated with UFFI? They are probably relying on what they were told by Mike, the previous owner. Was Mike absolutely certain the house was never insulated with UFFI? Was he in a position to know that? As properties change hands over time, and a pile of these "UFFI warranties" build up, it will be that much harder for subsequent owners to know conclusively — and warrant beyond question on a sale — whether UFFI was ever used as an insulator in a particular property. Over time, the UFFI warranty may become worth little more than the paper it is printed on. In fact, some offers today have watered down the UFFI warranty to the point where vendors state either a) "to the best of our knowledge and belief" the house was not insulated with UFFI or b) they never installed UFFI during their period of ownership. Both are virtually meaningless.

Furthermore, a UFFI warranty only allows a buyer like Teddy to sue Paul, the seller, for damages after closing, and not back out of the deal, if it is learned before closing that the house was insulated with UFFI. Unless Teddy can show that Paul's failure to disclose the presence of UFFI was a fraudulent misrepresentation, Teddy cannot cancel the transaction. Not only is fraudulent misrepresentation a very difficult standard to prove, it can only be established at a trial, held long after the scheduled closing date. So Teddy faces a real dilemma. Does he refuse to close, hoping he can establish fraudulent misrepresentation when he sues Paul? If Teddy does that, he also runs the risk of being sued by Paul for not closing the deal as scheduled. Or does Teddy close the transaction for the UFFI-filled home (to avoid being sued by Paul), and then sue Paul for damages after closing? It's a real quandary.

Many homes insulated with UFFI have safe and acceptable levels of formaldehyde gas. Tests can be performed to establish the exposure limit and whether it meets acceptable UFFI standards (0.1 parts per million for dwellings). Anyone knowingly and willingly buying a UFFI home might want to make his or her offer conditional on acceptably safe readings being taken immediately after the offer is signed, right before closing, and perhaps even in the interim.

To increase their marketability, some owners of homes insulated with UFFI have had it removed from the walls, with the house then retested for acceptably safe levels. An inspection report can be issued by a federally approved inspector if the home now conforms with government standards. As in the case of UFFI insulated homes, the offer should be made conditional on acceptably safe levels being attained at the same three intervals. But this is where the offer's wording regarding UFFI is critical. The vendor can honestly state that the house does not have urea formaldehyde foam insulation. But he or she cannot state that it "never did have" UFFI.

Even homes not insulated with UFFI will have levels of formaldehyde when tested. Formaldehyde is found in the glue of particle board, aerosol products, dry cleaning chemicals, natural gas furnaces, tobacco smoke and new carpeting. No one can live in a formaldehyde-free environment. It's all a question of degree.

Despite what many people think, a home inspector cannot tell conclusively whether UFFI is present in the walls of a house without opening up all the walls. Of course, that is not practical. Often, though, a visual inspection will indicate if UFFI was used as an insulator. Home inspectors look for drill holes in the exterior brickwork, where UFFI was injected into the walls. Evidence of the foam may be found near electrical outlets, or around the foundation wall. In many cases, home inspectors can reliably detect the presence of UFFI in a home. Yet they still generally qualify their reports by saying that "no evidence of UFFI was noted upon visually inspecting the home."

Buyers prepared to spend extra money can have the air quality tested in the wall cavities. This requires the seller's consent (an unlikely option), as it involves drilling directly into the wall cavities. Only this test can absolutely guarantee whether UFFI has been used as an insulator.

Potential buyers of properties built before 1981 who are anxious to establish that the property is not and never has been insulated with UFFI should do the following: 1) insert a condition (not a warranty, as is usually done) into the offer that the property is not and never has been insulated with UFFI (because this is a condition and not a warranty, discovery of UFFI before closing will enable the purchaser to back out of the transaction without penalty); and 2) ask the home inspector to investigate the property for UFFI, recognizing the limitations noted earlier.

Over the years the thinking on UFFI has changed. At one time lenders invariably insisted that a mortgage on a UFFI home be insured with Canada Mortgage and Housing Corporation, no matter how much equity the buyer had in the property. In 1993 CMHC announced that it would no longer require a statutory declaration from the borrower about UFFI. Many lenders today do not require any information about whether a house is, or ever was, insulated with UFFI. That followed an eight-year court battle in Quebec over UFFI that was finally decided in December 1991. A Quebec Superior Court judge dismissed the claims of six home owners who had UFFI injected into the walls of their homes, as they failed to prove conclusively that UFFI caused their health problems.

Still, the stigma associated with UFFI lingers in the public's mind. And UFFI continues to have a perceived (if not an actual) impact on property values. Therefore, prudent buyers as part of their home-buying strategy will always inquire about the existence, past and present, of UFFI in a home, and insert the appropriate clause into their Offer to Purchase.

35

Tax and the Canadian Home Owner

Most Canadians know that the sale of a principal residence is exempt from capital gains tax. A number of other, less well-known provisions of the Income Tax Act of Canada could also be relevant, depending on a buyer's particular circumstances. Everyone owning a home must have a basic understanding of the impact our tax laws can have on home ownership.

Besides income tax, there's the GST. It is more of a concern when buying a house than when owning or selling it. For more information on GST issues when buying a home, see chapter 25.

While the information in this chapter reflects the current state of the law, how it is applied may vary depending on your specific situation. Professional guidance from a chartered accountant or a tax lawyer should always be obtained when dealing with tax matters.

Principal Residence Exemption

Profit made on the sale of a principal residence is exempt from capital gains tax. The term "principal residence" includes a housing unit (house, apartment in a duplex, apartment building or condominium, cottage, mobile home, trailer or houseboat) or a share of a co-operative housing corporation, whether owned alone or with another person. To be tax-exempt in any given year, it must have been "ordinarily inhabited" that year by the taxpayer, his or her spouse, former spouse or child. The taxpayer also must have been resident in Canada each year in which the exemption is claimed. Qualifying for the exemption are both the building and the land immediately surrounding the building that could reasonably be regarded as contributing to the use and enjoyment of the housing unit. The maximum amount of land generally allowed to qualify this way is half a hectare (about 1.23 acres).

Technically, a form designating your home as a principal residence should be completed when filing your income tax return for the year it is sold. That one designation would cover all the years it was a principal residence. However, it is Revenue Canada's policy only to require that the designation be filed if there are any taxable capital gains after using the principal residence exemption.

What does the expression "ordinarily inhabited" mean? According to Revenue Canada, it depends on the facts in each particular case. There is no minimum time period during which the property must be owner-occupied. Nor must the property have been ordinarily inhabited for the entire year. Where a home is only occupied for a short period of time in a given year, Revenue Canada will accept it as being ordinarily inhabited provided that the principal reason for owning the property was not to gain or produce income. Receiving incidental rental income from a seasonal residence won't taint the property, either.

To meet the test of being "ordinarily inhabited," the typical and accepted signs of occupancy must exist, involving both the property and the owner. Therefore, actual physical use and enjoyment of the property to the knowledge of others is crucial. For example, home owners normally have their mail, bills and magazine subscriptions directed to the property. They update the address on their driver's licence, and get to meet neighbors on the street or in the complex. Usually, it is not too difficult for a person who is actually occupying a home to establish that he or she ordinarily inhabits it.

Starting in 1982, only one housing unit could be designated each year as a principal residence per "family unit," even if more than one property was owned and inhabited during the year. In addition to a taxpayer, "family unit" includes his or her spouse (unless they are separated) and children (except those who are married or age 18 or older). This killed the pre-1982 scheme where two spouses could have two separate principal residences, Carol owning the cottage and Larry owning the city home, each home being exempt from capital gains tax when sold. (By the way, the definition of "spouse" includes both married couples and persons of the opposite sex living in a common-law relationship who i) are the natural or adoptive parents of a child or ii) have lived together for at least 12 straight months.)

If only one home is "owner-occupied" in a year, this will be the principal residence for that year. Is there a problem when home owners sell their home and move to another during the year? No. The formula in the Income Tax Act for calculating the principal residence exemption recognizes this, by including a so-called "bonus year." For most taxpayers, their gain on the sale of their principal residence is reduced by the following formula:

$$\text{Exempt gain} = \frac{1 + \text{the number of years in which the property was a principal residence, and during which the taxpayer resided in Canada}}{\text{The number of years during which the taxpayer owned the property}} \times \text{Capital gain}$$

Jeff bought a house in 1993, lived in it continuously, sold it in 1997 for a $15,000 gain, and bought another owner-occupied house that same year. According to the above formula, Jeff should designate his old home as his principal residence for the years 1993, 1994, 1995 and 1996. Although only one property can be designated as a principal residence each year, Jeff can designate his new home as his principal residence for 1997 without incurring any capital gains tax on the sale of his old home. Using the formula, Jeff's $15,000 gain is reduced by $15,000 to zero, allowing him to claim the full principal residence exemption, as follows:

Exempt gain = $\dfrac{1 + 4 \text{ (years 1993, 1994, 1995 and 1996)}}{5}$ x \$15,000

= \$15,000

The effect of the "1 +" in the formula is to treat both properties as a principal residence in the year of sale, even though only one house can technically be designated as a principal residence per year.

Interspousal transfers of a property (from one spouse to the other, from both spouses to one spouse, or from one spouse to both spouses) do not trigger immediate capital gains tax. Any tax payable is deferred until the property is sold to a third party, following which tax is collected for the combined period of ownership. If the property was always a principal residence during that time, no capital gains tax is payable. Peter bought a house in 1987 and transferred it to Lydia in 1992. She sold it in 1997. Because it was a principal residence for the entire 10-year span, the \$30,000 capital gain was totally exempt from tax. And if it was continuously a principal residence, the "attribution" rules that affect future capital gains on interspousal transfers of income-producing property don't apply.

Whether a transfer of property to an adult child triggers capital gains tax depends on how it was used by the parent prior to its transfer. In the most common situation, a parent like Lou transfers his home to his son, Ted, who also uses it as his own principal residence by living there. No tax is payable on the transfer by Lou, it having been his principal residence. And no capital gains tax will be payable by Ted either, as long as it continues to be Ted's principal residence. Capital gains tax would be payable by Lou if the property had not been Lou's principal residence before the transfer. And capital gains tax will be payable by Ted if the property is not his principal residence after the transfer.

The Income Tax Act is a two-sided coin. Profits from the sale of a principal residence are not subject to capital gains tax, but any loss incurred on the sale of a principal residence is not a capital loss. Sorry, you can't have it both ways!

Divided (or Mixed) Use Deduction

Some houses are used for more than one purpose at the same time. Often, home owners like Annie use the main and second floors as a principal residence while renting out the basement, an income-producing use. When that happens, all rent received from the basement must be included in Annie's income, while expenses *specifically incurred* earning that rental income are deductible from her income. These include bookkeeping costs and the cost of newspaper ads. In addition, that portion of the expenses incurred for the building *as a whole* (such as realty taxes, insurance, mortgage interest, heating and utilities) which can reasonably be attributed to the rental use of the property, can also be deducted from Annie's income. Deciding how much of the property is used for rental purposes (and therefore the proportion of the building expenses that are deductible from other income) is commonly based on either the total number of rooms rented or the total square footage that is rented, as a percentage of the whole house.

Irv rented two rooms in his eight-room house for a monthly charge of $300 each. During the year, he spent $200 in advertising to rent the space. Therefore, Irv's gross income will be $300 monthly for each room, or $7,200 for the year. His net income will be that $7,200 less the $200 in direct expenses, less a further 25% of the overall expenses for the house.

When part of a home is rented out, the principal residence exemption for the whole house can be maintained, provided that no capital cost allowance (depreciation) is claimed on the rented portion of the house. Revenue Canada permits this arrangement even though part of the property is being used for a non–principal residence purpose — to produce rental income. If depreciation is claimed on the rental portion of the property, capital gains tax may be payable on the portion of the house rented out, when the house is sold. So if you rent out part of the house, don't claim depreciation, plain and simple.

Change of Use Exemption

Sometimes property used as a principal residence is converted into income-producing property for a limited period of time. Often this happens when a home owner like Gary temporarily moves out of a house (perhaps for a short-term job placement out of town) but plans to move back in after several years. This change of use from principal residence to income-producing property normally results in a "deemed disposition" of the property (land and buildings) at fair market value and its deemed re-acquisition for the same amount. Therefore, any future capital gains would be taxable, while the reverse is true for any future capital losses. Despite this, the Income Tax Act provides a limited exemption for a complete change of use, when a former principal residence is temporarily converted into income-producing property.

On his tax return for the year the use was changed, Gary must file a special election which deems the change of use not to have occurred. To do this, Gary must sign a letter that contains a description of the property, and state that he is making the change of use election. Gary can then designate his former home as his principal residence for that year, and three more years after that, even though Gary does not live there any more. While this change of use election is in effect, Gary cannot claim capital cost allowance (depreciation) for the property against the rental income received. If Gary moves back in before the four-year period is up, his temporary move from the house has not "tainted" it for purposes of the principal residence exemption. If Gary sells the house during that four-year period, the total capital gains will be exempt from tax, the property still being recognized as his principal residence, despite this change of use.

To be able to continue the principal residence designation this way despite a change of use, Gary must continue to be a resident of Canada. In addition, Gary's "family unit" can only have one principal residence, be it the "change of use" property or any other property they own. Therefore, Gary can't buy another home while relocated elsewhere and designate both it and the "change of use" home as his principal residence for those four years. Only one or the other, but not both.

Mortgage Interest Deductibility

Interest paid on a mortgage arranged to finance the purchase of a principal residence is not deductible from other income. However, interest paid on a mortgage arranged to finance the purchase of rental property is a deductible expense. If part of a house is rented out — the "divided use" situation — a proportionate share of the mortgage interest will be deductible against rental income.

Canadians in some situations can also deduct the interest expense on their home mortgages. To do this, the mortgage proceeds must be used for an unequivocal and unambiguous business or investment purpose. Further information on making mortgage interest deductible in Canada appears in *Hidden Profits in Your Mortgage.*

Home Office

Expenses that are incurred to earn income are normally deductible against other income. For years, Revenue Canada allowed the cost of operating a home office, including a secondary location at home, to be deductible in this fashion. But it has since tightened the rules, imposing a number of conditions and restrictions on the deductibility of "work space in home" expenses. For example:

- Self-employed people can only deduct such expenses if the home office is used either a) as that person's principal place of business, or b) exclusively to earn business income, and on a regular and continuous basis to meet clients, customers or patients. If Jerry, a self-employed accountant, has a downtown office, he can't deduct any of his home office expenses, even though he may do some work there or meet the occasional client at home. To satisfy the criterion of being used "exclusively to earn business income," the home office must be totally segregated, and not be used for any other purpose. The den or family room just won't do; nor will infrequent meetings or frequent meetings at irregular intervals.

- Only expenses related to the home office can be deducted — e.g., the prorated portion of mortgage interest, property insurance, realty taxes, heating and other utilities — and they cannot exceed the income from the business. Therefore, home office expenses cannot create a loss for income tax purposes, or increase one that already exists. In determining how much of the property is used as work space in home (and therefore the proportion of expenses that are deductible from other income), similar principles apply as with the divided use deduction.

- Be very careful depreciating a property with a home office. While capital cost allowance (the technical term for depreciation) can technically be claimed for a home office (subject to the limitations on tax losses described above), the principal residence exemption does not apply to a work space where depreciation has been claimed. Therefore, like in the divided-use situation, you may be better off not claiming any depreciation when calculating home office expenses. Unused expenses can be carried forward indefinitely, provided that the criteria for a home office continue to be met.

Moving Expense Deduction

Canadians who move to a new community may be able to deduct their moving expenses from income earned at the new location. To do this,

- your move must be employment related, to a new location in Canada, even if for the same employer (e.g., a company transfer, change of job, or moving your place of business);

- your new residence must be at least 40 kilometres (25 miles) closer than your old residence to the new place of business or employment; and

- your employment or business at the old location ceases.

Ian moved from Calgary to Montreal for a new job. All reasonable amounts that Ian paid in moving himself, his family and his household effects can be deducted from his income earned at the new location. These include travelling costs, meals and lodging en route, transportation and storage costs, temporary board and lodging near either residence, costs incurred in breaking an unexpired lease, costs incurred in selling a former home (including legal fees and disbursements, real estate commission and any prepayment penalty incurred), plus legal fees and disbursements incurred on the purchase of the new home, provided that the old property is sold. Receipts must be kept, in case an audit is conducted.

Where an employer picks up the full cost of the move or reimburses the employee for the full cost, no amount is deductible. Any partial reimbursement must be applied to reduce the amount of the income tax deduction. Marvin recently incurred $5,000 in expenses when moving from Vancouver to Toronto. Because he received $3,500 from his employer, Marvin can only deduct $1,500 from the income earned at the new location.

Moves into and out of Canada do not qualify for the moving expense deduction.

Buying from a Non-Resident Vendor

Anyone buying property must determine the residency status of the vendor for income tax purposes, as non-resident vendors are taxed differently when selling property. When a resident Canadian sells real estate (be it a principal residence or income-producing property), usually this is satisfied by the vendor delivering an affidavit to that effect on closing.

When the vendor is a non-resident, purchasers have a legal obligation to protect the interests of Revenue Canada. For the transaction to proceed as scheduled, the non-resident vendor must deliver a prescribed certificate from Revenue Canada on closing. Otherwise, the purchaser is obligated by law to withhold 1/3% of the total purchase price and send it to Revenue Canada. There it will be applied towards any income tax and capital gains liability the non-resident vendor may have. Buyers who do not comply with this requirement face a very onerous penalty. Although the entire purchase price may have been paid to the non-resident vendor, the purchaser will have to pay an additional one-third of the purchase price to the government, presumably from his or her own pocket! Ignorance of the law is no defence. Buyers cannot afford to turn a blind eye to the issue of non-resident vendors, because of the penalty involved.

Most standard form offers state the rights and obligations of both seller and buyer when a non-resident is selling a piece of real estate. Whenever you know or suspect that the seller is or will be a non-resident on closing, notify your lawyer immediately. Let him or her set the wheels in motion early, so that the appropriate certificate relieving the purchaser from liability will be available for closing.

Making Mortgage Payments to a Non-Resident Lender

Purchasers who buy a house from a non-resident vendor must also be careful if the vendor takes back a mortgage on closing. The same is true where the mortgage lender is known to be a non-resident. A little red flag should begin waving, warning of possible dangers.

By law, Canadians who borrow money from a non-resident lender must remit a "withholding tax" to the federal government. Failure to do so makes the borrower responsible for any shortfall in the amount of tax payable to Revenue Canada on those mortgage payments. If the full amount of the mortgage payment was previously forwarded to the non-resident lender, this means double jeopardy for the resident borrower. The obligation to pay the money to the government rests with the borrower, not the lender!

Depending on whether a tax agreement exists between Canada and the country where the non-resident lives, the withholding tax can be 15% or more. This withholding tax only applies to the *interest* portion of a mortgage payment; the principal portion of a blended mortgage payment is not affected. So when the monthly interest payable is $1,000, upwards of

$150 must be sent by the resident borrower to Revenue Canada as the withholding tax. The remainder can then be forwarded to the non-resident lender. (With blended mortgage payments, the interest component will be shrinking each month, meaning a different amount of withholding tax must be remitted each month.)

Whenever payments are made to a non-resident lender, be extremely cautious. Contact Revenue Canada to learn the amount of applicable withholding tax for the country involved. The first time money is withheld from the mortgage payment to pay this tax, send it to Revenue Canada with a covering letter, detailing the circumstances of the payment and how it was calculated. Also request that a non-resident account be established. In time you will receive a proper remittance form from Revenue Canada, which should accompany future payments of withholding tax. Besides this, be sure you explain to the non-resident lender what you have done, why, and how the deduction was calculated.

Paying Revenue Canada its due is not the end of the story. As a Canadian borrowing from a non-resident lender, you must also file an annual return with Revenue Canada regarding this withholding tax. Do not take this obligation too lightly! Remember, the penalty for noncompliance will come out of your pocket, not the lender's.

36
Now That You Own Your Own Home

Isn't it wonderful! The deal has closed and the home is yours. Perhaps you have already started to settle into the house. What a feeling!

Buyers who developed and applied their own HOBS should have gone from start to finish with a minimum of surprises and disruptions. Although the transaction was complex and had its difficult moments, you were fully prepared for every step of the way. You knew exactly what you were looking for, in terms of needs and wants, communities and neighborhoods. Your real estate professionals were lined up well before any contract was signed. Your finances were in order before any commitments were made, and you knew how much money would be needed to close before proceeding into the marketplace. Having done your homework, you were also able to recognize the right house when you viewed it — the one that satisfied all of your needs and as many wants as possible, the one you could afford to buy and carry each month. In short, by developing your own, unique home-buying strategy and sticking to it, you knew precisely what you were committing to, before making that commitment. And that allowed your enthusiasm for the new home to flourish, reaching a crescendo on closing.

A house is more than a mere structure; it is a rare opportunity that allows you to display your unique lifestyle. No matter how much the property may be in "move-in" condition, much remains to be done to mould it to your individual taste, to make that house into your home. Some tasks may be more pressing than others — painting and wallpapering the house, or possibly ordering drapes and window coverings. Minor or even major repairs and renovations may be necessary. Floors and carpeting may require replacing as well.

Now that you own a place of your own, apply this same winning approach to improving and upgrading it over time. Once again, establish a strategy, a master game plan, to repair and spruce up the house over time as a true expression of your taste. Decide what you want to do, and when you want to do it. Then budget for that work over the course of the next few years. Knowing what will be done next spring or summer, and the year after that, and properly planning for it, will keep your personal excitement and love for the house at its highest level. You will keenly anticipate those upcoming changes, because they have been so well planned, and because you know they can be afforded. So convert your successful home-buying strategy to a home-owning strategy, and start implementing it immediately.

Remember that the interest paid on your mortgage is not deductible in Canada against other income in most cases. As part of your home-ownership strategy, take advantage of the prepayment privileges you have negotiated in your mortgage. Apply the POPS principle — Pay Off your Principal Sooner, described in *Hidden Profits in Your Mortgage* — to save thousands of dollars in interest costs and cut years off the time needed to retire that mortgage. Money saved can then be applied elsewhere as part of your home-owning strategy.

Almost two-thirds of Canadians own their own home. Welcome to the club. You have proven that home ownership is an old-fashioned virtue, one that appeals to Canadians of all ages and backgrounds. You have worked hard, in many ways, to get to this stage. So enjoy your new home in good health. Congratulations! You deserve it.

Appendix A

Items of personal property that might be included in a resale offer. Remember to be specific.

— Refrigerator
— Stove
— Washer
— Dryer
— Dishwasher
— Storms and screens
— Drapes and drapery tracks, blinds, window coverings and shutters
— Air-conditioning (central or window units)
— Light fixtures (those the seller will *remove* from the home are listed; otherwise all accompany the house)
— Hot water heater (if owned or rental)
— Gas/electric/oil furnace and equipment
— Broadloom where laid
— Garage-door opener and hand-held unit
— Fireplace accessories
— All other permanent fixtures on the premises belonging to the seller, to be in good working order on the date of closing, free of liens and encumbrances.